world cultures: japan

helen gilhooly

For over 60 years, more than 40 million people have learnt over 750 subjects the **teach yourself** way, with impressive results.

be where you want to be
with **teach yourself**

The publisher has used its best endeavours to ensure that the URLs for external websites referred to in this book are correct and active at the time of going to press. However, the publisher has no responsibility for the websites and can make no guarantee that a site will remain live or that the content is or will remain appropriate.

For UK order enquiries: please contact Bookpoint Ltd, 130 Milton Park, Abingdon, Oxon OX14 4SB. Telephone: +44 (0) 1235 827720. Fax: +44 (0) 1235 400454. Lines are open 09.00–18.00, Monday to Saturday, with a 24-hour message answering service. Details about our titles and how to order are available at www.teachyourself.co.uk

For USA order enquiries: please contact McGraw-Hill Customer Services, PO Box 545, Blacklick, OH 43004-0545, USA. Telephone: 1-800-722-4726. Fax: 1-614-755-5645.

For Canada order enquiries: please contact McGraw-Hill Ryerson Ltd, 300 Water St, Whitby, Ontario L1N 9B6, Canada. Telephone: 905 430 5000. Fax: 905 430 5020.

Long renowned as the authoritative source for self-guided learning – with more than 30 million copies sold worldwide – the *Teach Yourself* series includes over 300 titles in the fields of languages, crafts, hobbies, business, computing and education.

British Library Cataloguing in Publication Data: a catalogue record for this title is available from the British Library.

Library of Congress Catalog Card Number: on file.

First published in UK 2002 by Hodder Headline, 338 Euston Road, London NW1 3BH.

First published in US 2002 by Contemporary Books, a Division of the McGraw-Hill Companies, 1 Prudential Plaza, 130 East Randolph Street, Chicago, IL 60601, USA.

This edition published 2004.

Typeset by Graphicraft Limited, Hong Kong.

Printed in Great Britain for Hodder & Stoughton Ltd., a division of Hodder Headline, 338 Euston Road, London NW1 3BH, by Cox & Wyman Ltd, Reading, Berkshire.

Papers used in this book are natural, renewable and recyclable products. They are made from wood grown in sustainable forests. The logging and manufacturing processes conform to the environmental regulations of the country of origin.

Impression number 10 9 8 7 6 5 4 3 2 1
Year 2010 2009 2008 2007 2006 2005 2004

contents

About the author

Helen Gilhooly has lived and worked in Japan and has extensive experience of teaching Japanese and writing materials for learners of all ages. She has an MA and PGCE in Japanese and is currently the Language College Director of Aldercar Community Language College in Derbyshire. She is also a teacher trainer of Japanese at Nottingham University. Other publications with Hodder & Stoughton include *Teach Yourself Beginner's Japanese*, *Teach Yourself Beginner's Japanese Script* and *Teach Yourself Instant Japanese* (Japanese Language Consultant).

Acknowledgments

Thank you to Niamh Kelly of Dublin City University for reading and giving feedback on the manuscript; to Robert Gilhooly of the *Japan Times*, Hugh Levinson from the BBC and Masae Sugahara of Sheffield University for giving advice and information; to Phil Turk (series editor), Rebecca Green and Sue Hart of Hodder & Stoughton for reading and commenting on each unit; to Mavis Pilbeam for feedback on the original proposal; but most of all to John and Jefferee.

introduction

This book is designed to give you as full a basic overview as possible of the main aspects of Japan: the country, its languages, its people, their way of life and culture and what makes them tick.

You will find it a useful foundation if you are studying for examinations which require knowledge of the background of Japan and its civilization, or if you are learning the language in, for example, an evening class and want to know more about the country and how it works. If your job involves travel and business relations it will provide valuable and practical information about the ways and customs of the people you are working with. Or if you simply have an interest in Japan for whatever reason, it will broaden your knowledge about the country and its inhabitants.

The book is divided into three sections:

- **The making of Japan**
  Units 1 and 2 deal with the forces – historical, geographical, geological, demographical and linguistic – that have brought about the formation of the country we know as Japan and the language we known as Japanese. Unit 2 also takes a look at the role of Japanese language outside the immediate frontiers of Japan.
- **Creative Japan**
  Units 3–7 deal with the wealth of creative aspects of Japanese culture from the beginnings to the present day. These units take a look at the main areas or works of literature, art and architecture, music, traditions and festivals, science and technology, fashion and food and drink, together with the people who have created and are still creating them.

- **Living in Japan now**
  Units 8–11 deal with aspects of contemporary Japanese society and the practicalities of living in present-day Japan: the way the political structure of the country is organized, education, work and leisure, and modern Japanese people and their customs and attitudes. The final unit looks at the country's political, economic and social relations with the wider world, and takes a glance at the future.

Taking it further

Each unit ends with a section entitled 'Taking it further', where you will find useful addresses, websites, suggested places to visit and things to see and do in order to develop your interest further and increase your knowledge.

The language

Within each unit you will encounter a number of terms in Japanese, whose meaning is given in English when they are first introduced. If you wish to put your knowledge into practice, we have provided in each unit a list of useful words and phrases to enable you to talk or write about the subject in question.

We have been careful in researching and checking facts, but please be aware that sources sometimes offer differing information. Of course a book of this length cannot contain everything you may need to know on every aspect of Japan. That is why we have provided so many pointers to where you can find further information about any aspect that you may wish to pursue in more depth. We trust that you will enjoy this introductory book, and that it will provide leads to further profitable reading, listening and visiting.

Phil Turk
Series Editor

author's note

Japanese words and phrases used in this book are written in **rōmaji** (the Roman alphabet: a, b, c etc.) and the pronunciation guide here will help you to be able to pronounce the words correctly. Key words are also given in Japanese script, both within the text and in glossaries at the end of each chapter.

Japanese names

This book follows the Japanese order: surname followed by first name. For example, the famous Japanese fashion designer known as **Issey Miyake** in Western countries, is referred to as **Miyake** (surname) **Issei** (first name) in Japan.

Pronunciation guide

The Japanese 'alphabet' is made up of a number of sounds created by combining the five vowels (a, e, i, o, u) with a consonant. These sounds are always pronounced in the same way.

The five Japanese vowels in order are:

a as in m<u>a</u>n
i as in h<u>i</u>t
u as in bl<u>u</u>e
e as in <u>e</u>nd
o as in h<u>o</u>t

Here is a bizarre 'headline' to help you remember these sounds:

M<u>an</u> <u>hi</u>ts t<u>wo</u> <u>e</u>xtra sh<u>o</u>ts!
a **i** **u** **e** **o**

A sound chart of the Japanese syllables follows. Bearing in mind the pronunciation of the five vowels as just explained, try working through the chart line by line, speaking out loud. Pronunciation of Japanese is very straightforward and there are pointers at the side of the chart to help you.

SOUND CHART

a	i	u	e	o	
ka	ki	ku	ke	ko	
sa	shi	su	se	so	
ta	chi	tsu	te	to	
					* **tsu** is an unfamiliar sound for English speakers; it is only one syllable (or beat); run the **t** and **s** together as you say them
na	ni	nu	ne	no	
ha	hi	fu	he	ho	
					* **fu** is a soft sound, between **f** and **h**. Your front teeth don't touch your lips as you say it; air is let out between your teeth and lips
ma	mi	mu	me	mo	
ya		yu		yo	
ra	ri	ru	re	ro	
					* **r** is a soft sound, somewhere between **r** and **l** and not like the French **r** sound
wa				n	
					* **n** has a full beat and has an **un** sound
ga	gi	gu	ge	go	
					* **g** as in *get* not *gin*
za	ji	zu	ze	zo	
ba	bi	bu	be	bo	
					* There is no **v** sound in Japanese and **b** is substituted for foreign words: the name *Valerie* becomes *Ba-ra-ri-i*, for instance
pa	pi	pu	pe	po	
da			de	do	

The final set of sounds in the sound chart consist of a consonant plus **ya, yu** or **yo**. These also have a single beat (i.e. they are one syllable) although English-speaking people sometimes mistakenly pronounce these sounds with two beats. For example, the first sound of the city name **Kyoto** is often wrongly pronounced **ki-yo** instead of **kyo**. Practise saying these sounds too:

kya	kyu	kyo	
sha	shu	sho	
cha	chu	cho	* **ch** as in *chance* not *character*
nya	nyu	nyo	
hya	hyu	hyo	
mya	myu	myo	
rya	ryu	ryo	
gya	gyu	gyo	
ja	ju	jo	* **ja** as in *jam* not German *ja*
bya	byu	byo	
pya	pyu	pyo	

How to pronounce words

Every syllable in Japanese is given equal stress, whereas in English we give more stress to some parts of the word than others. Look at this example:

(English)	a-**me**-ri-ca	stress is on **me**
(Japanese)	a-me-ri-ka	each syllable has equal stress

English-speaking people often add stress to Japanese words. For example:

Hi-ro-**shi**-ma rather than Hi-ro-shi-ma

To make your accent sound more authentic, try not to stress parts of words in the English style; instead give equal stress to each syllable.

Long syllables

In this book, a macron is used over vowels to indicate where the sound is a long sound. Let's look at an example to illustrate this:

Jūdō

The syllables with macrons are twice the normal length (two beats) but you say the word smoothly. However, macrons are not used in the case of placenames and other Japanese words when the name appears within an English context.

Double consonants

A double consonant indicates that you should pause slightly before saying it, as you would with this English word:

headdress (pause after 'hea' – not 'head dress')

You will come across these double consonants in Japanese: **kk, ss, tt, pp**. For example: Hokkaidō (north island of Japan).

Silent vowels

Sometimes **i** and **u** become almost unvoiced. For example:

Itadakimas(u) *I humbly receive* (said before eating)

Brackets are used to point out the unvoiced part.

Helen Gilhooly

the making of Japan

In this unit you will learn

- **about Japan's beginnings – the myths and the facts**
- **about the origins of the Japanese people**
- **about the geography and the climate**
- **about the main events and people of Japanese history**
- **about the world wars and Japan's post-war occupation**

An overview of Japan's history and geography will help to set the scene before exploring other aspects of Japanese life and to identify important influences on the development of a specifically Japanese heritage. It is inevitably an overview but the information at the end of this unit will provide pointers for those of you who wish to explore these topics further. There is also a timeline in Appendix 1 which gives an 'at-a-glance' view of Japanese history and the main players, events and places. Refer to this and the map on page 3 during your reading to help you get a feel for where the pieces of the Japanese 'jigsaw' fit.

Beginnings

The creation myths . . .

The earliest written records of the history of Japan date back to the 8th century. The mythical account of the creation of Japan recorded in these chronicles is as follows: A male god, Izanagi, and a female god, Izanami, dipped a heavenly jewelled spear into the sea from a floating bridge in the heavens. The drops of water from the spear fell to form the islands of Japan. Izanagi and Izanami stepped onto this land and went on to create the gods of the sea, river, mountains, fields, trees, water, fire, stone, metal, earth, sun, moon and so on. One of these, Amaterasu, the sun goddess, is regarded as the great great grandmother of the first (legendary) emperor of Japan, Jimmu. The word for emperor in Japanese, **tennō**, means *heavenly sovereign*. This myth was used increasingly from the late 19th century and in the years leading up to World War II to establish the emperor as '*sacred and inviolable*'.

. . . And the evidence

Geological and fossil evidence shows that the Japanese islands were formed at least 400 million years ago. Archaeological evidence indicates that they have been inhabited from 30,000 years ago or more. The map shows the islands of modern Japan in their setting on the east edge of the Asian continent.

During the Ice Ages the low sea levels made it possible for people to migrate to Japan from the Asian mainland (present-day Russia, China and Korea). From 10,000 BC (the end of the last Ice Age) the Japanese islands were finally separated from the Asian mainland.

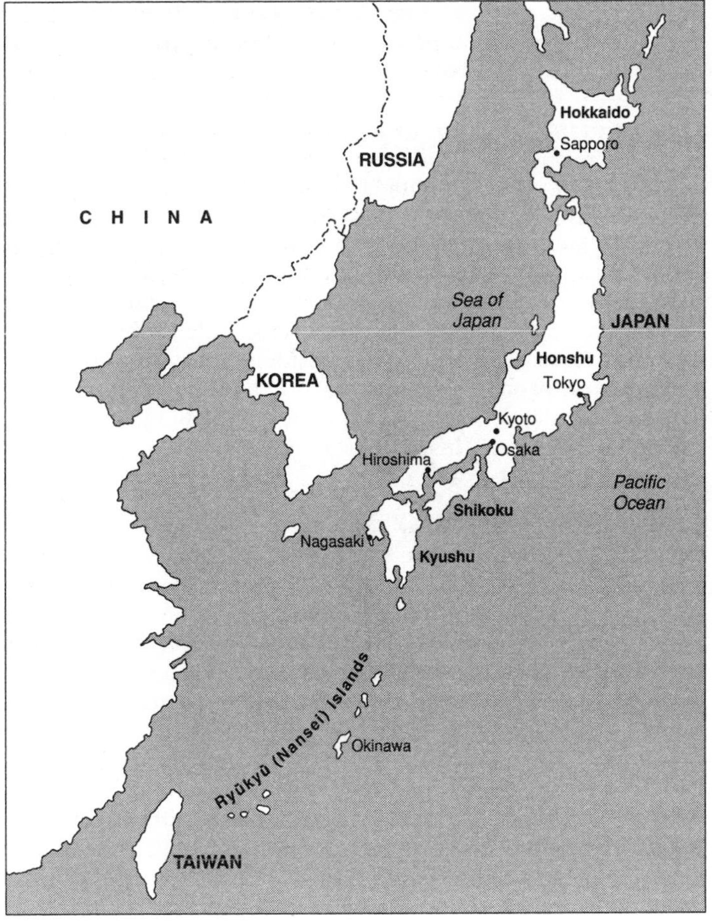

Map of modern Japan

The land (kokudo 国土)

Japan is a group of islands called an archipelago which stretches some 3,200 km (about the distance from London to Moscow) in a long arc and in area is about the size of California and 1.5 times the size of Britain. In total there are about 3,600 islands, some no more than a rock and many inhabited only by birds and other wildlife. The majority of the population lives on the four main islands, particularly the largest, **Honshū**. Seventy-five per cent of Japan is mountainous or hilly and 70 per cent is covered in forests. The mountain ranges mainly run along the middle of the island chain, forming Japan's 'backbone'. The majority of the population live in the flatter coastal areas which are predominantly urban.

Natural disasters (shizen saigai 自然災害)

Legend has it that a **namazu** (large catfish) lives under the islands of Japan and from time to time flicks its tail, causing **jishin** (earthquakes) and **tsunami** (tidal waves). The geological explanation is that Japan lies in an area where three tectonic plates meet and move against each other causing land subsidence, earthquakes, volcanoes and tidal waves. Japan, then, has to contend with a high incidence of natural disasters and Japanese people throughout history have had to adapt their lives to these dangers and rebuild their homes and livelihoods in the wake of them. This will certainly have played a part in shaping the Japanese way of life and thinking.

Earthquakes (jishin 地震)

On average, there are three **jishin** (earthquakes or tremors) every day somewhere in Japan but most are too slight to feel. The last big earthquake to hit Japan was in Kobe in 1995 when 5,000 people were killed and 300,000 left homeless. Tokyo, one of the largest cities in the world, lies over an earthquake-sensitive area and has had a major earthquake about every 70 years. The last, in 1923, killed over 100,000 people, with many deaths caused by house fires which the earthquake triggered off. If the 70-year pattern continues, another earthquake is long overdue in the Tokyo area. The **tsunami** which often accompany **jishin** can cause more damage. For example, the Chile earthquake in 1960 sent out a tidal wave across the Pacific which killed or injured over 1,000 Japanese.

Volcanoes (kazan 火山)

There are about 200 **kazan** in Japan, and more than 40 remain active today. In fact, Japan has about one-tenth of the world's active volcanoes and there were more than 30 volcanic eruptions in Japan in the 20th century alone. Even Japan's highest and sacred mountain, Mt Fuji, is a dormant volcano which last erupted in 1707. There are advantages to volcanoes, too, for the land around them contains naturally hot water which people can use in their homes and **onsen** (hot springs) for bathing.

Typhoons (taifū 台風)

Taifū, which often hit at the end of summer, can cause major flooding and property damage. Problems with flooding have been made worse by changes to rivers and surrounding plains. In the past, rivers were wide and formed Japan's plains but human intervention has created narrow, high-banked rivers which, during rainy months, flood frequently. Much of the previously marshy land around rivers has been reclaimed as residential areas which are also frequently under threat of flooding.

Climate (kikō 気候)

Japan enjoys a temperate climate with a wide range of temperatures from the subarctic zone in Hokkaido to the subtropical zone of Okinawa and the **Ryūkyū** islands. The average temperature of Hokkaido's warmest month is the same as the average temperature of Okinawa's coldest month! There are four distinct seasons with reasonably predictable weather. Spring (**haru**) is warm and mild and marked by Japan's famous **sakura** (cherry blossom) season. From March, the progress of the cherry blossom from south to north of the country is shown every night on the television. The reverse process starts in autumn (**aki**) when, from September, the leaves begin to change to splendid reds, oranges and yellows (called **kōyō**) and the progress once more is followed on TV, this time from north to south. The main rainy season called **baiu** or **tsuyu** begins at the end of spring and when it stops after two or so weeks, the skies clear and summer (**natsu**) begins. South-easterly winds from the Pacific mean that the summer is hot and very humid, especially in the cities. **Taifū** often arrive towards the end of the summer and there is also a weaker rainy season in October. Finally, north-westerly winds from the Asian continent create very cold winters (**fuyu**) with severe snow fall (**yuki**) on the Japan Sea side and cold winds on the Pacific Ocean side (the mountain ranges in between form a barrier between the two different types of weather).

FACTS AT A GLANCE

Total area	377,688 km^2	
Longest river	367 km (228 miles)	**Shinanogawa** (central Honshū)
Highest mountain	3776 m	Mount Fuji
Largest city	11.4 million	Tokyo (number includes Yokohama)
Population	127 million (year 2000)	
Dangerous animals		**mamushi** (viper), **kuma** (bear)

Origins of the Japanese people

From the archaeological evidence, the earliest inhabitants of Japan appear from about 30,000 BC on, but Japan was still connected to the Asian mainland and so a specific Japanese culture or people is not particularly clear. From the **Jōmon period** (10,000–300 BC) the Japanese islands were separate and in this and the next period – the **Yayoi period** (300 BC–AD 300) – there are a very small number (about 1,000 in total) of human bones which give some indication of the characteristics and origins of the earliest inhabitants of Japan. On such scanty evidence, however, archaeologists have been cautious to make definitive claims but some interesting theories have emerged.

The Ainu people

Frequently described as the '*indigenous people of Japan*', the Ainu are said to be the earliest inhabitants. They are thought to have no direct links with native Japanese people and had a separate language with different dialects (see p. 33). They lived over a wide area in the north part of Japan (North Honshu, Hokkaido and Sakhalin) but suffered much persecution and alienation from the Japanese, particularly during the 19th century, and because of this and disease their numbers declined. There are currently estimated to be about 24,000 Ainu living mainly in Hokkaido.

Archaeologists and physical anthropologists studying human bones from the Jomon period have identified characteristics which incorporate both Ainu and modern Japanese features whereas bones from the later Yayoi period are close in similarity only to Japanese physical features. This has led to one theory that the Jomon people were ancestors of the Ainu (but not exclusively) and the Yayoi were ancestors of the Japanese people. The places of origin also appear to be different because the Ainu lived in the north suggesting they originally came from North Asia (e.g. Siberia) whereas Japanese people of the Yayoi period clearly had connections with China and Korea. These connections are shown by the appearance in the Yayoi period of rice cultivation, iron and bronze which were all introduced from the Asian mainland. There is also a wealth of Yayoi archaeological findings with Korean features and influences.

Rulers and power: the beginnings

The Jomon people were hunter-gatherers who had a diet of plant foods, deer, wild pig, fish and shellfish. With the development of rice cultivation and the use of bronze and iron implements in the Yayoi period came the beginnings of a class society in the form of clans ruled over by chieftains. Evidence for this comes from both Chinese documents of the time and the appearance of large tomb mounds indicating the burial of important leaders.

FAMOUS PEOPLE
Queen Himiko

Chinese documents from the 3rd century AD talk about a religious female ruler in Japan (or *Wa* as Japan was called in China at the time). Her life and rule are shrouded in mystery but what can be said is that there were leaders emerging with considerable power and influence over ordinary people. Queen Himiko appears to have been surrounded by religious taboos which limited her movements and power. She had 1,000 female slaves, only one male was allowed to see her to take messages to her and she ruled through her younger brother who met with Chinese diplomats of the time. She ruled over an area known as Yamatai which was probably either North Kyushu or the Nara area.

Unification of Japan

The tomb building of the Yayoi period continued into the **Kofun** (tomb) period (AD 300–710) when huge keyhole-shaped and round tomb mounds were built. The tombs clearly indicate a class society and some of the largest ones would certainly have been the burial places of the imperial family and other high-ranking people. The dead were protected by burial goods and sculptures known as **haniwa** which were made using Korean and Chinese styles and craftsmanship. The biggest change of this period was the formation of the Yamato Court, the first unified state in Japan with its centre in Nara prefecture. There are still remains of palace buildings and clusters of keyhole tombs in this area today.

FAMOUS PEOPLE

Prince Shōtoku (AD 574–622) was an important figure during the Kofun period and the unification of Japan. He was a member of the imperial family and responsible for strengthening the power of the emperor at that time. He also promoted Buddhism and supervised the building of a number of Buddhist temples (see p. 96).

The imperial system and the sun goddess

The two earliest Japanese historical documents, *Kojiki* (AD 712) and *Nihon Shoki* (AD 720), were commissioned by emperors (male and female) during the Nara period (AD 710–794) to document the descent of the imperial line from Amaterasu, the sun goddess. These documents included legendary emperors and creation myths. In earlier times the emperor or empress was thought to have magical powers symbolized by three items known as the imperial regalia – a mirror, sword and jewels. In legend these were given by Amaterasu to her grandson who passed them on to the first emperor, Jimmu, and they were then successively passed on from emperor to emperor. The originals of the mirror and sword are allegedly kept in two Shinto shrines, one being the Ise Shrine, the centre of Shinto religion. The present emperor, Akihito, was handed the jewels and replicas of the other two items when he became emperor and they are kept in the imperial palace.

From 1889 onwards, with the creation of the constitution of the Empire of Japan, the emperor's divine powers were re-emphasized and he was described in the constitution as 'sacred and inviolable' although political power still remained with the government. In the 1920s and 1930s, ideas of the emperor's divinity and the superiority of the Japanese race over others grew. Extreme displays of devotion to the emperor and the Empire of Japan were shown during World War II in the suicidal actions of Japanese soldiers but on 1 January 1946 Hirohito declared to the Japanese people (and to the world) that the divinity of the emperor was ensconced in 'legends and myths' and denounced his divinity. The emperor is now a symbol of the state. There is a small minority who believe that the emperor should have his full status restored and another minority who believe the system should be abolished completely.

DID YOU KNOW?

The Japanese imperial system is the oldest hereditary monarchy in the world and the rule that only males can inherit the position is recent.

The first capital cities in Japan

With the unification of Japan came the building of capital cities from where the imperial court ruled. A new city and palace was built for each new emperor. One of the earliest known cities was **Fujiwarakyō** (AD 694–710) in Nara prefecture which was the first city to be built using the Chinese grid system (with streets running at right angles to each other in north–south and east–west directions). In AD 710 the capital moved to **Heijōkyō** (modern-day Nara City), marking the beginning of the Nara period (AD 710–794) when Buddhism became fully established and cultural achievements flourished. Nara City today is an important and fascinating historical site with temples and works of art and, an easy day trip from Kyoto, it is widely visited by Japanese and foreign tourists.

DID YOU KNOW?
Nara Daibutsu (Great Buddha of Nara)

16.2 metres high and made from gilt bronze, this was the largest statue in Japan when it was completed in AD 752. It is housed in the **daibutsuden** (Great Buddha Hall within the Tōdaiji Temple) which is the largest wooden building in the world and a national treasure.

LANGUAGE POINT

The word **kyō** (京) used in **Fujiwarakyō** and **Heijōkyō** means *capital city*. It forms part of the names of the cities of **Kyōto** (京都) meaning *Capital City* and **Tōkyō** (東京) meaning *Eastern Capital*.

A courtly culture – the Heian period (AD 794–1185)

The Heian period saw imperial rule at its height, the rise and fall of the powerful Fujiwara family and the blossoming of native Japanese culture and arts. The period began with the Emperor

Kammu who founded his capital in **Heiankyō** (modern-day Kyoto) and ended with the establishment of the first of the **shogunate** or military governments. During this time, a feudal system of private landownership gradually developed and the emperor's power weakened.

The Fujiwara family

This family was the first of a number of powerful families in Japanese history. By marrying daughters to future emperors and establishing members of their own family as regents they were able to rule through young, inexperienced emperors. They exerted great influence over the Heian Imperial Court and the most influential person was Fujiwara no Michinaga (966–1028). He ruled the imperial court as regent for more than 30 years, had four daughters married to emperors and was grandfather to three emperors.

FAMOUS PEOPLE
Murasaki Shikibu

Murasaki Shikibu is often referred to as the writer of the world's first novel. She was a lady-in-waiting at the imperial court in the 11th century and wrote her novel *The Tale of Genji* (***Genji Monogatari***) here as well as volumes of poetry and a diary. She portrays a fascinating picture of courtly life through her writings and we are drawn into a world of intrigue and romance, hinted at through allusions to meetings of lovers at night, the sending and receiving of love poems and the tread of a step outside a lady-in-waiting's room. She and her book are featured on the 2,000-yen bank note (see p. 21).

The rule of the shogun (1185–1868)

Shogun were military dictators who ruled Japan by establishing a system of law and order, supported by a strong and loyal military class. Their fortunes came and went and, over a period of almost 700 years, there were three shogunate governments, begun by three different powerful families, **Minamoto**, **Ashikaga** and **Tokugawa**. The title of shogun (military dictator) was given to **Minamoto no Yoritomo** and his descendants by the emperor in 1192. From then on, the emperor was at best a spiritual and cultural leader and at worst no more than a figurehead. Three key features of shogunate rule were **bushi** (the warrior class), **samurai** and **daimyo** (great landowners).

Bushi (warrior class 武士)

The first shogun, **Minamoto no Yoritomo,** created a three-part ruling class of warriors, designed to ensure loyalty from his followers. At the top were the vassals or **gokenin,** a small group of his most loyal followers who enjoyed many rewards for their loyalty such as the bestowing of land. Second in line were the samurai who in the Kamakura period (1185–1333) had a specific role and rank and, though not as high in rank as the **gokenin,** were well equipped and provided for by the shogun. Finally, there were the **zusa** or foot soldiers whose numbers grew over the period as wars increased.

The samurai (侍)

Samurai means '*one who serves*' and they were part of the ruling class from the 12th century until 1872 when the samurai class was abolished by the Meiji government. Their origins date back to the 8th century when they were an elite warrior class created by the emperor to keep peace in the provinces. By the 10th century they had control of the provinces and had built up substantial landownership and armies. During the first two shogunates, the samurai were essentially warriors but the peace brought about by the Tokugawa shogunate meant they no longer had a military role, although they continued to receive an allowance from the shogun. Some became government officials but many had no particular role and they were not allowed to be farmers. As a result, they had a great deal of leisure time and many began to pursue intellectual and cultural activities such as martial arts, Zen Buddhism and the tea ceremony. It was during this time that the Code of the Warrior (**bushidō**) reached its highest form with its emphasis on self-discipline, meditation, selflessness and absolute loyalty.

FAMOUS PEOPLE

The 47 ronin

This story is much loved and known in Japan even today. It is a great example of the absolute loyalty of samurai to their lord. A ronin was a masterless samurai. These 47 believed that their lord had been wrongfully dishonoured when he was forced to commit suicide by a retainer of the shogun. They swore that they would avenge their master and, in 1703, assassinated the retainer. The shogun had a dilemma because, although the samurai had broken the law, they had also shown loyalty, a virtue held in great esteem by the shogunate. However, they had challenged the authority of the shogun and so were ordered to commit suicide. They obeyed the order.

Samurai armour

The samurai were distinguished by their elaborate armour. The horned helmets and fierce-looking face masks were designed to frighten their enemy. Their weaponry consisted of a long sword (seen as the very soul of the samurai), a short stabbing sword, a long bow and a spear. The armour was made up of plates of iron and leather joined together and decorated with leather cords and silk.

DID YOU KNOW?
Swords and swordsmiths

The Japanese art of sword making dates back to the 8th century and the development of steel. Swords from this period onwards are still in existence today due to their fine craftsmanship and the high quality of the steel. Even the earliest swords were made from up to 100,000 layers of steel and were hammered to create extraordinary hardness and extremely sharp edges. Swordsmiths were held in high esteem and each school of swordsmiths would have their own individual markings on the swords they produced and would inscribe their name, the date and the place where the sword had been made on the blade. Swords were decorated with lines and patterns which became increasingly ornate during the Edo period. The samurai wore two swords, a short and a long one, and this was a distinguishing feature of their armoury. The Meiji government banned the wearing and making of swords although a few smiths were allowed to keep the art alive. After World War II many swords were destroyed or exported overseas but interest in sword making has grown in the post-war era.

The daimyo (大名)

The word **daimyo** means literally *large land* and it came to be applied to landholding military lords who were the masters of the samurai. **Minamoto no Yoritomo**, the first shogun, was a daimyo and samurai leader. Under the authority of the shogun, they were assigned land known as domains and held local power. They were the provincial military governors, keeping law and order at a local level and building castle towns where their samurai followers had residence. By the end of the second shogunate (Muromachi) they had become very powerful within their domains. Under the third shogunate (Tokugawa), their powers were restricted but in return for their absolute loyalty to the shogun, they were given considerable autonomy within their domains.

The Kamakura shogunate (1185–1333) (鎌倉幕府)

Towards the end of the Heian period, disputes over land and general unrest increased and the powers of the imperial and Fujiwara families declined. Between 1180–85, two warrior families, **Taira** and **Minamoto** fought to gain absolute power and finally, Minamoto no Yoritomo defeated the Taira family and established his headquarters in eastern Japan, at Kamakura (south of modern-day Tokyo) and became the first shogun. He established a dual ruling system with himself at the head of government and the emperor in Kyoto (west Japan) as spiritual and cultural leader. Yoritomo established a kind of centralized feudal system across the country through the appointment of provincial military governors who kept law and order in their area and land stewards who collected land taxes. Whereas the Heian period had been marked by the creative output of the imperial court in the areas of literature and arts, the Kamakura period was defined by the cult of the warrior with its ideals of self-discipline and achievement through action not writing.

DID YOU KNOW?

The word **kamikaze** used to describe the actions of World War II Japanese suicide pilots, means *divine wind* and was first used to describe the sudden storm which drove Mongol invaders back from the shores of Japan in 1274. The Mongol Empire in China was under the leadership of Kubilai Khan who declared war on

Japan when the Kamakura shogunate refused to recognize him as Emperor of China. He sent troops again in 1281 and, after two months of fighting, a typhoon once more brought the battle to a sudden end. The Buddhist and Shinto priests claimed the credit for such 'divine intervention' and made demands, not met, to be rewarded for their role.

The Muromachi shogunate (1333–1568) (室町幕府)

The Kamakura shogunate became increasingly unpopular and in 1333 was finally destroyed by the emperor. He in turn was challenged and overthrown by **Ashikaga Takauji** and so began the dominance in power of the Ashikaga family and the creation of the **Muromachi shogunate** (also known as the **Ashikaga shogunate**).

The Muromachi shogunate was marked by both important cultural developments and also increasing social unrest and loss of centralized power. The Ashikaga family were great patrons of the arts, and noh theatre, poetry, Zen Buddhism, painting and garden design flourished under them. They built such magnificent structures as the golden and silver pavilions. The headquarters of the shogunate were now based in Kyoto in order to keep control in west Japan with the emperor no more than a figurehead and a branch shogunate in Kamakura. The daimyo in the provinces became increasingly powerful and political power was fragmented. There were great advances in merchant trade and agriculture during this period, an increasing use of coins and the emergence of more towns especially around ports, markets and castles (built by daimyo to control their vassals).

FAMOUS PEOPLE

Oda Nobunaga (1534–82), Toyotomi Hideyoshi (1539–98) and Tokugawa Ieyasu (1543–1616)

These three men are known as the great unifiers of Japan in the time between the second and third shogunates after a century of civil war. The rise of powerful daimyo in the provinces had weakened the rule of the central shogun and, in 1573, **Oda Nobunaga** finally defeated the shogun and forced him to commit suicide, burning down much of Kyoto at the same time. He was a brilliant but ruthless leader who, at the height of his powers, had under his control over one-third of Japan. His life came to a violent end when, in 1582 he committed **sempuku** (or **harikiri** – death by disembowelment) rather than be captured by enemy troops. A famous **haiku** poem of the time summed up his ruthless character as follows: **Nakanunara**, **Koroshiteshimae**, **Hototogigu** which means 'The cuckoo won't sing? Then kill it'!

Toyotomi Hideyoshi who had been in the service of Oda Nobunaga continued the unification of Japan. He was a shrewd and ambitious leader who, by 1591, had reunified the whole of Japan through a series of brilliant military campaigns. Hideyoshi's ambitions reached beyond Japan and in 1592 and 1597 he launched two unsuccessful invasions of Korea which damaged relations with both Korea and China for many years after. In his last years he became increasingly suspicious of family and followers around him, convinced that there were plots against him. He made his nephew commit suicide and, suspicious also of the growing numbers of Westerners and Christian converts in Japan, he had 26 Christians put to death. Hideyoshi's relentless drive and ambition were summarized by a haiku poem as follows: **Nakanunara**, **Nakasetemise yo**, **Hototogisu** which means 'The cuckoo won't sing? Well then, I'll make it sing.'

Neither Hideyoshi or Nobunaga called themselves shogun, believing this title to belong only to descendants of the Minamoto family as originally decreed by the emperor. Instead, they ruled as regent through weak shoguns whom they put in power. **Tokugawa Ieyasu**, however, declared himself shogun with the agreement of the emperor and began the last and longest of the shogunates. He had been an ally of Oda Nobunaga and had to show him absolute loyalty by killing his own wife and forcing his eldest son to commit suicide. He created an alliance with Hideyoshi by sending him a son to adopt and in return was allowed to marry Hideyoshi's sister. After the death of Hideyoshi in 1598, he formed alliances with four powerful military families and won a victory over Hideyoshi's followers at the battle of Sekigahara in 1600. His greatest achievement was to bring peace and unity to Japan and, when he died in 1616, he was canonized as a Buddhist saint and buried at Nikko (to the north of Tokyo) which remains today as a fantastically ornate and sumptuous temple complex and mausoleum. Ieyasu's patience and strategic thinking were summarized by this haiku poem: **Nakanunara**, **Naku made matou**, **Hototogisu** which means 'The cuckoo won't sing? Then I'll wait until it does.'

The Tokugawa shogunate (1600–1868) (徳川幕府)

Ieyasu demanded the complete loyalty of the 260 daimyo under his control and in return he allowed them to keep their domains to rule over and keep peaceful. This was known as the **bakuhan** style of government with the shogun having national and the daimyo local authority. He expected absolute loyalty to be shown by adherence to his laws, provision of military service when needed, contribution to often expensive large-scale building projects and the keeping of law and order. He established social stability through the creation of a four class society – **shi-nō-kō-shō** – with the samurai as the ruling class at the top, then the farmers, craftsmen and, finally, merchants who were given low status because they did not produce anything themselves. They nevertheless became very rich during this period and formed a new bourgeois-style class who developed their own interests in culture and entertainment including **bunraku** (classical puppet theatre) and **kabuki** (classical theatre). There were other classes below this including teachers, lawyers and doctors and there were even two outcaste groups of people: **eta**, who did unclean work such as slaughtering animals and cleaning animal hides; and **hinin** (non-human), who guarded criminals, worked in the entertainment trade or begged.

Ieyasu set up his headquarters at Edo (modern-day Tokyo) and the era is called the Edo period. The imperial court continued to be based in Kyoto. Edo became a bustling commercial centre with a population of over 1 million by the 18th century, making it the largest city in the world at that time. (London had a

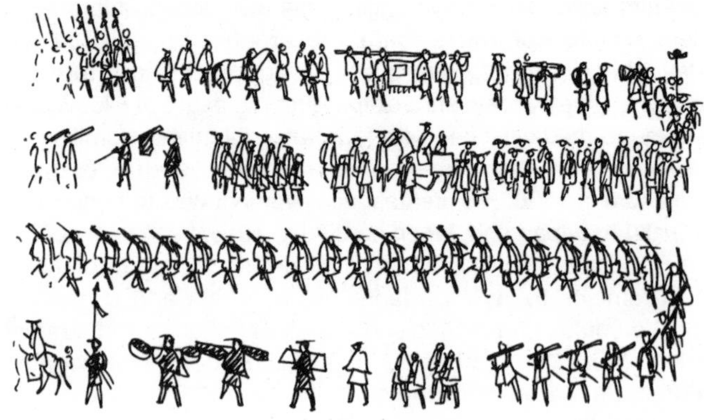

Daimyo procession

population of about 750,000 at this time.) The Edo period was also marked by the growth in number and size of cities as the daimyo established themselves and their followers in castle towns within their domains. Edo itself had at its centre a castle in which the ruling class were based. Around it were merchant and craftsmen's quarters as well as temple and shrine precincts. There are still a few remains of Edo buildings in Tokyo today and the imperial palace is built on the site of the castle with the remains of the moat and stone perimeter wall around it.

DID YOU KNOW?
Daimyo processions

Ieyasu devised a clever plan for ensuring daimyo loyalty and preventing them from accumulating too much wealth and power. All daimyo had to live in Edo every other year. They were allowed to return to their domain in alternate years to see to their affairs there but had to leave their wives and children in Edo effectively as hostages to ensure their loyalty to the shogun. The cost of moving family and followers between two places and keeping two residences ensured that the daimyo could not get too rich and while they were in Edo they were under the scrutiny of the shogun and his followers.

There were five transportation routes out of Edo, all of which had surveillance points to check that wives were not being smuggled out of Edo or guns being smuggled in. Such acts would have been interpreted as disloyalty and the daimyo would be disgraced and have his domain taken from him. The most famous route was the **tokaidō**, the Eastern Sea Road, which stretched 303 miles down to Kyoto. It has been immortalized through the woodblock prints of **Hiroshige** who captured many scenes of travel and travellers along the road and at its 53 station points. The modern-day **shinkansen** (bullet train) now follows this route although there are also a few remains of the original road and some of its stations.

Foreigners in Japan

Foreigners had visited and influenced Japan from the very earliest times, the earliest visitors being the Chinese and Koreans. The first Western visitors to Japan were shipwrecked Portuguese sailors in 1543. After this many missionaries, merchants and travellers began to arrive in Japan from Portugal, Spain, the Netherlands and England. Christianity was first introduced by Francis Xavier, a Spanish-born missionary working for the Portuguese, in 1549. The Portuguese and Dutch established trading treaties with Ieyasu and created trade posts in Nagasaki. However, from 1623, the shogunate became increasingly suspicious of Christians and the threat they might be to national government and in 1639 a policy of national seclusion was established in Japan. The Portuguese were banned completely because of their attempts to convert Japanese to Christianity. The Dutch and Chinese were allowed to stay but could only trade from a manmade island, **Deshima**, in Nagasaki bay. Japanese people were not allowed to travel abroad, with very few exceptions. This policy is also called the 'closed door' policy because effectively Japan cut off all contact with the outside world for over 200 years.

FAMOUS PEOPLE
William Adams (1564–1620) and Lafcadio Hearn (1850–1940)

William Adams was an English sailor who was shipwrecked off the coast of Kyushu in 1600 when serving on a Dutch ship. He became a friend and confidant of Tokugawa Ieyasu who bestowed on him a large estate in Miura near Edo. He was given the Japanese name **Miura Anjin** and his travels and adventures around Japan and South-east Asia have been written about in several Japanese and English books including ***Shogun*** by James Clavell, which was also produced as a film although criticized for its lack of historical fact.

Lafcadio Hearn was brought up in Ireland and went to Japan in 1890 where he married the daughter of a samurai. He was the first foreigner to become a Japanese citizen and took the Japanese name **Koizumi Yakumo**. He introduced the West to Japan through his writing and translations (see Taking it further, p. 27).

The Meiji restoration (明治維新) and the Meiji era 1868–1912 (明治時代)

The Meiji period is known as the beginning of Japan's modernization. Pressure began to be exerted on Japan from the 1850s to open up to foreign trade and in 1853 Commodore Matthew Perry sailed into Edo bay with a letter from the American president requesting the opening up of diplomatic and trade relations between America and Japan. The arrival of his black ships equipped with cannons made the request rather more of a demand but internal dissatisfaction with the government also played an important role and in 1854 the first of many treaties with Western countries was set up and Japan ended its 200 or so years of seclusion.

Changes after this were rapid and dramatic. The samurai leaders began to rise up against the weakened shogun and in 1868 they restored the emperor's powers and established him in the shogun's palace in Edo. Edo was renamed Tokyo (*Eastern Capital*) and the era was named Meiji (*Enlightened Rule*). Many samurai took on important roles in the new Meiji government and were instrumental in bringing about the modernization of Japan. In 1872 the daimyo domains were replaced with a centralized prefecture system and in 1872 the samurai class was abolished and class equality established. There was some opposition to this by rebel samurai but these revolts were quickly put down.

DID YOU KNOW?

Burakumin – Japan's outcaste community

Although the Meiji restoration abolished the class system, the outcaste group who worked, for instance, as undertakers, butchers and leather workers were still considered unclean and separate from the rest of society. They were called 'new commoners', but their status remained and the title **burakumin** endures today. Although now their jobs and roles are not limited to animals and the dead, it is the hereditary links to the old unclean class which are the subject of deeply embedded discrimination and they continue to have difficulties finding work or marrying outside of their own group. **Buraku** lists have been used by companies to check whether a person is of **buraku** descent and detectives can be hired to check a person's potential **burakumin** link before a marriage is agreed to. There are an estimated 3 million **burakumin** in Japan today and they form the largest minority group. Most Japanese do not admit openly to their existence and are not well informed about them but they continue to be discriminated against.

In the enthusiasm to 'modernize', leading figures of the Meiji government visited Europe and the USA from 1871–1873 as part of the **Iwakura** Mission, to find out more about the West and to take ideas back to Japan. A parliamentary system based on the German model was established (see p. 141), a national army system with conscription based on European models replaced the old samurai system and a national education policy was put into place. A massive westernization process gained momentum in all aspects of life including transportation, postal system, electricity, music, clothes, food, architecture and the arts, and the slogan **bunmei kaika** (*civilization and enlightenment*) was widely promulgated, particularly in the major cities. There are some fascinating photographs, pictures and woodblock prints of this time, capturing the rapid changes and sometimes incongruous mixture of Japanese and Western influences and fashions.

The impact of such rapid and momentous changes on Japanese people and lifestyles cannot be underestimated. This was a country which had been virtually closed for 230 years to all the major industrial, social and economic changes that had swept through the Western world. The only forms of transport had been horses, rickshaws, boats and foot. Within four years of the Meiji restoration, there was a steam-powered train between Tokyo and Yokohama followed by steam boats, the first car imports in 1899 and the first aeroplane in 1911. Buddhist beliefs and other superstitions had restricted the eating of meat but with the Meiji restoration came the demand for chicken, pork and dairy products which the majority of Japanese people would never have tasted before. And, as more and more Westerners appeared in Japan and Japanese began to visit Europe and the USA, the aura of mystery and fear surrounding foreigners began to lift, at least in the major cities.

FAMOUS PEOPLE
Three prominent Meiji figures

Of the many 'movers and shakers' of the Meiji period, three have been honoured with their faces printed on three of the Japanese bank notes. On the 1,000-yen note is **Natsume Sōseki** (1867–1916), on the 5,000-yen note is **Nitobe Inazu** (1862–1933) and on the 10,000 note is **Fukuzawa Yukichi** (1835–1901).

Natsume Sōseki was a novelist who went to England as a government student in 1900. In his writing he explored the dilemmas and contradictions posed by the new modern Japan and the remaining elements of the previous feudalistic society (see also p. 52).

5000
Y634682F 子供銀行券
五千円
子供銀行
Y634682F
5000

10000

1000

NIPPON GINKO
2000
2000
2000 YEN

(see p. 10)

Nitobe Inazu was a writer and educator, his writings were widely translated into English and he was the best-known Japanese writer in the West of that time. He spent three years each in the USA and Europe. His most famous work is *Bushido: The Soul of Japan*, written in 1899, which laid out the principles of traditional Japanese moral thinking. His famous saying, now the motto of Hokkaido University, was **Boys, be ambitious**.

Fukuzawa Yukichi was an educator, writer and a great promulgator of Western thought in Japan. His father had been a low-ranking samurai and Fukuzawa had been born into an impoverished family. He hated all that feudalism stood for and studied Dutch and later English. In 1860 he joined the first Japanese study missions to the USA and then Europe. He was a firm advocator of human rights, an idea previously unknown to Japanese people and a famous quote from his writings was **All men are equal under the sun**. His works were highly acclaimed in Japan and he is considered to this day as one of the founders of modern Japan.

Events leading to World Wars I and II

The modern world which Japan entered was one where exploration, colonialism and imperialism had featured very prominently over a long period of time. When Commodore Perry arrived in Edo Bay in 1854, the treaty which the Japanese subsequently signed was widely held to be unequal and weighted in the favour of the Americans. Other such unequal treaties followed with Germany, Britain, the Netherlands and Russia. There was much dissatisfaction in Japan with this 'second class' treatment but, as Japan made rapid changes and developed its own national army, it began international power policies of its own starting with an unequal treaty with Korea in 1875. This was followed by the Sino-Japanese war (1894–5) with China from which Japan emerged the victor and China signed a treaty acceding land to Japan. At this point, however, Russia, France and Germany interfered and persuaded Japan to give some land back, leading to domestic unrest and accusations by the Japanese that their government was weak. Japan then entered into the Russo-Japanese War (1904–5) with Russia over land in China and Korea, resulting in the Russo-Japanese Alliance in which each agreed to respect the other's territories in Asia. These wars, however, were to set the scene for Japan's military activity over the next 50 years.

Colonization and World War I

In 1910 Japan invaded Korea and it remained a colony until 1945. The Koreans were forced to learn and speak Japanese as their first language, they had to have Japanese names, the teaching of Korean history was banned and hundreds of thousands of Koreans were moved to Japan as labourers (by the end of World War II there were more than 2 million Koreans in Japan). In 1914 Japan entered World War I as an ally of Britain and, after capturing German territory in China and the Pacific, forced China to sign treaties recognizing Japan's gains. By 1918, Japanese military, imperial and economic power had reached new strengths and the production of munitions to support the war effort had given Japanese exports a huge boost.

Increase of militarism and extreme nationalism

The 1920s saw recession, cuts in wages and the end of the prosperity enjoyed during the war. There were many movements and demonstrations calling for democracy in Japan, the Communist Party was established in 1922 and it was a time of great growth in radical political parties and thinkers. At the same time, much of Japan was still rural and in these areas traditional and conservative values were deeply rooted. A growing number of right-wing activists believed that the social order was being weakened by this new left-wing thinking and in the same year (1925) that all men over the age of 25 were given the vote, a peace preservation law was passed to control the spread of 'dangerous thinking'. On one day in 1929, about 700 suspected Communists were arrested and more than half were charged. By the 1930s, reaction against intellectual and left-wing movements had spread and a secret political police organization was used to track down and remove any kind of political dissent. Ideas of democracy were gradually being removed by militarism and an authoritarian government, as Japan increasingly isolated itself from the West and from Asia.

Japan enters World War II

Japan's policies in Asia became increasingly militaristic and aggressive and, following its conquest of the Chinese state of Manchuria (renamed by the Japanese as **Manchukuo**) and the establishment of the last Chinese emperor as the puppet head of state, it withdrew from the League of Nations under increasing criticism of its actions. The Nanking massacre of 1937–8 when an estimated 140,000 Chinese were killed, was publicly condemned, even from within Japan, but any 'liberal' or 'leftist' objectors were now quickly silenced by arrest or worse. In 1940, Japan signed a tripartite pact with Germany and Italy then moved into Indo-China (now Vietnam) in 1941. In response, the USA blocked all shipments of raw materials, including oil, to Japan and the Japanese military, desperate to protect the territory it had already gained and to gain access to oil resources in South-east Asia, decided the only way forward was to take US naval forces in the Pacific by surprise, then move swiftly to capture American, British and Dutch-occupied territory including oil-rich Indonesia (then Dutch East Indies). And so, on 7 December 1941, under Prime Minister Tōjō Hideki, the Japanese bombed the US naval forces at Pearl Harbor, Hawaii, and declared war against the USA, Britain and the Netherlands although never with the military backup of Germany and Italy which had been hoped for.

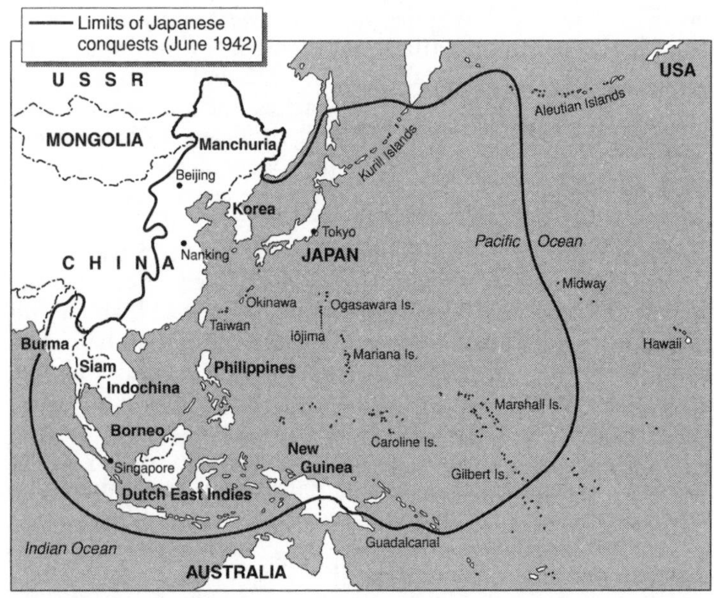

Extent of the Japanese empire by 1942

Prisoners-of-war

Japan always knew that their military strength could not match that of the Americans or the Allied forces but their surprise tactics worked and they marched through South-east Asia, taking soldiers and civilians prisoner as they went. Many thousands of prisoners died at the hands of the Japanese, some exhausted from being forced to walk hundreds of miles, some from starvation or disease contracted in the internment camps, others were executed by the Japanese soldiers. Perhaps most infamous was the Burma–Thailand (Siam) Railway, planned by the Japanese to carry raw materials and supplies through South-east Asia and known as the Death Railway because of the thousands of British, British Commonwealth and American POWs and forced local labourers who died building it.

The Japanese people and the war

In the 1930s and 1940s, Japan's military leaders had control of the government, the cabinet and the emperor, and made political decisions based on military assessments, increasingly without consulting the government. Any civilian cabinet minister who objected ran the risk (frequently carried out) of assassination. As with other countries at war, the Japanese people were urged, through nationalist and patriotic slogans, to do their duty for their country, but more extreme steps were taken to ensure absolute loyalty and unquestioning obedience. In 1941 **kokumin gakkō** (compulsory schools) were introduced to indoctrinate the young in allegiance to the emperor and country. The militaristic education included military drills and factory work and children even had to have their hair cut in the close-cropped style of Japanese soldiers. The spirit of **bushidō** (code of the warrior) was instilled in every soldier and the belief was promulgated that Japan could win the war because of its fighting spirit and its position as a divine nation. When the fortunes of war turned against Japan, the military government filtered 'selected' information through to the people which spoke of the heroic deeds of the Japanese soldiers and the aggressive actions of the enemy. The young men chosen to carry out the kamikaze attacks towards the end of the war were treated as heroes and there was much footage of soldiers being cheered on by friends and family as they walked to their planes. In fact, some of those who survived the attacks have talked since about their fear and unwillingness, the deep sorrow of their families and the certainty of death if they disobeyed orders. At the end of the war, with almost 1 million civilians dead because of the fierce bombing raids, the ordinary Japanese person felt both ashamed at the defeat and cheated by those in power.

Setbacks and resistance

The turning point of the war was in June 1942 when the Japanese were beaten by the Americans in the naval battle of the

Midway, north of Hawaii. The Japanese did not have the men or material resources to control the territories they had captured and the USA used submarine blockades to prevent oil and metal ores being carried back from South-east Asia to Japan. The Japanese were forced to give up the territories they had won and to concentrate on protecting their homeland which was now the target of Allied fire bomb attacks. By 1945 most of Japan's major cities had been destroyed by air raids and on 19 February, American forces landed on **Iōjima** Island, 48 km (30 miles) south of the Japanese mainland. They needed this island as a base for B-29s carrying out bombing raids on Japan but it was a hard-fought battle, lasting almost a month and resulting in the deaths of 20,000 Japanese and 7,000 Americans. The people of **Iōjima** had been urged to fight to the death because the US soldiers would act like barbarians and show no mercy. This pattern continued in Okinawa with the deaths of virtually the entire Japanese force of 110,000 men, 150,000 civilians and 50,000 Americans. When the Japanese government refused to accept the terms of the Potsdam Declaration which demanded '*unconditional surrender*', the US government decided that atomic warfare was necessary to avoid even greater loss of life.

Hiroshima and Nagasaki

Japan is the only country to have had **genshi bakudan** (atomic bombs) used against it. Several possible cities, all with substantial munitions factories, were chosen and President Truman stated specifically that the aim was '*to make a profound psychological impression*'. On 6 August 1945, the weather was clear over Hiroshima and so the B-29 bomber *Enola Gay* flew over the city and dropped the uranium-235 atomic bomb. When Japan did not immediately surrender, a second plutonium bomb was dropped over Nagasaki on 9 August. About 140,000 people in Hiroshima and 70,000 in Nagasaki died immediately or within a few months of the bombing, amounting to about 50 per cent of the population of each city (compared to a 17 per cent loss in the heaviest conventional bombing). **Hibakusha** (atomic bomb survivors) continue to suffer the after-effects of radiation-related diseases and many thousands have died in the years since the bombing. Both Hiroshima and Nagasaki have peace parks and museums dedicated to the memory of those who died and to peace. Both museums give very balanced accounts of the war and the atomic bombs (although Hiroshima's museum for many years almost ignored the fact that Japan had been involved in a war) and both cities are very active in caring for **hibakusha** and campaigning for world peace. Mayors of both cities have several times been the target of attacks by extreme right-wing groups.

Surrender and occupation

Even after the bombing of Nagasaki, the military were still resistant to surrender but the emperor intervened and, although army officers tried to stop the broadcast, Emperor Hirohito announced Japan's surrender in a radio broadcast on 15 August 1945. People were shocked to hear the emperor's voice which had never been heard before in public and many found it difficult to understand his formal court style of language. Japan was occupied by US forces for nearly seven years during which time war crime trials were held (see also p. 94), 948 military and political leaders were executed, including the notorious wartime prime minister Tōjō Hideki, the emperor publicly renounced his divinity and Japan's democratization process was put into motion (see also p. 154).

FAMOUS PEOPLE
Tōjō Hideki (1884–1948)

Tōjō was Japan's prime minister during World War II (1941–4) and a key player in Japan's military expansion and wartime aggression. Immediately after the war he attempted suicide but he was eventually tried as a Class A war criminal and hanged on 23 December 1948.

Altogether, 3 million Japanese people died during World War II and in 1945 the outlook was bleak as Japan came to terms with its humiliating defeat, the devastation of cities and industry, a severe shortage of food and an economy in crisis. The units that follow, in particular 7–12, will explore the ways in which post-war Japan rose to the challenge and rebuilt itself to become the second biggest economy and an important participant on the world's stage but will also examine issues about the war which continue to affect Japan's international relations and the perceptions of those who suffered under Japanese occupation.

Taking it further

There is a wealth of Japanese information, generally updated on a regular basis and some of the main website addresses are listed here. These will be referred to again in later units and you will need to come back to the addresses in this unit. Some are English-only or Japanese-only sites and for some you can choose your language from the menu. You can also search for your own information using a good search engine or site – **Yahoo.com** has a Japan-dedicated site (enter **Japan** in the Search box) and gives you the opportunity to use it in Japanese or English.

Japanese embassies all over the world have JICC (Japan information and cultural centres) and these are a great source of information on all aspects of Japan. You can also borrow videos and audio materials, and can subscribe to a number of monthly newsletters and magazines, some free, including a monthly update of Japan-related events and exhibitions in your country. Go to **http://www.embjapan.org** and there are links to every Japanese embassy and JICC in the world.

http://www.jinjapan.org/ or **http://jin.jcic.or.jp** will take you to JIN (Japan Information Network) which has a number of very useful links. From the menu select **Japan Atlas** for information on historic sites, nature and regions; take a virtual tour of Japan by selecting **regions and cities**; or search for further websites on Japan by selecting **Japan Web Navigator**.

Books

Introducing Japan, Donald Richie (Tokyo and New York, Kodansha International, 1992)

The Roads to Sata: A 200-mile Walk through Japan, Alan Booth (New York and Tokyo, Weatherhill, 1985)

Glimpses of an Unfamiliar Japan, Lafcadio Hearn (1894)

Matsuo Basho's 1689 travel diary (*Oku no Hosomichi*, *The Narrow Road to the Deep North*, Harmondsworth, Middlesex and Baltimore, MD, Penguin Books, 1966)

The Tale of Genji, Murasaki Shikibu (tr. Edward Seidensticker, Penguin Books, 1976)

The Tale of Murasaki, Liza Dalby (Vintage, 2001). A novel about the writer of *The Tale of Genji* and Heīan court life

A Book of Five Rings, Miyamoto Musashi (New York, Overlook Press; London, Allison and Busby, 1974). About bushidō (warrior code) and swords

For detailed general information

Cultural Atlas of Japan, Martin Collcutt *et al.* (Oxford, Phaidon; New York, Facts on File, 1988)

Japan: An Illustrated Encyclopedia (Tokyo, Kodansha, 1993) (CD-ROM version also available)

GLOSSARY

自然災害 **shizen saigai**	*natural disasters*
地震 **jishin**	*earthquake*
津波 **tsunami**	*tidal wave*
火山 **kazan**	*volcano*
台風 **taifū**	*typhoon*
気候 **kikō**	*climate*
春 **haru**	*spring*
夏 **natsu**	*summer*
秋 **aki**	*autumn*
冬 **fuyu**	*winter*
桜 **sakura**	*cherry blossom*
紅葉 **kōyō**	*autumn colours*
梅雨 **tsuyu** or **baiu**	*rainy season*
古事記 **kojiki**	*8th-century historical document*
日本書記 **nihon shoki**	*8th-century historical document*
大仏 **daibutsu**	*Great Buddha*
将軍 **shōgun**	*shogun, general*
幕府 **bakufu**	*shogunate*
武士 **bushi**	*warrior, samurai*
武士道 **bushidō**	*way of the warrior*
侍 **samurai**	*samurai*
大名 **daimyō**	*feudal lord*
維新 **ishin**	*restoration*
時代 **jidai**	*era*
世界第二次大戦 **sekai dainiji daisen**	*World War II*
原子爆弾 **genshi bakudan**	*atomic bomb*

02 the Japanese language

In this unit you will learn

- **about the origins of the Japanese language**
- **about its links with other languages**
- **about its main features**
- **about the three writing systems**

Nihon meaning *Japan* and **go** meaning *language* are combined into the word **nihongo** – *Japanese language* 日本語. And when the Japanese themselves learn their language at school they call it **kokugo** meaning *mother tongue*. This unit will outline some of the main features of **nihongo**.

Is Japanese difficult?

This is a question often asked either by people considering taking up Japanese or by people impressed that someone is learning Japanese. Sixteenth-century European missionaries to Japan described Japanese as *'the Devil's tongue'*. Actually, answering the question depends on how you view language learning in general. You could argue that every language has its difficult features and certainly English is a good example with its huge number of irregular verbs and its complex (and seemingly illogical) grammar and spelling rules. By comparison, Japanese has fairly straightforward grammar rules, very regular verbs and it is spelt and pronounced phonetically. Of course, there are features of the language which are difficult or unfamiliar to the non-Japanese learner, such as the use of respectful language, the very wide vocabulary and the sentence structure. However, learners of Japanese often comment that the comparatively simple grammar rules and pronunciation make Japanese an easy language to begin to master and that the main difficulty or challenge is the writing system, although it is also extremely interesting. It is worth remembering that many Japanese people find English a hugely complicated language to speak and find it difficult to know, for example, when to use *the* or *a* or a plural because features like these do not exist in Japanese.

Who speaks Japanese?

Approximately 127 million people in Japan as well as Japanese emigrants around the world, in particular in North and South America. During the Meiji period (1868–1912) when there was a shortage of work in Japan and overpopulation problems, about 850,000 Japanese emigrated to the USA (in particular, California and Hawaii), about 12,000 to Canada (mainly British Columbia) and, until World War II, about 190,000 to Brazil. The **issei** (first generation) spoke Japanese as their first language and many of the **nisei** (second generation) did so too, mainly attending Japanese schools and mixing only with the

Japanese communities. By contrast, most **sansei** and **yonsei** (third and fourth generations) have been assimilated into their countries of birth, do not speak Japanese and have never visited Japan. In recent years, countries such as Australia have become emigration destinations for well-off retired Japanese couples and, as Japanese communities have grown in areas such as Queensland, Australians have expressed concerns about caring for this elderly Japanese population.

Japanese is also the second language of older Chinese and Korean people who are either resident in Japan or were forcibly taught Japanese during the occupation of their countries (see pp. 22–3, 34). Since the 1970s, and in line with Japanese industrial growth abroad, more and more people around the world have begun to learn Japanese as a foreign language. This is particularly so in countries around the Pacific Rim such as East Asia, South-east Asia, Australia, New Zealand and North America. It has become the fifth most popular foreign language in the USA, it is the first modern foreign language on the curriculum in many Australian and New Zealand secondary schools and in the UK it is now the most popular minority language (after French, German, Spanish and Italian) taught in secondary schools. The Japanese government is encouraging more foreign students to study in Japanese institutions of higher education and in 2000 there were over 50,000 foreign students in Japan with the highest number from Korea, China and Taiwan but substantial numbers from the USA and Brazil too. An estimated 3 million people around the globe, including 2 million Chinese, are currently learning Japanese.

What are the origins of Japanese?

Japanese is part of a family of languages known as the Altaic languages and its origins can be traced back to Central Asia. Included in this group is Korean to which Japanese is closest in structure. For example, the Japanese sentence order (subject object verb, see p. 35) is the same in Korean. Both languages have several layers of polite language (see p. 36), and both have a phonetic writing system of consonants and vowels grouped into syllables. Interestingly, Japanese also has some similarities in vocabulary with the Malayo-Polynesian group of languages which cover a wide area from Taiwan to Easter Island in the South Pacific, perhaps as a result of ancient Polynesian explorations and even migrations around the Japanese coast.

Examples of vocabulary include words for coastal plants and sealife which would not have been part of Central Asian languages. Chinese and Japanese languages do not share common origins but the Japanese writing system originated in China, a country which has had a very important influence on Japanese culture (see Units 3, 4 and 5).

Are there other languages in Japan?

The only other indigenous language is Ainu, spoken by the Ainu people. The origins of this language are unclear and up to now it has been grouped with some north-eastern Asian languages. There is no evidence of ethnic links between the Ainu and the Japanese people and although there are many similarities with Japanese (for example, *god* is **kami** in Japanese and **kamui** in Ainu), these are most probably the result of close contact between the two peoples and a two-way exchange between the languages. The Ainu language has the same five vowels as Japanese but only 12 consonants whereas Japanese has 19. The sentence order of SOV (subject, object, verb) is the same as Japanese (whereas English is SVO) and, like Japanese, there is no plural or gender. Ainu dialects were once very numerous but, by the time people began studying Ainu from the end of the 19th century, only two remained, that of the Hokkaido Ainu and the Sakhalin Ainu (an island north of Hokkaido). These two dialects were so different that speakers of each could hardly understand the other. There has never been a written Ainu language and stories and songs were passed down orally from generation to generation. The Ainu language today is spoken by only a small number of Ainu people living on the north island of Hokkaido and very few of these use it as their main language. It has essentially been a dying language, disappearing rapidly as the Ainu people are assimilated more and more into the general population but there have been moves recently to preserve both Ainu language and culture. Evidence of the Ainu language can be seen in place names, for example, **betsu** means *river* and, if you look at a detailed map of Hokkaido, you will find many places around the coast which end in **betsu** (Noboribetsu, Mombetsu and Shibetsu for example).

There are also the **ryūkyū** dialects (**ryūkyūgo**), spoken by inhabitants of Okinawa and neighbouring islands in the far south of Japan. These are closely related to Japanese but cannot be understood by speakers of standard Japanese. The **Ryūkyū** people lived on the Okinawan islands from at least 3000 BC and had contact with both Japan to the north and Taiwan to the south. A number of dialects appear to have developed but one, the **shuri** dialect, became dominant from the 15th century AD. This was gradually replaced from the Meiji period by **hyōjungo** (standard Japanese). Main differences between the dialects and **hyōjungo** are the pronunciation of the syllables and the endings of verbs and adjectives. For example, **tokoro** (*place*) is **tukuru** in **ryūkyūgo, tori** (*bird*) is **tui** and the **masu/masen** (*do/don't*) verb endings become **biin/biran**. **Ryūkyūgo** dialects are still in common use today but all users are also fluent in standard Japanese.

Finally, older Korean and Chinese residents in Japan, brought over to Japan as a result of Japanese colonialism from 1910 onwards, still use their native language although their children and grandchildren mainly speak Japanese as their first language (but there are Korean schools where the first language is Korean). English is the first foreign language taught in Japanese schools although many Japanese are not confident in using it. The largest numbers of foreign residents in Japan are (in descending order) Korean, Chinese, Brazilian, Philippino, American and Peruvian.

Main features of the Japanese language

Japanese is relatively easy to learn to speak at beginner's level and the language has some interesting features.

Regular grammar rules

There is no masculine and feminine in Japanese, no specific plural (although there are a few exceptions such as the addition of **tachi** when talking about people in the plural, for example, **watashi** means *I* and **watashi**<u>**tachi**</u> means *we*) and no conjugation of verbs. In other words, the verb ending remains the same regardless of who does the action (compare with English, *I go*, *he goes* and so forth which are all covered by **ikimasu** in Japanese). There are only two main tenses, the past and the present/future, with a 'probably' used for future events which are not certain (e.g. the weather). There is no definite article (*the*, *a*, etc.) and instead of prepositions (*in*, *to*, *from*, etc.), Japanese has postpositions (that is, the word is placed after not before – **gakkō kara** means *school from*). One unusual feature (for Western learners) of Japanese is that adjectives as well as verbs change their endings according to tense, negative or affirmative statements as well as other forms. Look at the following table.

English adjective	**Japanese adjective**
It is delicious	**oishii**
It is not delicious	**oishikunai**
It was delicious	**oishikatta**
English verb	**Japanese verb**
I eat	**tabemasu**
I don't eat	**tabemasen**
I ate	**tabemashita**

Sentence order

Japanese sentence order has the basic pattern of SOV (subject object verb) with the verb spoken at the end of the sentence, as sometimes in German. English, by way of contrast, has the pattern of SVO (subject verb object). For example, in English we would say '*I* [subject] *eat* [verb] *meat* [object]' which in Japanese translates as **watashi wa niku o tabemasu** meaning literally '*I meat eat*'. In addition, the subject is not used in Japanese if it is clear who or what the subject is and so **niku o tabemasu** also can be translated as '*I eat meat*'. This means that, essentially, Japanese sentence order is the reverse of English and the main point to remember is that the verb comes *at the end* of the sentence.

Pronunciation (hatsuon 発音)

Japanese has relatively easy pronunciation rules. Sounds are created by combining the five standard vowel sounds, **a**, **i**, **u**, **e** and **o**, with one of the 19 consonant sounds (e.g. **ka**, **ki**, **ku**, **ke**, **ko**). These sounds are always pronounced in the same way and so, once learnt, are easy to remember and use. Unlike English, there is no stress accent; in other words, every syllable has equal stress. For example, the city name **Hiroshima** should be pronounced Hi-ro-shi-ma and not Hi-**ro**-shi-ma or Hi-ro-**shi**-ma as it is often mistakenly pronounced by foreigners. One interesting point about pronunciation is that, unlike English, there is no separate *l* and *r* sound and the Japanese can only pronounce these as a single sound, somewhere between the two. This has led to a number of confusions and misunderstandings for Japanese people when trying to distinguish between, for example, the English words *lamb* and *ram*, *lice* and *rice* or *election* and *erection*. The foreign learner of Japanese should aim to keep the *r* sound soft (not like the French *r*) and aim at a sound somewhere between *r* and *l* (see p. ix for more on pronunciation).

One other important feature of Japanese pronunciation is that of pitch. For example, words using identical sounds are distinguished in pronunciation through use of high and low pitch. The word **hashi** can mean either *bridge* or *chopsticks*. **Háshi** means *chopsticks* and **hashí** means *bridge* (the acute accent above a syllable shows it has high pitch). Of course, context will also usually indicate the meaning of a word, and pitch is neither as strong as stress accent nor as complex as tonal languages (e.g. Chinese).

Standard Japanese (hyōjungo 標準語)

Although there are a large number of local dialects (**hōgen**) in Japan, they do not vary as greatly as some of the European regional languages and, as a result of centralized compulsory education and the influence of television and radio, the vast majority of Japanese people speak **hyōjungo** or standard Japanese (based on the Tokyo dialect) alongside any local dialect. One dialect which is still widely used today is the kansai dialect (which includes the cities of Kyoto and Osaka). An example of this is the word **okini** meaning *thank you* (in standard Japanese the word is **arigatō**).

Levels of speech

A more complicated feature of Japanese is the use of different levels of language depending on the status, age and sex of the person being addressed. Before looking at this in greater depth, here is a simple example of how it works. In Japan, shop assistants in department stores are trained to show extreme respect for all customers. After all, the saying goes **O-kyakusama wa kamisama desu** – *the customer is god*. Therefore, when speaking to customers (e.g. in the elevator or over the tannoy system) they use humble language to refer to themselves and the store and respectful language to address the customer. Customers, however, because of their higher status, only need to speak to the assistant in neutral polite or plain language.

Now let's take this apart a little. There are three main levels of polite language (also called honorific language or **keigo**). These are humble (**kenjōgo**), respectful (**sonkeigo**) and neutral polite (**teineigo**). Humble and respectful language is used when the person being addressed is of a higher ranking (age, sex and work status can all be factors). In our example, this was the customer. Humble language is used by the speaker in referring to themselves or their in-group (e.g. family or company). In our example, this was the shop assistant and the store. It has the effect of lowering the speaker's status and deepening respect for the person being addressed. Respectful language is used by the speaker in referring to the person being addressed and anything connected with them. In this situation, the person being addressed (the customer) would usually reply using more informal language to reflect their higher status.

Neutral polite language is used when there is no need to show specific respect to someone. For example, it would be used by two people who didn't know each other very well but were of the same social status. And finally, plain language is used in more informal situations (e.g. between two friends) or by a higher ranking person to a more junior person.

In case you still feel baffled by these levels of speech, take comfort in the fact that young Japanese people today are using honorific language less and less. In fact, some companies have taken steps to train new employees in the correct use of honorific language because they are no longer using it naturally. In any case, as a foreign speaker of Japanese, it is perfectly acceptable to use the neutral polite forms (**masu/desu**) and, if you are unsure, you could be in danger of using honorific language inappropriately. There are certain set phrases, however, which you can gradually add to your repertoire and feel safe in using. (There are a few at the end of this unit.)

Feminine and masculine language (joseigo 女性語 danseigo 男性語)

There are particular words, language structures and conventions used specifically by women or men which add another dimension to the Japanese language. There are two types of feminine language (**joseigo**). First, there are specific words, grammar and ways of speaking which are used by females. These date back to the language of the court ladies (**nyobo kotoba**) in 14th-century Japan (but there are even earlier references to feminine language). Examples used in today's society include the addition of **o** and **go** before certain words to make them sound more genteel. For example, **o-hashi,** *chopsticks* and **o-tearai**, *toilet* (literally '*the hand-washing place*'). Men also use these additions but not to the same extent as women. There are also feminine words for saying *I* – **atashi** and **atakushi** – and the use of the sentence ending **wa**. A final example is the use of higher pitch when speaking. These all have the effect of making women's speech seem more genteel, gentle and non-challenging. It is interesting to note that women nowadays sometimes use masculine language in situations where they need to appear more assertive and strong.

Second, women tend to use more polite forms of the language in a wider set of situations than men. Therefore, this isn't specifically feminine language as both sexes use it and it is true to say that in most societies around the world there is a tendency for women to speak more politely in given situations.

Masculine language (**danseigo**) is distinguished by specific words only used by men (e.g. **boku** meaning *I*), distinctive sentence endings, low pitch and a greater use of plain forms. Traditionally it is used when the speaker wishes to express his authority and strength towards juniors or women. Interestingly, in recent times men (and women) are judging the appropriateness of specific situations rather than simply social standing to decide whether to use assertive, neutral or more gentle language.

Swearwords (nonoshiri no kotoba) and taboo expressions (imi kotoba)

The Japanese language does not have swearwords in the same tradition as Western countries, with strong religious or sexual associations. Japanese swearwords are fewer and milder – words such as **baka** and **bakayaro** translate as *idiot* or *fool*. Even the word **kuso** does not have the same impact as the English *shit*. A visit to the cinema exemplifies these differences because a subtitled American film, rich in a wide range of expletives, is translated using a tiny range of words (mainly the three just mentioned) and often the swearword is not translated at all. However, insults can be given in different ways and, in particular, through the use of plain or masculine language in Japanese. This can be very insulting in situations when more polite language would normally be used. Be careful if you do pick up any swearwords – Japanese people tend to be very polite towards foreigners but could be offended if you use such words because they do not have the casual usage that English swearwords can have.

Taboo expressions are words avoided because they are thought to bring bad luck and also refer to the words used in their place (a parallel example in English is the expression '*break a leg*' rather than '*good luck*' used by actors). For example, traditionally the word **shio** (*salt*) is avoided after nightfall because it is close in sound to the word **shi** meaning *death* and instead the euphemism **nami no hana** (*flowers of the waves*) is used. This was first used by court ladies who had secret words for all areas of domestic life which would not be understood by the uninitiated.

They speak too quickly!

This is often the complaint of learners of Japanese when they first hear a Japanese tape or meet a Japanese person. Actually, it is the most common complaint of learners of any language but the fact is that all languages are spoken at more or less the same speed! The habit to develop is to train the ear to pick out key words and information and even more importantly, not to panic. And don't forget, you can always say **motto yukkuri itte kudasai** – *please speak more slowly*.

Written Japanese

When confronted with a page of Japanese writing, you could be forgiven for thinking that to unravel and comprehend it would be an impossible task. There is a sample of a Japanese headline from a cookery magazine on p. 41. I will refer back to this later but look at it now to gain a flavour of written Japanese.

In fact, many foreign learners of Japanese become fascinated by the script and find it challenging, exciting and ultimately very satisfying to master. And your Japanese friends will always be very impressed by your grasp of their written language, however basic this may be.

There are three scripts in Japanese (four if you include **rōmaji** or romanized script, in other words, the Western alphabet). These three scripts are **kanji, hiragana** and **katakana**. Each has its own specific function and the three are used in combination (plus **rōmaji** for some foreign words and acronyms, e.g. NATO) within whole texts. Let's look at each individually, beginning with **kanji**.

サラダのアレンジが広がる
シンプルサラダと相性のいい
ソース三種
3
3
2
1

Japanese cookery magazine text

Kanji (Chinese characters 漢字)

The ancient Chinese developed a writing system in the 14th century BC which spread to the Korean peninsula and from there to Japan in the 4th and 5th centuries AD. Before this time, there had been no form of written Japanese and **kataribe** (*messengers*) travelled around to convey important information to people orally. Both Korea and Japan adapted kanji to fit their own language and, even in China, the kanji developed over 3,000 years ago have been revised, changed and abbreviated over time.

Kanji are ideographs which convey a specific meaning, word or idea. The simplest and earliest of these were pictographs. These were pictures drawn by the Chinese of the world around them, such as the sun, moon and trees, which were gradually standardized into the kanji used today. Here are three examples of this process.

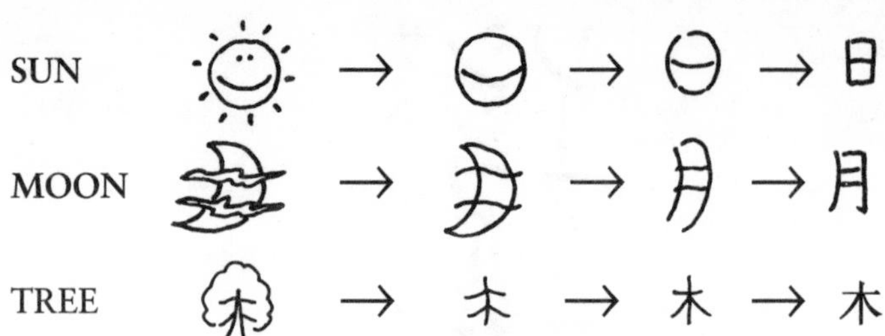

Sun, moon, tree – progression to Chinese script

These are very simple examples but there are kanji to represent all aspects of language including concepts, feelings and ideas and extensive kanji dictionaries can contain as many as 40–50,000 kanji. However, the former Japanese Ministry for Education, **Monbushō**, in 1981 produced an approved list of 1,945 kanji for daily use known as the **jōyō kanji**. These are the kanji needed to read texts such as newspapers thoroughly. The learning of these 1,945 kanji is spread throughout the nine years of compulsory education. In addition, there are a further 284 more unusual kanji which are used in names and Japanese parents may look even beyond these additions to find auspicious kanji when naming their children (as parents in the West might consult a naming book to find more unusual names). The rules for writing kanji are very precise and the correct order for writing each kanji is learnt and practised repeatedly at school (as in the West the rules for correctly writing the alphabet are taught at school).

DID YOU KNOW?
Shodō (way of writing or calligraphy)

Shodō was introduced to Japan with kanji from China and many styles have developed since. As in China, it is considered to be one of the fine arts in Japan and the mark of a cultured person. **Shodō** is written using kanji and/or kana and the main implements are the **futofude** (thick brush) used for the main part of the text and **hosofude** (thin brush) for the signature or fine writing. **Sumi** (Chinese ink) is made from wood or oil soot mixed with fish bone or hide glue. In some styles, such as **kaisho**, the characters are easily recognizable but in others such as **sōsho** (*grass writing*) the characters are often abbreviated or linked to each other in a rounded and flowing style. A post-war avant garde development has produced styles which are totally abstract and bring calligraphy close to the principles of modern art.

Kana (仮名)

Hiragana and katakana are collectively known as **kana**. They are phonetic alphabets or syllabaries. This means that each symbol represents a sound or phoneme. This is different from the roman alphabet system where each symbol is a letter and these letters are grouped into sounds. Here is an example of this difference:

In English the word *goodbye* is made up of seven letters: G-O-O-D-B-Y-E
In Japanese *goodbye* is **sayōnara** and is made up of five syllables: SA-YO-U-NA-RA
These are represented by five hiragana symbols. さようなら

Kana was originally developed in the 9th century in order to be able to write the Japanese language phonetically. Kana symbols were created by simplifying kanji and so their shape derives from kanji. The first set of phonetic characters were called **man'yōgana** which were kanji chosen, regardless of their meaning, because their pronunciation was the same as the sounds of the Japanese language. For example:

加 *pronunciation* **ka** (*meaning*: **increase**)

The **man'yōgana** were eventually simplified from these kanji into the hiragana and katakana systems. Here is how the sound **ka** was simplified:

hiragana: 加 → か katakana: 加 → カ

The Buddhist priest, **Kūkai** (774–835), is credited with the invention of the kana syllabary. Both hiragana and katakana represent the same set of 46 basic sounds (plus other combination and modified sounds) but the symbols are written differently. This is not an alien idea to English speakers for there are essentially two alphabets, capital and lower case, which both represent the same letters but in Japanese the two kana scripts exist for different purposes. Let's look at each in turn.

Hiragana (平仮名)

The word **hiragana** means *cursive/rounded/easy to use* and indicates both the shape and relative simplicity of the script. The hiragana symbols were developed by simplifying the **man'yōgana** kanji which represented the sounds of the Japanese language. An example of this process is shown in the preceding section. Hiragana was necessary in order to adapt the Chinese writing system to the Japanese language.

It was during the Heian period (794–1185) that hiragana developed to allow for a more pure expression of the Japanese language. Before this, written expression had been very limited in Japan, with the use of lots of Chinese words and phrases, and restricted mainly to official documents written by men. The Chinese system continued to be used for official matters but the kana system allowed for more creative writing and became essentially the writing system of the imperial court and, more importantly, of aristocratic court ladies and their female attendants. The Heian court women used the kana writing system to express themselves through poetry, prose and diaries and so it is that the heights of creativity in Heian literature were achieved mainly through women writers using hiragana which was given the name **onnade** meaning *women's hands*.

Today, hiragana symbols are used to write the grammatical parts of words and sentences and Japanese words which don't have a kanji. For example, when writing verbs, the kanji expresses the main idea or meaning and hiragana are used to indicate the tense (e.g. past or present) or function of the verb. Here are the first five symbols:

あ い う え お
a i u e o

Katakana (片仮名)

This word means *partial* because katakana symbols were developed from part of kanji characters. There is an example of this use of one part of a kanji to form katakana **ka** on p. 43. Here are the first five katakana symbols (pronounced **a, i, u, e** and **o**):

ア イ ウ エ オ

In overall appearance, katakana symbols are more angular in shape and hiragana are more rounded. Compare the two sets of symbols and see if you can identify these features.

Katakana was thought to have been invented by the Buddhist priest **Kūkai** in order to write out Chinese and Sanskrit Buddhist texts phonetically. Today, the main use is for writing non-Japanese words which have been introduced into the language. These fall into two categories:

1 *Loan words* (**gairaigo**) For example,
コンピュータ(**kompyūta**) means *computer*.

2 *Foreign names* such as countries, cities and personal names. For example, アメリカ (**amerika**) is *America.*

Here are some examples of shop signs written in katakana:

McDonald's hamburger

Curry house

There are also three ways in which katakana is used for writing Japanese words:

1 *For emphasis/To make words stand out*, e.g. in advertising.
2 The classification of plants and animals.
3 To write onomatopoeic words.

Now look back to the Japanese text sample on p. 41. Some parts have been underlined and numbered 1, 2 or 3. Each of these numbers relates to kanji, hiragana or katakana. Can you work out which number relates to which script? Remember: hiragana is more cursive (rounded), katakana is more angular and kanji characters are more complex. Check your answers at the end of this unit.

And finally in this section, Japanese is traditionally written vertically (**tategaki**) and you begin reading from the top right of a page. This means that books are opened from what we would consider to be the back. Nowadays, however, books, newspapers and magazines are often written Western style, in horizontal lines (**yokogaki**) from left to right and in these cases the book is opened from what we would consider to be the front.

Loanwords (gairaigo) into and out of the Japanese language

The Japanese language has a rich and varied vocabulary. Historically, it has borrowed and adopted words from many languages beginning with Chinese, then European languages from the 16th century onwards and more recently from America, Britain and other European countries. Early examples of loanwords include **pan** (*bread*) and **tempura** (*battered food*) both deriving originally from Portuguese but now part of the Japanese vocabulary. In this century thousands of words have been adopted in a wide range of areas such as those in the box.

Area	Japanese	English
technical	**monitā**	*TV monitor*
business	**pāto**	*part-timer*
electronics	**terebi**	*television*
computer technology	**mausu**	*mouse*
sports	**sakkā**	*soccer football*
fashion	**wanpīsu**	*one-piece* or *dress*
food	**hanbāgā**	*hamburger*
social issues	**sekuhara**	*sexual harassment**

*shortened from ***seku*****sharu** ***hara*****sumento**)

This last example highlights ways in which the pronunciation of words is clipped to fit Japanese pronunciation rules. It is also fashionable to take parts of two words and fit them together to make a new word as with **sekuhara** and also, a buzzword of the late 1990s, **pokemon** (from ***poke*****t** ***mon*****sters**).

Foreign languages have also been used to create Japanese-made product names. Examples include **walkman, discman, tamagotchi** (**tamago** is Japanese for *egg* and **chi** is variously explained as the first part of *chicken* or the last part of **tomodachi** meaning *friend*) and **pokemon**. These words have then entered our own language, setting up an interesting 'borrowing-back' scenario. Many of the loanwords used in Japanese today are **ryūkōgo** (trendwords) which will be fashionable for a while and then will disappear. Many others are a fixed part of the Japanese language.

Finally, can you work out what these words mean in English? (Answers at end of the unit.)

1 **sutēki**
2 **kēkī**
3 **tenisu**
4 **kamera**
5 **resutoran**

Taking it further

There are a number of Teach Yourself books for Japanese published by Hodder & Stoughton including:

- *Teach Yourself Beginner's Japanese* – an easy introduction (Helen Gilhooly, 2003)
- *Teach Yourself Japanese* – the complete course (Helen Ballhatchet & Stefan Kaiser, 2003)
- *Teach Yourself Beginner's Japanese Script* (Helen Gilhooly, 2003)

There is also a wide range of Japanese learning software including:

- Euro Asia Software
- Kanji Sensei (Pacific Rim software)
- Japanese Master
- **http://diamond.intersc.tsukuba.ac.jp/~jacop/index.html** – a collection of digitized video clips containing short conversations for Japanese conversation practice

You can find and sample many more on the internet. Here are some useful addresses:

- **http://www.kanjicards.com**
- **http://www.instantlanguages.com**
- **http://www.infortech.co.jp/kurobi/**
- **http://www.sabotenweb.com/bookmarks/language.html**
- ePALS Japanese language at **http://www.epals.com/index_jp.html**
- **http://www.members.aol.com/writejapan/** Japanese writing tutor site for practising hiragana and katakana

The cultural section of the Japanese embassy in your country should also be able to supply you with a list of Japanese classes or at least with suggestions of who to contact.

And a final suggestion, the 10th-century female writer, **Sei Shonagon**, wrote ***Makura no soshi*** – *The Pillow Book* (tr. Ivan Morris, New York, CUP; London, OUP, 1967) which is a brilliant collection of short essays and eye-witness accounts of court life in which she talks, among other subjects, about distinctions between feminine and masculine language.

Some useful honorific phrases

Itadakimasu Said before eating (lit. *I humbly receive*)

Gochisōsama deshita Said after eating (*it was a feast!*)

Tetsudatte kudasaimasen ka *Could you possibly give me a hand?*

Watashi wa ____ to mōshimasu *I am called ____* (your name)

Suzuki-san wa irasshaimasu ka? *Is Mr/s Suzuki there?*

GLOSSARY

日本語 **nihongo**	*Japanese*
国語 **kokugo**	*native language, mother tongue*
文法 **bunpō**	*grammar*
標準語 **hyōjūngo**	*standard Japanese*
発音 **hatsuon**	*pronunciation*
方言 **hōgen**	*dialect*
敬語 **keigo**	*honorific language*
謙譲語 **kenjōgo**	*humble language*
尊敬語 **sonkeigo**	*respectful language*
丁寧語 **teineigo**	*polite language*
女性語 **joseigo**	*feminine language*
男性語 **danseigo**	*masculine language*
漢字 **kanji**	*Chinese characters*
仮名 **kana**	*kana syllabary*
平仮名 **hiragana**	*hiragana syllabary*
片仮名 **katakana**	*katakana syllabary*
外來語 **gairaigo**	*loanwords*

Answers

Text samples: **1** = hiragana **2** = kanji **3** = katakana

Loanwords: **1** steak **2** cake **3** tennis **4** camera **5** restaurant

03 literature, art and architecture

In this unit you will learn

- about key types of Japanese literature
- about some of Japan's most celebrated writers and poets
- about Japan's most influential art and craft movements and artists
- about important traditional and contemporary buildings and where to see them

Japanese literature (bungaku 文学)

This overview of Japanese literature mentions only a few of Japan's many great writers but a more extensive list is given in Taking it further (p. 67).

Eighth century AD

Before there was a writing system in Japan there was a strong oral tradition of recounting and passing down tales, songs and legends. The first major published works in Japan were the **kojiki** and **nihon shoki**, 8th-century writings which traced the descent of the imperial family back to mythical times. Many of the myths and songs in these writings were much older and had been passed down in oral form. The late 8th century saw the beginnings of a style of 31-syllable poetry called **waka** or **tanka** (short poem) and the first anthology of **tanka** poetry was called the *Man-yōshū*.

Heian literature: 9th–12th centuries

The use of kana in literature led to an outpouring of high-quality prose writing particularly by aristocratic and court women (see p. 44). **Murasaki Shikibu** is famous for writing the world's first novel, *The Tale of Genji*, and her well-known contemporary, **Sei Shonagon**, wrote ***Makura no Sōshi*** (*The Pillow Book*).

FAMOUS PEOPLE
Sei Shonagon (AD 966–1025)

Sei Shonagon was a lady-in-waiting at the imperial court and her book is an observation, often very witty, of court life and the lives of the aristocracy. She was reputed to be very self-confident and competitive and her book contains a number of rather self-opinionated claims and boasts. She and **Murasaki Shikibu** were great rivals and **Murasaki** made some very unflattering remarks about **Sei** in her diary. Nevertheless, they were both great writers and *The Pillow Book* contains vivid and vibrant accounts of life at that time (see p. 47).

Literature of the 12th–16th centuries

The new warrior class and commoners began to write literature during this period and a new type of prose writing was **gunki monogatari** or *war tales*, a famous example being ***Heike Monogatari*** which tells the story of the fighting between the **Taira** and **Minamoto** families from AD 1180 to 1185. A new form of poetry writing also emerged called **renga** or linked verse. Poets gathered together to write the 100-verse **renga** poems, each writing one verse on the spot which they would read out loud and which would be linked into the next verse. The verses alternated between three lines of 5-7-5 syllables and two lines each of seven syllables. The poets would write about nature, the seasons, the beauty of flowers and blossoms, and love. Towards the end of the 15th century, another form of poetry emerged out of the **renga** form of 5-7-5 syllables and dominated the poetry scene for over 200 years. It was called **haiku** and today it is popular worldwide. A **haiku** is a 17-syllable poem with three lines of 5-7-5 syllables. The main subjects for traditional **haiku** were observations of nature or human life.

FAMOUS PEOPLE
Matsuo Bashō (1644–94)

Bashō established haiku as a serious art form and is considered to be one of Japan's greatest writers. During his lifetime many pupils and disciples studied under him and set up their own haiku schools. Towards the end of his life he travelled with a pupil around the north-eastern part of Honshu and wrote haiku about both his actual journey and on the theme of life as a journey. He died from food poisoning while travelling down to the southern island of Kyushu.

Here are examples of haiku by four of the most well-known haiku poets, three of the Edo period and one, Shiki, of the Meiji period. They have not been translated into the 5-7-5 syllable pattern in these translations.

Bashō (1644–94)	**Furuike ya** **Kawazu tobikomu** **Mizu no oto**	*An old pond* *a frog jumps in* *the sound of water*
Buson (1716–84)	**Yūkaze ya** **Mizu aosagi no** **Hagi o utsu**	*The evening breeze* *water laps against the* *legs of a blue heron*

Issa (1762–1826)	**Aki no yo ya** **Tabi no otoko no** **Hari shigoto**	*An autumn night . . .* *a travelling man's* *needlework*
Shiki (1867–1902)	**Suzushisa ya** **Aota no naka ni** **Hitotsu matsu**	*The coolness* *in the middle of a* *green ricefield* *a single pine tree*

Literature of the Edo period (1600–1868)

The art of writing spread from the aristocratic and warrior classes to the increasing number of merchants and commoners living in towns. The development of commercial printing also made literature available to a much wider audience than previously. There were a number of important writers in this period including **Ihara Saikaku** (1642–93) who created a new type of novel called **ukiyo-zōshi** (*novels of the floating world*) which were observations of the merchant class and of townspeople and were often very amusing. His style of writing had a great influence on modern Japanese literature. There was also **Jippensha Ikku** (1765–1831) who was extremely popular as a comic book writer and wrote a series of books over 21 years describing the adventures of two men as they travelled around Japan.

Modern literature

Modern Japanese literature begins with the Meiji restoration (1868) when the introduction of Western culture and technology brought about massive social changes in Japan. Translations of European novels flooded the country and the novel began to be seen as a serious form of writing. A modern literary form of writing was developed to replace the classical Japanese style which no longer corresponded to spoken Japanese. One leading novelist of the Meiji period was **Natsume Sōseki** (see also p. 20), particularly famous for his novel ***Wagahai wa neko de aru*** (*I am a Cat*) which was originally published in instalments in a newspaper between 1905–6. The novel's central character is a cat which makes satirical and humorous observations of his master and others who visit the house. It is considered to be a criticism of Meiji society and also shows **Sōseki**'s disapproval of Japan's rapid assimilation of

Western culture and technology. The novelist **Nagai Kafū** (1879–1959) also wrote many critical works of Meiji Japan and his novel, ***Furansu Monogatari*** (*A Tale of France*, 1909) was banned for being too critical. The poet **Shimasaki Tōson** (1872–1943) is held to be the founder of modern Japanese poetry which was influenced by European poetry styles. A second great Meiji poet was **Ishikawa Takuboku** (1886–1912) who had a huge influence on the writing of modern **tanka**. His poetry has been translated into many languages.

Watakushi shōsetsu (the I-novel 私小説)

The I-novel dominated Japanese literature throughout the 20th century and remains popular today. It is an autobiographical style of writing, usually with the author at the centre, who explores ideas and thoughts in a very honest and confessional manner. There is usually very little plot or characterization and the emphasis is on realism and the description of everyday happenings however trivial. The first I-novel, ***Futon***, written by **Tayama Katai** in 1907 is a frank confession of the writer's feelings towards a young female pupil. **Dazai Osamu** (1909–48) wrote the masterpiece ***Ningen Shikkaku*** (*No Longer Human*, 1948) shortly before he committed suicide after several attempts throughout his life. The novel features episodes from Dazai's life and is in the form of a set of notes written by a young man with a distrust of people which eventually leads to a mental breakdown, two suicide attempts and reliance on morphine.

War literature

War literature was a result of Japan's involvement in war from the late 19th century onwards. The Sino-Japanese War (1894–5) and the Russo-Japanese War (1904–5) resulted in many writings which glorified war and had a strong nationalistic air although some published works were more critical. However, by the time of the second Sino-Japanese War (1937-45) and World War II, freedom of speech was restricted and writers faced imprisonment and torture if they wrote literature with anti-war sentiments. A policy called **tenko** (*change of direction*) was introduced which gave anti-war writers and other activists the opportunity to sign a declaration that they had changed their view and were now fully supportive of the war effort. Many writers signed these rather than face imprisonment and so very few critiques of the war were written during that period.

Writers were often sent to the front to report on the war and they were expected to glorify the work of the Japanese soldiers. **Ishikawa Tatsuzō** (1905–85) wrote a criticism of the behaviour of Japanese soldiers in China in a short novel called ***Ikiteiru Heitai*** (*Living Soldiers*, 1938). This was banned by the government and Ishikawa was convicted under the wartime censorship rules.

Once censorship was lifted at the end of the war, writers were free to reflect on and expound their true views of the war. This resulted in a proliferation of excellent war writings which give valuable insights into the feelings of the Japanese people following the war and the effects of war on both the country and the individual's psyche. Many writers suffered an acute sense of guilt because they had not spoken out during the war and others felt despair at what they saw as a ruined country with no future. Some explored the negative effects of the military propaganda on soldiers (and their families) who were dehumanised by the war effort and devastated by defeat. Such reflection and analysis led to a wide variety of thought-provoking and informative writings which help to give a balance to the picture of Japanese involvement in the war. A selection of these are given at the end of this unit in Taking it further.

Hidashi no Gen (*Barefoot Gen*)

Barefoot Gen by **Nakazawa Keiji** is a set of two books written in **manga** (cartoon) style on the subject of World War II and, in particular, the events leading up to and the immediate aftermath of the dropping of the atomic bomb on Hiroshima. Gen, the hero of the story, is a young boy whose father has been imprisoned because of his stance as a conscientious objector and the events which unfold are seen through Gen's eyes. The books are a very moving account of the atomic bomb explosion on Hiroshima and have been a huge success throughout the world and translated into many languages.

Modern writers

As well as those writers already mentioned, there follows a short list of some of the most famous names in fiction writing of the 20th century.

Akutagawa Ryūnosuke (1892–1927)

He is considered to be one of Japan's most eminent short story writers. His stories explore the complex psychology of the human mind and he often used old Japanese tales which he rewrote with modern interpretation. In 1915 he wrote ***Rashomon*** and this, along with another of his stories, ***Yabu no naka*** (*In a Grove*, 1922) was used as the script for the film *Rashomon* (1956) directed by **Kurosawa Akira** (see p. 130). Towards the end of his life he suffered ill-health and eventually committed suicide in 1927. The **Akutagawa** Prize for new prose writers is the most important literary prize in Japan and was set up in his memory.

Miyazawa Kenji (1896–1933)

Renowned in Japan as a children's story writer and a poet, he received great acclaim only posthumously, after World War II. He was a devout follower of the **Nichiren** sect of Buddhism and throughout his life tried to follow its strict rules of celibacy, self-denial and freeing of oneself from material possessions. His most famous children's story is ***Ginga tetsudō no yoru*** (*Night Train to the Stars*, 1927, translated in 1987).

Tanizaki Jun'ichiro (1886–1965)

He played a major role in moving literature away from the I-novel. He wrote fiction as entertainment and was particularly concerned with the relationships and sexual tensions between men and women. His novel ***Sasameyuki*** (*The Makioka Sisters*) appeared in serialization form in 1943 but was banned by the war authorities for being 'too frivolous'. It tells the story of four sisters living in Osaka in the 1930s and took its inspiration from *The Tale of Genji* which **Tanizaki** translated into modern Japanese.

Kawabata Yasunari (1899–1972)

Japan's first winner of the Nobel Prize for Literature which he won in 1968 for his novel ***Yukiguni*** (*The Snow Country*). The story tells of the hopeless love between a geisha girl and an older man, tired of life, and is set in the snowy landscape of the area along the sea of Japan. His style of writing is considered to accentuate the exquisite beauty of the Japanese language. He appears to have committed suicide by gassing in 1972, although some people believe it was an accident.

Mishima Yukio (1925–70)
He has won wide international acclaim although his manner of dying is at least as well known as his writings and was made famous by the film *Mishima* directed by Paul Schrader. His first book, ***Hanazakari no mori*** (*The Forest in Full Bloom*) was published when he was only 16 and sold out within a week. He wrote about the emptiness of post-war Japan and explored the complexities of the human mind. He was fascinated by words and the ways they could be portrayed in prose and poetry. His greatest work is considered to be ***Kinkakuji*** (*The Temple of the Golden Pavilion*, published 1956, translated 1959) which explores the psychological processes leading a young priest, fascinated with the beauty of the Golden Temple, to burn it down. **Mishima**'s views became increasingly extremist right wing in his later years and on 25 November 1970 he attempted a *coup d'etat* at a Japanese self-defence base which failed. He then committed **harakiri** (*death by disembowelment* – normally referred to as **seppuku** in Japan) which ended with one of his followers beheading him with a sword in the samurai tradition of honourable suicide.

Ariyoshi Sawako (1931–84)
One of a group of outstanding female writers who came to prominence in Japan particularly in the latter part of the 20th century. She wrote about contemporary social issues, especially those which affected women's lives. Her 1972 novel ***Kōkotsu no hito*** (*The Twilight Years*) is a very honest and often disturbing account of the care of the elderly in Japan and the enormous burden it can place on women and their families.

Oe Kenzaburo (1935–)
He has written many politically provocative and searching novels and is Japan's second winner of the Nobel Prize for Literature (*A Personal Matter*, 1994).

Japanese art (bijutsu 美術)

This section concentrates on the general areas of religious art, painting, prints, ceramics and sculpture. Japanese art has developed its own unique styles through a range of historical, cultural and geographical influences. Chinese and Western cultures have been imitated, assimilated and innovated into new art styles. Nature has also had a strong influence and flora such as plum, cherry, chrysanthemum and maple appear in a range of art forms.

Religious art

Buddhist art which spread from India via China and Korea has had a profound influence on Japanese art, both religious and secular. Buddhist and Shinto (Japan's native religion) art items include paintings and sculptures of Shinto **kami** (gods), human and animal guardians and various Buddha and bodhisattva (see p. 94). Sculptures were initially in gilt bronze, then in wood carved from one block. The famous sculptor **Unkei** (1148–1223) invented a new technique in which individual wooden parts were carved and then assembled into one sculpture. Many of his statues remain today including one on the great south gate of the **Tōdaiji** Temple. Buddhist art also influenced **suibokuga** (*ink paintings* – see next section).

Important painting styles of the pre-modern age (before 1868)

Paintings were produced on a variety of media such as temple walls and wooden panels, sliding and folding screens, hand scrolls, castle murals and woodblock prints on paper. In the 14th century **suibokuga** (ink painting) in black and white was introduced from China and became very popular with Zen painters. The most popular form was **sansuiga** (landscape painting) and the Zen priest **Sesshū** (1420–1506) was a master of this form. From the 16th century a more decorative and grandiose style of landscape, figure and **kachōga** (bird and flower painting) was developed within the **Kanō** School of painting which became patronized by the Tokugawa shogunate (1603–1868). One great name was **Kanō Tanyū** (1602–74) who started painting at the age of four and whose work was greatly admired by the shogun. He had a bold, unconventional style and specialized in black and white landscape paintings. His greatest work of five scrolls depicting the life of the shogun, **Tokugawa Ieyasu**, is displayed at **Ieyasu**'s mausoleum in **Nikkō**. Outside of the **Kanō** School, the artist **Ogata Kōrin** (1658–1716) was a very prominent artist who specialized in screen and scroll paintings of flowers and blossom with a decorative and bold style. Many of his works are displayed at the **Nezu** Art Museum in Tokyo.

Ukiyoe (pictures of the floating world 浮世絵)

An ukiyoe print

Ukiyoe were prints produced by carving pictures into woodblocks (normally made of cherry wood), painting the images produced in the wood and printing them onto paper. The artist would design the original image and then a group of expert carvers (**horishi**) would carve them into the wood, putting their own unique style and carving technique into the production. Printers (**surishi**) would use brushes and other instruments to paint on the colours according to the instructions of the artists. Many of the woodblock prints were very complex and made up of a series of woodblocks printed in a particular order so that the picture and colours gradually developed. Printers might also be required to apply their own painting skills by adding shading or embossing to the final print. The name of the painter and publisher would be stamped onto the final print but a whole group of unaccredited carvers and printers were also crucial to the whole process.

The art of **ukiyoe** flourished in the Edo period (1603–1868) and mass production made it affordable and very popular with the middle classes. The subject areas were scenes of everyday life in Edo Japan, particularly the pleasure areas, courtesans and kabuki actors. The word *floating world* described an easygoing, pleasure-seeking way of life. Many of the artists also produced **shunga** (literally *spring pictures*) which were essentially sex manuals. In the 1800s landscapes became very popular and the landscape prints of great artists such as **Hokusai** had an important influence on the French Impressionists and the

English Pre-Raphaelites. In the late 19th century **ukiyoe** prints enjoyed enormous popularity in Europe and the USA and thousands were bought and exported abroad. Artists such as Van Gogh and Gauguin were keen collectors of **ukiyoe**. There are many great collections in museums across the world and some are given in the Taking it further section.

DID YOU KNOW?
Japonisme

This term describes the impact of Japanese art on Western artists in the late 19th century. Artists such as Monet, Degas, Van Gogh, Gauguin, Klimt, James Whistler and Bonnard were deeply influenced by Japanese approaches to composition such as close-up views of a subject (the Impressionists adopted this approach) and by the use of two-dimensional and elevated perspectives, bold colour and patterns from nature. Japonisme transformed Western art and this can be seen most clearly in the works of the French Impressionists.

Famous ukiyoe artists

Hishikawa Moronobu (1618–94) was famous for his **bijin-e** (*beautiful women* pictures); **Kitagawa Utamaro** (1753–1806) invented the **ōkubi-e** (prints of the head and shoulders of women) but after producing prints for only six years was imprisoned by the shogun for portraying him surrounded by beautiful women and drinking sake and died two years later; **Sharaku Tōshūsai** (dates unknown) was famous as a portrait painter of Kabuki actors and his works were widely exported to Europe; **Hokusai Katsushika** (1760–1849) was famous for his landscapes and bold style and produced two particularly well-known series **Fugaku Sanjūrokkei** (*36 views of Mt Fuji*, 1823) and **Fugaku Hyakkei** (*100 views of Mt Fuji*, 1834). One print which is reproduced on many modern products such as coasters and bags is *Beneath the Waves at Kanagawa* which shows a huge blue wave curving upwards with boats caught within it and a distant Mt Fuji visible at the base of the curve (see p. 58); **Hiroshige Andō** (1797–1858) was famous for his use and portrayal of light, weather and atmosphere. One well-known series is **Tōkaidō gojūsantsugi** (*The 53 Stations of the Tokaido Road*, 1833–4) which depicts many everyday scenes along the highway from Edo to Kyoto.

Painting in the modern age

The Meiji period (1868–1912) marked the beginning of the modern age in Japanese art. Two general styles of painting emerged, **yōga** (Western-style painting) and **nihonga** (Japanese-style painting). There was initial great enthusiasm for copying Western styles followed by a renewal of interest in traditional Japanese styles and then experimentation between both traditions. In post-war times, Japanese artists have experimented with a wide range of forms and have made very important contributions to the international scene.

Nihonga artists use traditional Japanese techniques, materials and styles. Paintings are normally produced on **washi** (Japanese paper) or silk although canvas is also used nowadays. Black and white pictures are produced using **sumi** (Chinese ink) which is made by mixing soot with **nikawa** (a glue made from hide or fish bone). Colours are produced from pigments of natural materials such as plants, minerals or insects. These are made into powder then mixed with **nikawa** and water. Traditionally, **Nihonga** was a separate art form to yōga (Western style) but artists increasingly have been experimenting with Western techniques and styles. The **nihonga** artist **Yokoyama Taikan** (1868–1958) was a founding member of the Japan Fine Arts Academy in Yokohama and used light and space (a Western concept) in his paintings.

Yōga was a term used to distinguish Western-style painting from **nihonga** and describes paintings which are created using Western techniques and materials such as oils, pastels, water colour and canvas. Japanese artists have experimented with the whole range of styles and schools. The **yōga** artist **Kuroda Seiki** (1866–1924) went to France at 18, fell in love with European paintings and, with other artists, formed the Meiji Fine Arts Society. His style was called the Purple School because of his great use of this colour in his work. **Yasui Sōtarō** (1888–1955) and **Umehara Ryūzaburō** (1888–1966) were key players in moving **yōga** on from imitating Western styles to developing unique styles, which included the use of **nihonga** techniques and styles.

Modern sculpture

During the Meiji period many Japanese sculptors went to study in Europe. Great sculptors began to emerge such as **Ogiwara Morie** (1879–1910) who moved Western-style sculpture on from imitation to individual and interpretative styles. He studied in France and was influenced by Rodin and romantic realism and brought these ideas back with him to Japan. One of his great works, **Onna** (*Woman*, 1910, bronze) can be seen at the National Museum of Modern Art in Tokyo. **Takamura Kōun** (1852–1934) had trained as a Buddhist sculptor and **netsuke** carver and he combined these traditional styles with Western ones to create realistic images in ivory, wood and bronze. One work of note is **Rōen** (*Aged Monkey*), a wooden sculpture which can be seen at the Tokyo National Museum. Post-war sculptors began to explore the whole gamut of styles and schools in the international sphere (see section on contemporary art).

DID YOU KNOW?
Netsuke

Netsuke were a type of carved toggle used with a cord to secure belongings to the belts and sashes of Japanese kimono. They became particularly popular in the Edo period (1603–1868) as smoking increased and people began to carry tobacco. Netsuke produced in Japan show clear Chinese influences. They were generally carved from wood or ivory, with inlays made from tortoiseshell, gold, amber, lacquer, glass and ebony. Popular subjects were gods, animals, mythical creatures and humans and they ranged in size from 2.5–15 cms (see illustration). The art form reached its height in the first part of the 1800s but from the 1850s, with increased contact and demand from the West, they began to be mass produced and of much poorer craftsmanship. Then, as Japanese people began to wear Western clothes, the need for netsuke diminished.

Example of netsuke

Contemporary art

In post-war Japan, artists in all fields have increasingly had the freedom to express themselves and explore the possibilities of art in every direction. They have entered and been accepted into the international scene and have made many important and innovative contributions. Examples of art and artists include **Shiraga Kazuo** (1924–) who followed the **gutai** (concrete or definite) art movement which explored new ways of expression. In 1955, he famously immersed himself in one ton of cement! A well-known sculptor is **Miyawaki Aiko** (1929–) who experiments with large abstract sculptures made out of brass pipes. One of her works is displayed in front of the Plaza Tower in Costa Mesa, California. Artists who have recently made a name internationally include **Tatsumi Orimoto**, a live performer, famous for cycling around with loaves of bread tied to his head; and a pair of artists called **Maywa Denki** who masquerade as the presidents of an electronics company and produce music and strange surrealist objects.

Ceramics (tōjiki 陶磁器)

The art of ceramics is a highly developed and revered art in Japan. Since its creation in 1950, the designation of **ningen kokuhō** (*living national treasure*) has been bestowed on many notable potters, illustrating the importance and reverence that is attached to ceramics. Pottery has been made in Japan for more than 12,000 years beginning with the cord-decorated pottery of the **Jōmon** period around 10,000 BC. Pottery items are admired for their shape, decoration, design and their feel, with imperfections seen as part of the overall effect.

Major ceramic styles

The technologies of wheel-thrown pots and glazing were introduced by Korean potters from the 5th century onwards. A new ware called **seto**ware was developed in Nagoya in the 12th century which was distinguished by green and amber ash glazes with a style influenced by ceramics from the Song dynasty in China. From the 15th century **seto**ware was also made with dark brown iron glazes and, with the introduction of Western technologies in the Meiji period, **seto**ware went into mass production and became the biggest pottery producer in Japan.

The 15th and 16th centuries also saw a resurgence of interest in unglazed pottery, especially **bizen**ware, which was considered particularly suitable for tea ceremony items because of its simple and rustic style. At the same time, more formal, decorated wares began to appear, such as **raku**.

DID YOU KNOW?
Rakuware (楽)

This is a low-fired soft ceramic with a lead glaze which is said to have been invented by a tile maker, **Chōjirō**, in the second part of the 16th century. He was asked by the great tea ceremony master, **Sen no Rikyū** (see p. 98) to produce tea ceremony ware using this method and **raku** has been associated with tea bowls ever since. The glaze is usually red or black, sometimes white, and each item is individually handmade. The shogun, **Toyotomi Hideyoshi**, is supposed to have given **raku** its name by presenting **Chōjirō**'s son with a gold seal with the word **raku** (*pleasure*) stamped on it. Today the word **rakuyaku** is used more generally for pottery that has been quick fired at low temperatures, producing the soft ceramic finish of traditional **raku**ware.

Korean potters again brought their influence to the development of Japanese ceramics in the early 17th century when a potter named **Ri Sampai** discovered porcelain clay in the **Arita** region (modern-day Saga prefecture in Kyushu), turning the Arita area into a major producer of ceramics as it remains to this day. Early porcelain was influenced by Chinese Mingware and used milky white and blue glazes. The introduction of **kakiemon**ware (see next section) introduced new colours and influences and these became very popular for export to Europe.

FAMOUS PEOPLE
Three potters

Sakaida Kakiemon (1596–1666) is famous for inventing colour glazes for use on porcelain wares. After experimenting for 20 years using pigments from China he produced glazes of reds, greens, yellows, blues and browns. The wares were exported first to China and then to Europe and are included under the general title of **Arita**ware. His name was bestowed on him by a feudal lord who greatly admired the red of an ornamental persimmon he had made (the word for persimmon in Japanese is **kaki**). The name has been passed down to his descendants and **Kakiemon** XIII (1906–82) was a **ningen kokuhō** (living national treasure).

Bernard Leach (1887–1979) and Hamada Shōji (1894–1978)

Modern ceramics from the 1900s onwards saw an increase in the number of studio potters with individual styles and diverse influences. Bernard Leach was an English potter who lived in Japan from 1909–20 and introduced Japanese ceramics to the West. He met the Japanese potter, **Hamada Shōji**, while in Japan and together they returned to England in 1920 and established the Leach Pottery at St Ives in Cornwall. **Hamada** returned to Japan in 1924 and established a pottery at **Mashiko** in Tochigi prefecture. He was a great promoter of the folk crafts movement which started up in 1926 and he turned **Mashiko** into a renowned centre of ceramics, using simple glazes and local clays to produce a wide range of designs and styles. He was made a **ningen kokuhō** (living national treasure) in 1955 and received the Order of Culture in 1968.

Folk crafts (mingei 民芸)

Yanagi Muneyoshi (1889–1961) led the folk craft movement in Japan which began in 1926. He noticed a decline in the production of local, handmade objects and produced a catalogue of **mingei** (*folk crafts*) which he defined as everyday, handmade objects created by unnamed craftsmen who continued the craft traditions handed down over generations. **Mingei** objects were both utilitarian and beautiful, created on a large scale but not by machine and totally separate from **bijutsu** (*fine art*) which had no practical use. **Mingei** objects are categorized as lacquerware; textiles (including weaving and dyeing); wood and bamboo work; metal and leather work; ceramics; painting and sculpture. **Bernard Leach** and **Hamada Shōji** were great supporters of the movement and it was seen as a reaction against Western influences and modernization and an appreciation of regional and ethnic cultures. In 1936 the Japan Folk Craft Museum was opened in Tokyo.

Japanese architecture (kenchiku 建築)

Traditional architecture

The designs of traditional Japanese houses (see p. 171) were very simple and designed to fit with the climate and environment. Hot, humid summers and relatively long, cold but dry winters had a strong influence on design and wood was the main building material because it breathed better in humid environments, was flexible in earthquakes and was easy to obtain. Homes were raised off the ground to improve airflow and the roof was low hanging and covered in thatch or ceramic tiles in order to protect the whole house, including the veranda, from heavy rain. Screens and paper panels (**shōji**) were used to partition off parts of the house for privacy and to let in light. The inside and the outside of the house were seen as a whole and the veranda was key in achieving this. Houses were built by **daiku** (*architect–carpenters*) who would first build the wooden frame and then create the walls using bamboo lattice and clay. These basic styles and techniques still exist today alongside concrete apartment blocks and houses built from more modern materials. (More details on houses are given in Unit 9.)

Buddhist and Shinto architecture

Shinto shrines were built in keeping with the natural surroundings with the purpose of honouring a beautiful place or natural object such as a rock or waterfall. The building style was similar to homes with natural wood, a raised floor and a low hanging roof. The entrance to the shrine was marked by an impressive **torii** gate (see p. 92).

With the introduction of Buddhism, Shinto shrine design changed and evolved. Chinese red began to be used on the wooden columns of the buildings and white on the walls and the styles of roof changed too, the most popular being the **nagare** style in which one side of the roof swept down much lower to cover the stairs.

Buddhist temple complexes were introduced from China and Korea. There are seven main buildings, the most important being the main hall, the pagoda for keeping Buddhist relics and the lecture hall. Buddhist temples went through a number of styles including the 12th-century **daibutsuyō** (*Great Buddha*) style which combined Chinese and traditional styles. A good example of this is the great south gate of the **Tōdaiji** Temple in Nara and the whole temple complex shows Buddhist architecture at its best. A great example of Pure Land (see p. 97) Buddhist architecture is the **Byōdōin** Phoenix Hall in **Uji** which is near Kyoto and pictured on the 10-yen coin.

Contemporary architecture

In the Meiji period, Western designs and technology were absorbed and assimilated with traditional Japanese architectural styles. Good examples of the two extreme building styles of the early 20th century are **Tatsuno Kingo**'s Tokyo Station (1914) which is very much a Western-style design and **Itō Chūta**'s Meiji Shrine in Tokyo (1920) which is a traditional Japanese design. There was an explosion of building in the post-war period which led to later criticisms of concrete box and soulless designs. Out of this came a desire for purer designs free of commercial or economic 'quick gain'. Such designs have given Japan the image of a futuristic country, with parts of Tokyo and Osaka often likened to scenes from the film *Bladerunner*, and post-war Japanese architects have won international acclaim. Modern buildings normally have earthquake-proof features such as huge weights on the roof which counteract the swaying caused by tremors.

FAMOUS PEOPLE
Tange Kenzō (1913–)

He has an impressive record of monumental building in Japan and abroad. His style combines traditional Japanese within modern contexts and his buildings are boldly shaped. He designed the Yōyogi National Sports Stadium (Harajuku, Tokyo) in 1963 as part of the 1964 Tokyo Olympic Games which is a complex of two oval buildings with steel suspended roofs (see p. 180). He also designed the Hiroshima Peace Memorial Hall and Museum in 1955 and has recently won international acclaim accompanied by some controversy for his 1991 Tokyo Metropolitan Government Offices which have captured the Shinjuku skyline once dominated by the world famous skyscrapers of the 1970–80s with their massive twin towers and luxurious frontage of marble and glass. He has also designed abroad including the OUB Centre in Singapore and was a planner for the new urban design of Skopje in Macedonia following the earthquake in 1965.

A walk around areas in Tokyo such as **Shinjuku, Shibuya, Harajuku, Akasaka** and **Asakusa** can be a truly breathtaking experience and will bring you face to face with some of the most spectacular architecture of the late 20th century, including some very controversial buildings such as the Super Dry Hall in Asakusa (*super dry* is the brand name of Asahi beer), which has the giant golden froth (open to interpretation!) of the beer as its roof. A trip by monorail to **Odaiba** in the Tokyo Bay area is also a fascinating experience. It is a huge area of reclaimed land, begun in 1989 and now complete, although when Japan's bubble economy burst in the 1990s, it was one of many ambitious projects which were stopped in full flow.

Taking it further

Reading Japanese novels in the original language can give you a wonderful insight into the workings of the Japanese language in literature. Twentieth-century writings are mainly written in modern Japanese and so are more accessible to the Japanese learner. There are also collections of short stories and essays, some with the English translation on the opposite page, which can offer a good starting point for those who wish to read original novels. Another way is to have both original and translation at hand so that you can check your understanding as you read. There are also some excellent translations and translators of Japanese and reading books in translation can still give many insights into Japanese society and viewpoints. The list which follows is in addition to texts mentioned in this unit and is a mixture of originals and translations.

Read Real Japanese, ed. Janet Ashby. Power Japanese (Japan, Kodansha, 1993). A collection of short stories and essays by modern writers with Japanese text, English translation and very useful grammar notes

Dondon yomeru iroirona hanashi. A collection of short stories in simplified Japanese by popular authors including Miyazawa Kenji, Natsume Sōseki and Akutagawa Ryūnosuke

Kuroi Ame, Ibuse Masuji (*Black Rain*, Tokyo, Kodansha International, 1965) which looks at the horror of the atomic blast in Hiroshima against the background of the beautiful landscape

Modern Japanese Literature, ed. Donald Keene, includes war writers and other 20th-century writers such as Dazai Osamu and Hayashi Fumiko (New York, Grove Press; London, Allen and Unwin, 1955)

The Catch and other War Stories, ed. S Saeki. A collection of war writings by major authors such as Oe Kenzaburo and Umezaki Haruo

Two well-known contemporary writers are Murakami Haruki (*West of the Sun, South of the Border*) and Yoshimoto Banana (*Kitchen*)

A useful and extensive list of Japanese literature is given at the back of the Kodansha Illustrated Encyclopedia (see Unit 1).

Japanese bookshops also have a list of the 'must reads' of Japanese literature, known as The Yonda Club.

Art and architecture

Books

The Art of Japan, J. Edward Kidder (Tokyo, Shogakukan Publishing, 1981)

Living Arts of Japan, John Reeve (London, British Museum Publications Ltd, 1990)

What is Japanese Architecture? Kazuo Nishi *et al.* (Tokyo and New York, Kodansha International, 1985)

Websites

Japan Information Network (see Taking it further, Unit 1) select **Virtual Museum** for information about Japanese arts.

Places

The Tokyo National Museum, British Museum and New York Ethnographic Museum all have extensive Japanese art collections. The Adachi Bijutsukan in Shimane, Japan has a huge collection of woodblock prints and is also famous for its Japanese gardens. There are a host of other specialist Japanese museums around the world and the best place to find out more is through your Japan embassy's JICC (see Taking it further, Unit 1).

GLOSSARY

文学 **bungaku**	*literature*
美術 **bijutsu**	*art*
建築 **kenchiku**	*architecture*
俳句 **haiku**	*17-syllable poem*
物語 **monogatari**	*tale, story*
小説 **shōsetsu**	*novel*
書く **kaku**	*to write*
読む **yomu**	*to read*
山水画 **sansuiga**	*landscape painting*
水墨画 **suibokuga**	*ink painting*
浮世絵 **ukiyoe**	*woodblock prints*
日本画 **nihonga**	*Japanese-style paintings*
洋画 **yōga**	*Western-style paintings*
和紙 **washi**	*Japanese paper*
陶磁器 **tōjiki**	*ceramics, pottery*
民芸 **mingei**	*folk crafts*

04 music and the performing arts

In this unit you will learn

- about the characteristics which give Japanese music and dance its 'Japanese-ness'
- about traditional performing arts such as kabuki, bunraku and noh
- about modern music and performance trends including karaoke
- about famous traditional and modern musicians and performers

The four main traditional Japanese theatre forms are **noh, kyōgen, bunraku** and **kabuki**. Each of these will be explained in more detail in this unit but a brief history of the development of music, dance and drama will help to set the scene.

Features of Japanese dance and music

What makes Japanese dance and music different from Western forms? There are many types of traditional Japanese dance which have their own movements, styles and rules. However, a general feature of Japanese dance is that artistic and visual qualities are more important than the portrayal of symbolic or realistic meaning. The main movements are of the arms, head and lower legs and great importance is attached to the pauses and timing between movements.

Japanese traditional music (**hōgaku**) is very different in sound from Western music because, rather than emphasizing rhythm or melody, it stresses the tone and sound quality of the instruments and vocals. In addition, whereas in Western music the vocals and instrumental parts accompany each other, in Japanese music there is a time lag between the two and a singer is not expected to follow or 'cling' to the instrumental part. The idea behind this is that each part is of equal importance and the listener should not have to divide their attention between them. If you go to a performance of traditional Japanese music, you will notice that the instruments will usually pause during the vocal parts. Another feature of Japanese music is the use of unpitched sounds (these can sound out of tune to the untrained ear), a technique not found in classical Western music. Also there is no idea in Japanese music of theme and repetition, and the musical scale consists not of an octave but of five tones. To the unaccustomed ear, Japanese music can seem to be lacking in recognizable melody and rhythm, to be slow in tempo and to be monotonous in sound but an understanding of the differences mentioned here will help you to appreciate the qualities of Japanese music and there are suggestions of recorded music in Taking it further (p. 87).

Origins of performing arts

Dance, music and song developed from two sources – native performing arts linked to Shinto religion and Chinese and Korean forms linked to Buddhism. The oldest known arts date back to at least the 7th century. Legend has it that **Amaterasu**, the sun goddess, was tempted out of a cave (where she was sulking) because the rain god performed a **kagura** dance to music. **Kagura** dances are still performed today at Shinto shrines and festivals. The dancers are often masked and wear elaborate costumes including animals such as lions, dragons and giant serpents. Kabuki dances developed from **kagura** dance.

Dance and music from Asia also appear in the early 7th century. **Gigaku** came from China via Korea and was a masked dance–drama with music and singers, linked to Buddhist processions. One of the dances was a two-man lion dance from which **shishi-mai** (mythical beast dances) including those in kabuki are thought to have developed.

Gagaku (雅楽) and bugaku (舞楽)

Gagaku is the oldest Japanese music still performed today. When it is performed with dance it is called **bugaku**. Both were introduced from China and Korea in the 7th and 8th centuries. They became the music and dance forms of the Japanese court and reached their height of popularity in the Heian period when courtiers had the leisure time to enjoy and develop a cultural lifestyle. The dancers normally wore masks and very luxurious and colourful costumes. They are still performed today at the imperial palace and there are public performances every spring and autumn in Nara.

The use of vocals in traditional music

In traditional Japanese music vocals were more important than instruments and this was a common feature of music throughout Asia. **Hōgaku** (traditional Japanese music) was normally performed vocally. **Gagaku** (court music) was played with instruments but wasn't purely instrumental because it was performed with dance (**bugaku**). Even music written for instruments was not intended to be only instrumental. For example, **koto** (13-stringed harp) music generally included a vocal score and **shakuhachi** (bamboo vertical flute) players aimed at producing musical tones which resembled a singing voice. This emphasis on the voice for producing music led to the development of a wide range of vocal techniques. Songs accompanied by the **shamisen** (lute) are produced in a high register from the top of the head whereas noh chants (see p. 74) can only be sung by men because they are in a low register from the pit of the stomach.

Traditional musical instruments

There isn't space to describe all the traditional musical instruments but a small selection are described here with other suggestions in Taking it further.

The **shamisen** is a 3-stringed instrument which was developed in China. It is like a banjo in shape, the head is covered in cat or dog skin over a wooden frame and the strings are made of silk. It is plucked with a plectrum. **Shamisen** music has many unpitched sounds and is used in **bunraku** and **kabuki** plays.

The **koto** is a 13-stringed wooden harp, about two metres in length, which is laid out flat on the floor or a low table to play. The right hand plucks the strings using three plectra on the thumb, index and middle finger while the left hand presses the strings behind the bridges to change the tone. Techniques to produce unpitched sounds include slowly sliding the reverse side of the plectra along the strings.

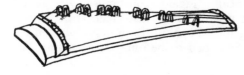

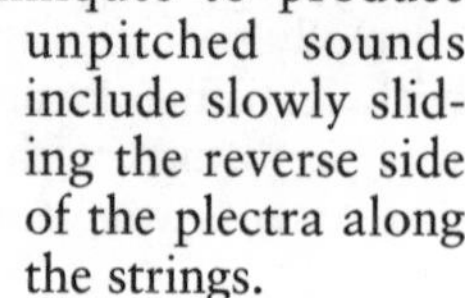

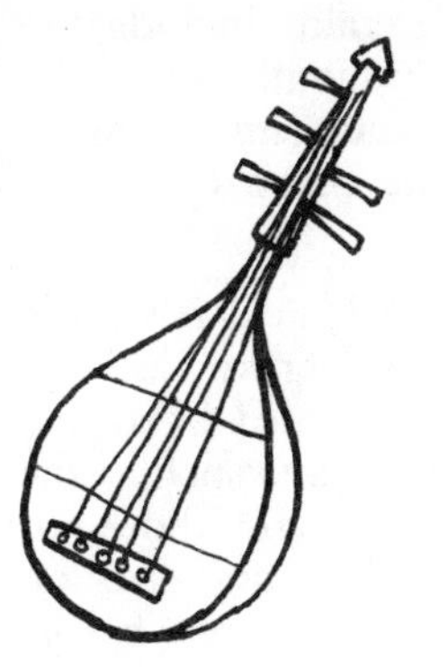

The **biwa** is a short-necked lute which has three, four or five strings. It can be traced back to the 8th century and was used in court music (**gagaku**) in the Heian period. The earliest players of the **biwa** were probably **biwa hōshi** (*lute priests*). These were blind storytellers who travelled around Japan performing their stories to the accompaniment of the **biwa**.

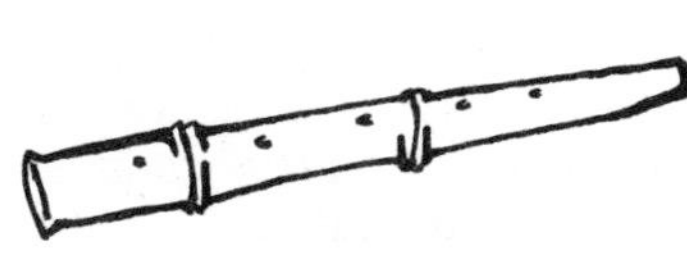

The **shakuhachi** is a bamboo flute played vertically with four finger holes and one thumb hole. It came from China in the 7th century as one of the court musical instruments. In the 17th century it became connected with Zen Buddhism and spiritual discipline and only **kumusō** (*nothingness priests*) were allowed to play it. Today, **shakuhachi** music has taken on many new directions and is a popular choice of contemporary musicians.

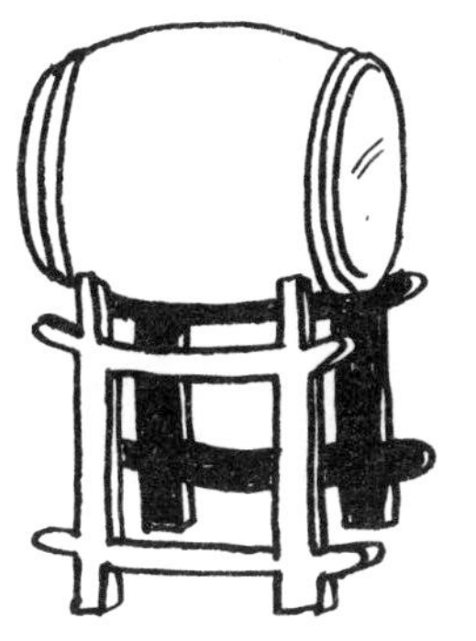

Taiko drumming has become well known outside Japan in recent years because of a number of Japanese and foreign **taiko** drumming groups who give spectacular and energetic performances in theatres around the world. **Taiko** refers to large drums which come in a variety of sizes, the largest being double-sided and positioned on a stand. **Taiko** drums are used in **gagaku** (court music), noh and kabuki drama, **kagura** dance and festival music.

Other instruments which originate in **gagaku** include the **yokobue** (side-blown flute), the **shō** (a type of mouth organ), the **hichiriki** (a type of short bamboo oboe), **tsuzumi** (small drums), **shakubyōshi** (wooden clappers) and **kane** (bronze bells of various sizes).

Today, most Japanese people have never played and rarely listen to traditional music or go to performances of **bugaku** although traditional dance and music are still performed at shrine festivals. However, some people learn instruments such as the **koto** and **shakuhachi**, and girls in particular might choose to attend classes in **buyō** (traditional dance). The music of **enka**, folk songs often sung in karaoke bars by older people, has its roots in **hōgaku** (*traditional music*).

Noh (能) and kyōgen (狂言)

Noh and **kyōgen** date back to the 14th century and are the oldest existing forms of stage entertainment in Japan. Noh was first performed in Kyoto and Nara with the backing of Shinto and Buddhist temples, and there were two types: **dengaku** noh (rice fertility dance–dramas) and **sarugaku** noh (*comedy dramas* – **saru** means *monkey*) which eventually were unified. Noh also drew on elements of older performing arts such as **kagura** dance music, **gigaku** masks and **bugaku** court dances.

What is noh?

Noh is a kind of opera which incorporates music, dance and poetic speech into a highly stylized and formulaic art form. The shogunate and warrior class considered it to be 'high-brow' theatre and were attracted by the ritual and inclusion of Zen Buddhist principles. The shogun, **Tokugawa Ieyasu** (1542–1616), standardized Noh theatre and, during the Edo period, rules and regulations governing acting styles, dress code and layout of stage were created. Commoners were forbidden by the shogunate to watch or take part in noh performances (although some did) and it was deemed suitable only for the aristocracy. It became open to the general public after World War II and today has a small but devoted following. Noh can appear slow and very formal to a newcomer and the language is classical Japanese but the following information will help you to understand this art form better and watching a performance of noh offers an insight into a fascinating and unique cultural tradition.

The stage and setting

Traditional noh stage

The noh stage is based on Shinto architecture and both roof and stage are made of cyprus wood. The five pillars mark the stage positions of the actors and there are no stage sets – only the backdrop of a single painted pine tree (**matsu**). The bridge (**hashigakari**) extends sideways from the changing rooms to the stage so that the walk to the stage is part of the whole drama. A good example of an outdoor noh stage is at the **Itsukushima** Shinto Shrine on the island of **Miyajima** near Hiroshima. Nowadays, noh stages are normally housed within concrete buildings such as the National Noh Theatre in Tokyo (see Taking it further).

The actors

There are two types of actor in noh plays – the **shi-te**, who is the main actor, and the **waki**, who is the supporting actor. The actors also have companions (**tsure**). All parts are played by men and the tradition of noh acting is passed down through families. Many actors begin training from the age of seven and take children's parts (**kokata**). Noh actors have a very stylized way of moving which is a type of 'sliding walk'. They move forward by sliding one foot forward, keeping it flat to the ground then lifting the heel and lowering it before repeating the same with the other foot. Steps are small and slow and noh has been described as '*moving sculpture*'.

Masks and costumes

Noh actors do not wear makeup but the **shi-te** (main actor) and his companions wear simply painted, wooden masks. There are a range of masks for different characters including old men, demons, gods and women. A second mask may be worn by the **shi-te** to reveal his true identity or character. Various stage props are used, such as fans which have symbolic meanings. The costumes are elaborate and bulky with many layers; headdresses and wigs make the actors appear taller. The **shi-te** wears white **tabi** (tight socks with a split between the big toe and the other toes).

Musicians and chorus

The musicians sit at the rear of the stage and the chorus at the side. The instruments used are **nohkan** (flute), **tsuzumi** (hand-held drums) and **taiko** (floor-standing drums). The chorus carry fans which they put on the floor in front of them and pick up when they begin to chant. The chorus have a number of functions which include describing the scene and time (remember that stage sets are not used) and filling in parts of the story.

Takasago: A noh play by Zeami

There are over 240 existing noh plays, all of which are performed according to very specific rules. The script consists of some prose but mainly poetry known as **utai** taken from classical Japanese and Chinese poetry. A synopsis of one play will help to give a flavour of noh drama. This play begins with the entrance of the **waki** who is a wandering priest. He sings of his travels as he walks across the bridge to the stage and he takes his set position at his pillar (lower stage left). The **shi-te** and companion enter next. They are an old couple who are sweeping the floor of the pine forest at Takasago. When they reach their pillar (upper stage right) they tell the **waki** that there is a pine tree in this forest which houses the spirit of a husband and, at a forest some distance away, there is another which houses the spirit of his wife. Although they are parted from each other, they are united at heart. The **shi-te** and companion then reveal their true identities – the spirits of those two trees – and the play ends with the **shi-te**, now wearing the mask of a god, performing a god dance (**kamimai**). The end of a noh play is normally marked by the **shi-te** stamping his foot and then walking slowly and silently across the bridge into the darkness.

FAMOUS PEOPLE
Kanami (1333–84) and Zeami (1363–1443)

As father and son actors and playwrights of the noh theatre they were largely responsible for establishing noh theatre as a serious art form rather than as mere street entertainment. In 1374, **Kanami** and **Zeami** performed in front of the shogun, **Ashikaga Yoshimitsu**, and he was so struck by the power of the play and the acting talents of **Zeami** that he became their patron and a keen sponsor of noh theatre. **Kanami** founded one of the main noh schools and **Zeami** wrote over 40 noh plays as well as the ***Fūshi-kaden***, considered even today as the bible of noh drama because it contains all the principles and rules of noh. Unfortunately, the next shogun took a disliking to **Zeami** and banned him from the stage then exiled him to Sado Island.

What is kyōgen?

Kyōgen is the comic interlude between noh plays or acts. It evolved from **sarugaku** (*monkey* comedy dramas) and is a type of pantomime, similar to the comic acts in Shakespeare plays. Where noh portrays formal characters who symbolize specific human (or other) qualities and uses largely poetic language, **kyōgen** is more down-to-earth with realistic characters who use colloquial language and humour to get their message across to the audience. **Kyōgen** offers light relief during a noh performance but also sets out in plain language to explain or enlarge on events and characters in the main noh play.

Kyōgen uses the same stage and setting as noh, all actors are male and the tradition is passed down through families. Like noh, there are specific schools of acting which have long traditions dating back to Edo and the actors have to be proficient in song, dance and dialogue. The costumes date back to those worn by commoners in medieval Japan such as large checked or striped undergarments, wide shouldered waistcoats and **hakama** (culotte-style trousers). The plays depict everyday life in medieval Japan and laugh at human weaknesses. Characters include the wily servant and his stupid and gullible master, the hen-pecked husband and the newly married son-in-law getting into embarrassing scrapes. The plays contain a lot of dialogue and the actors make their own sound effects which can be very funny.

Kyōgen had a big influence on kabuki (see below) and today offers a valuable insight into medieval lifestyle. It also contains a range of popular songs and music styles of its time. In recent years, it has become very popular in Japan and abroad and is performed independently of noh. You can see **kyōgen** performances at Gion Corner in Kyoto and **kyōgen** actors frequently tour abroad to enthusiastic audiences.

Kabuki (歌舞伎) and bunraku (文楽)

Where noh and kyōgen theatre were the pursuit of the nobility, kabuki and bunraku belonged to the common people of Edo period Japan. They both enjoyed enormous popularity and kabuki is still very popular today although bunraku has struggled more to be a commercial and artistic success. Both are a spectacular and colourful combination of music, vocals, dance and numerous special effects.

FAMOUS PEOPLE
Izumo no Okuni (16–17th century)

Little is known about the life of Izumo no Okuni but she is considered to be the creator of kabuki. It is believed that she was an itinerant dancer who travelled around Japan and it was from these dances that kabuki was born. It is also claimed that she and her female troupe performed in front of the second Tokugawa shogun in 1607 and that, because these dances were erotic, women were banned in 1629 from performing them. Since this time, all roles including those of women have been performed by male actors.

Origins of kabuki

Kabuki drew on kyōgen for its use of dialogue, its realism and its acting techniques. It took its stage layout from noh and added a different type of bridge, the **hanamichi** (this bridge leads from the back of the theatre through the audience to the stage so that actors can make dramatic entrances) and the curtain (to enable set changes), and disposed of the roof. It also drew on the texts and plots of noh and bunraku and used traditional folk dance styles to create a very varied repertoire of kabuki **odori** (*dance*). Kabuki music is created by the flutes and drums used in noh theatre and, from the 17th century, the **shamisen** which became the main instrument. The songs were taken from a wide range of folk and popular songs.

The kabuki stage

The kabuki stage has a front curtain of black, orange and green vertical stripes. It is used between acts and as a backdrop for short scenes. When the curtain is drawn, it is accompanied by the clacking sound of **ki** (wooden clappers) which become faster and faster and add to the dramatic excitement. The **mawaributai** (revolving stage) is a unique feature of kabuki and allows almost instant changes of scene as well as flashbacks within a play and the simultaneous performance of two scenes. The **seri** (trapdoor device) allows actors to vanish, appear suddenly, or reappear after a very swift costume change, adding to the tension and excitement of the performance. The **kuroko** (stagehand) who is treated as invisible by the audience, helps actors achieve almost instantaneous costume changes on stage to the great delight and almost disbelief of the audience. A famous example is the play ***Yoshitsune sembon-zakura*** (*The 1000 Cherry Trees of Yoshitsune*) in which a fox is able to take human form and the stunning costume changes between fox and human and back again make this play a great favourite.

Costumes and makeup

The costumes and wigs of high-ranking characters are very elaborate and luxurious and those of lower rank characters depict the everyday dress of Edo period Japan. **Kumadori** makeup is used on the face to express the mood or nature of a character. There are more than 60 patterns which express emotions such as anger, hatred, passion and jealousy. Red is used to express more positive or heroic traits whereas blue

Kabuki actor in costume

expresses more negative emotions. Brown and black are also used and the patterns are drawn over a whitened face. An example of a well-known (and photographed) pattern is **sujiguma** which is red jagged stripes across the actor's face with the eyebrows and eyes heavily accentuated in black. This serves to exaggerate the features of actors performing in the **aragoto** (*angry hero*) style of acting.

The actors

The art of kabuki acting is highly skilled and takes years to accomplish. It is handed down from father to son and actors belong to acting families whose head is a great actor. They take the name of the family they belong to and particular names are much sought after. Actors normally specialize in particular character types such as **onnagata,** the female roles played by men and develop very stylized vocal techniques. Dialogues run the full range from realistic to highly stylized and the lines are mainly in a 5–7 syllable pattern which gives the delivery a distinctive rhythm and tempo. There are also a wide range of set gestures, poses and acting conventions such as the **mie** (dramatic pose) in which the actor makes his appearance more dramatic by striking a pose at a moment of high emotion to the applause of the audience. Kabuki has retained its appeal today because particular actors are held in high esteem and have a keen following. Actors such as **Ichikawa Ennosuke II** and **Bandō Tamasaburō** will guarantee a full house.

The musicians

There are two sets of musicians in kabuki, those on stage who play the flute and drums (known collectively as **hayashi**) and **shamisen,** and those offstage who create the sound effects with **shamisen,** flute and percussion (including the wooden clappers). These sounds are stylized and prescribed, for example, the sound of falling snow. The onstage ensemble also includes a chanter and they sit on a revolving platform which carries them onto the stage to perform and then off again. The audience is an integral part of the performance and they shout and call out the names of famous actors.

Watching kabuki

Kabuki performances are still held regularly and can be seen in Tokyo at the National Theatre and **Kabukiza** in **Ginza**. A full kabuki performance can last five hours although the audience can come and go and there is a very relaxed atmosphere with people eating packed lunches as they watch. **Kabukiza** often shows favourite scenes rather than whole plays and is a good place to experience some of the more visually dramatic and elaborate kabuki acting.

Origins of bunraku

The earliest accounts of puppet theatre in Japan date back to the 11th century when itinerant entertainers performed plays with hand puppets. In the 15th and 16th centuries, the **biwa hōshi** (*blind priests*) travelled around Japan chanting stories from history to the accompaniment of the **biwa** (lute). In bunraku, the chanting is accompanied by the **shamisen** which replaced the **biwa** and the puppets move to it and act out the story.

The puppets and puppeteers

Bunraku puppets are just over half life size. They have no strings but are manipulated by various handles (**kozaru**) attached via bars (**sashigane**) to different parts of the face and body. The puppets are extremely lifelike and can move their eyes, eyebrows, eyelids, mouth, hands and fingers, head and legs. They wear very elaborate costumes and headdresses. They are manipulated by three puppeteers who appear on the stage, standing in a lower part and holding the puppets over a higher part. The two assistant puppeteers appear in black with hoods and are treated as invisible. The main puppeteer (**omozukai**), however, is often treated as a celebrity in his own right and may appear either in black or in a more elaborate costume depending on the play and his status.

The training to become a puppeteer is very long and is one of the main reasons why bunraku has suffered a decline in performance and popularity. It takes ten years to train as the **hidarizukai** (this assistant manipulates the left arm), another ten years to perfect the skill of the **ashizukai** (this assistant manipulates the legs) and a further ten to become an established **omozukai** (the main puppeteer, responsible for the eyes, mouth, head and right arm, he also supports the puppet).

The tayū (chanter)

The **tayū** recites the story and has to be highly skilled in order to cover the full vocal range of men, women and children. He is accompanied by a **shamisen** player and they sit stage left on the **yuka** (side platform). The three important elements of bunraku are the puppet movements, vocals and **shamisen** accompaniment.

FAMOUS PEOPLE
Chikamatsu Monzaemon (1653–1724)

Chikamatsu Monzaemon is considered to be Japan's greatest playwright and is also referred to as 'the Japanese Shakespeare'. He used the techniques of classical prose, drama and poetry in the writing of his plays and elevated bunraku from popular entertainment to a serious art form. He wrote for the famous **tayū**, ***Takemoto Gidayū*** and began by using historical events as the subject of his plays. He went on to use contemporary events (**sewa mono**) and rose to fame through the play ***Sonezaki Shinjū*** (*Love Suicides at Sonezaki*) in 1703. The play was so influential that it resulted in a spate of double suicides and the government had to step in and declare such suicides as crimes. **Chikamatsu** also wrote plays for kabuki and many are adaptations of bunraku plays. He explored the dilemma between social obligation and personal feelings and emotions.

Synopsis of *Sonezaki Shinjū* (*Love Suicides at Sonezaki*)

Chikamatsu wrote this play after hearing about an actual love suicide. Such suicides were not uncommon in Japan when families opposed the marriage of two lovers. In this play, **Tokubei** has fallen in love with a prostitute called **Ohatsu**. He is expected by his family to marry the girl they have chosen for him and, when he refuses, is thrown out of the family home. His situation worsens when a friend he trusted steals the dowry money intended for him from his uncle to set him up in business and the finger of accusation is pointed at **Tokubei**. He decides that the only way to prove his innocence is to kill himself. **Ohatsu** declares that she will kill herself too so that they can be reunited in the spirit world. The puppets express their love for each other through exquisite movements such as the gentle touching of their knees. In the final scene, **Tokubei** stabs **Ohatsu** in the throat then stabs himself. The play was also converted into a kabuki play.

Bunraku today is financially supported by the government and performances can be seen regularly at **Bunrakuza** in Osaka and also at the National Theatre in Tokyo. Bunraku performers also tour abroad from time to time.

Other performing arts

Rakugo (落語) dates back to the 16th century and is a comic monologue recited by a storyteller who uses voice and facial expression to convey different characters. Followers of **rakugo** are usually familiar with all the storylines because there are only a few and so it is the style in which the performer delivers the story which is most important. Today it is also popular on television and radio. **Odori** (踊り) are popular dances (as opposed to **bugaku** which are court dances) which thrived in the Edo period. They survive today in a number of forms including **bon-odori** which are performed as part of **Obon** (Festival of the Dead) and summer **matsuri** (*festivals*) and have many regional styles. In Kyoto, specific **odori** dance and dance styles have grown up around **geisha** and **maiko** (*apprentice geisha*). Performances of these dances can still be seen on specific dates at Gion Corner in Kyoto.

DID YOU KNOW?
Geisha (芸者)

Geisha (known as **geigi** or **geiko**) and **maiko** (*apprentice geisha*) are surrounded by many Western misconceptions. They are female entertainers who are highly skilled in Japanese arts such as classical Japanese dance, singing and the playing of the **shamisen** and **koto**. Their role is to entertain clients who have paid for their company at teahouses and restaurants. They are also trained to be interesting and witty conversationalists. The custom of geisha entertainment dates back to the 17th century. Girls would often be sold into the system by poor parents and would be adopted by a geisha house (**okiya**). They would work as servants until they were old enough to begin their **maiko** training, usually from about the age of 13. They would then wear the **maiko** uniform – a long-sleeved, colourful kimono with dangling **obi** (wide belt) and red collar at the neck, an elaborate hairstyle and white-powdered face. When a **maiko** became a geisha (traditionally at around the age of 18 but now when about 25) they changed their red collar for a white one, had a different hairstyle and no longer wore white powder.

Traditionally, geisha needed one important patron known as **danna** who would provide the financial support for them and their geisha house. They would have an emotional and sexual relationship with him and sometimes would retire and become his mistress or wife. In addition, they needed to gather a number of favoured clients known as **gohiiki** whom they would entertain at teahouses. The geisha profession offered a lifelong career for women because it did not depend on being young but on being skilled in arts and conversation. Retired geisha often managed bars and restaurants. In post-war Japan there has been a massive decline in the number of geisha, partly because of the increased popularity of Western-style hostess bars. However, girls do still enter the profession from the age of 15 (after they have finished compulsory education) but they no longer need to depend on a patron because wages are sufficient. A number of books about the geisha lifestyle have been published recently in English. (See Taking it further.)

Modern music

From the 1868 Meiji restoration onwards, Western music was adopted and adapted by the Japanese. Orchestras were formed all over Japan to perform Western music and particular types of music enjoyed great popularity such as military music, children's educational music and brass bands. Japan has also produced many first-rate musicians, composers and conductors of classical music who are well known internationally. Among these is **Ozawa Seiji** (1935–) who in his time has conducted the Boston Symphony Orchestra, and the pianist, **Uchida Mitsuko. Sakamoto Ryūichi** (1952–) is a classically trained musician and composer who won international acclaim through his soundtracks for the films *Merry Christmas, Mr Lawrence* (1983) (he also starred in this film) and *The Last Emperor* (1988), for which he won an academy award. He is renowned for his work with the synthesizer and formed the group Yellow Magic Orchestra in 1978. Jazz is also very popular in Japan with some musicians experimenting with traditional Japanese instruments such as the **shakuhachi.**

FAMOUS PEOPLE
Suzuki Shinichi (1898–1999)

Suzuki Shinichi's philosophy was that any child could develop their musical skills through training and education, and his method is famous and followed throughout the world. He is particularly well known for his success in training children from a young age on the violin by ear and rote practice (they learn to read music later). There are about half a million Suzuki Method pupils worldwide.

Pop music of all varieties, both Western and Japanese, is very successful in Japan. The teenage **aidoru** (*idol*) is big business for record companies in Japan. These somewhat cynical commercial ventures involve the auditioning of 'cute' potential pop stars often with minimal singing talents who are marketed aggressively to a hungry teenage audience and are stars for 6–12 months before the next face is launched. They are normally paid no more than a nominal salary and may even be continuing their school studies while being an **aidoru**.

DID YOU KNOW?
Karaoke (カラオケ)

Karaoke originated in Japan in the 1960s and still enjoys great popularity, particularly at work parties when everyone is expected to perform. The word comes from **kara** meaning *empty* and **oke** which is short for *orchestra*. *Empty orchestra* describes the music without lyrics which is central to karaoke. Home karaoke sets are also popular and are often used at picnics and outdoor parties.

Modern dance

Alongside traditional dance genres which continue to flourish in modern Japan, new forms of dance have also emerged. Classical ballet is very popular and Japan has produced international ballet stars such as **Morishita Yōko** who danced with Rudolf Nureyev. An important avant garde Japanese dance form which began in the late 1950s is **butō** which was made internationally famous by the group **Sankai Juku**. They shave their heads and paint their whole bodies white and their dance sequences create a spectacle of moving sculptures. Performances are often given in unusual places which enhance and complement the performance such as underground caverns and famous landmarks such as Stonehenge in Britain. Popular dance flourishes in all its forms and fads in modern Japan and all big cities have plenty of discos and nightclubs. If you visit Tokyo a 'must see' on the tourist route are the weird and wonderful dancers in Yoyogi Park who gather on Sundays in a variety of pop and rock costumes and perform dance routines.

Modern theatre

With the Meiji restoration in 1868 came a hunger for exploring new types of drama and theatre and a reaction against traditional forms such as kabuki. Kabuki playwrights themselves wrote new plays and a new form of drama called **shingeki** (*new theatre*) developed at the beginning of the 20th century. This was strongly influenced by playwrights such as Ibsen and Shakespeare and then, throughout the 20th century, by Marxism, socialist realism and other left-wing movements. Many of the plays performed were Western plays in translation. One of the major theatre companies was **Bungakuza** which is still active today. There was a reaction against **shingeki** in the 1960s and the rise of a new underground theatre movement called **shōgekijō undō** (*the little theatre movement*) which began to explore a wide range of styles, structures and subjects. The movement's name reflected the fact that performances were for small audience numbers of about 100 in small theatres, marquees or in outdoor settings. The plays were contemporary Japanese dramas and there was much experimentation and creativity.

Shimpa theatre grew out of kabuki but unlike **shingeki** had its roots in Japanese tradition rather than Western-style theatre. It began in 1888 and was revolutionary in using female actresses after a ban of more than 250 years. It also used female impersonators and focused on female roles in the areas, first, of politics then melodrama, Japanese history and contemporary life. It was especially successful at the beginning of the 20th century and some of the great plays explored female 'underworld' cultures such as geisha. It still exists but is less popular in modern-day Japan.

FAMOUS PEOPLE
Ninagawa Yukio (1935–)

The stage director, **Ninagawa**, became internationally famous through his work with the **shōgekijō undō** (*underground theatre movement*) and he ran one of its more successful theatre groups, **Gendaijin Gekijō** (Theatre of Contemporary Man) from 1969–71. He then moved into commercial theatre and has been particularly interested in converting Western plays to Japanese settings. Productions include *Romeo and Juliet* in 1974, a kabuki-style *Macbeth* in 1981 and *The Tempest* in 1987 which have all toured worldwide to great acclaim.

Takarazuka is a type of variety show with all-female casts who take both the male and female roles. The emphasis is on the spectacular with big numbers both in terms of song and dance. A show will include a variety of song styles including opera, pop and classical Japanese. Costumes and headdresses are big, glitzy and colourful and the women dressed as men are the main stars, admired for their beauty. **Takarazuka** theatre offers a unique insight into modern Japanese culture and is an alternative to West End and Broadway-style shows (Japan has these as well). Famous productions have included ***Kaze to tomo ni sarinu*** (*Gone with the Wind*).

Taking it further

Websites

Kabuki for everyone **http://www.fix.co.jp/kabuki/kabuki.html** has video clips of actors and dancers, music clips, colour pictures of actors and instruments.

The kabuki story **http://www.lightbrigade.demon.co.uk** includes history, dramatic elements, music, costume etc.

Elements of noh-kyogen **http://www.ijnet.or.jp/NOH-KYOGEN/** is an explanation of various aspects of noh and kyogen.

Bunraku fans' room **http://ing.alacarte.co.jp/~oichini06/P++café.html**

Music

Japanese Music and Musical Instruments, William P. Malm (Charles Tuttle Co., 1959)

Japanese Folk Songs with Piano Accompaniment, ed. Ryutaro Hattori (Japan Times, 1959)

The Wind Children and other Tales from Japan, Samira Kirollos (Andre Deutsch, 1989)

The Shining Princess and Other Japanese Legends, Eric Quayle and Michael Foreman (Anderson Press, 1989)

Recordings

The Japanese label Legacy–Dna produces a number of Japanese traditional musical recordings such as: *Gagaku – Ancient Japanese Court Music* by the Imperial Court Ensemble (1994); *Art of the Japanese Bamboo Flute*; and *Japanese Shinto Ritual*

Music. ARC have produced *The Art of the Japanese Koto, Shakuhachi and Shamisen* by the Yamato Ensemble, and the Sounds of the World label has produced *Japanese Favourites – Various Artists* (September 1999). You can find these and others on Amazon.com by searching for Japanese under **Music** and you can also listen to samples on this site. You can also check with retail outlets who will advice you on availability of Japanese music. Finally, the JICC (see Unit 1) loans videos and audio cassettes and will send you a list if you contact them.

Modern plays

Onna no isshō, Morimoto Kaoru (*A Woman's Life*, 1962)

Sono imōto, Mushanokōji Saneatsu (*The Sister*, 1936)

Yūzuru, Kinoshita Junji (*Twilight Crane*, 1956). Folktale shingeki play

Mishima Yukio rewrote noh plays in modern interpretation, exploring psychology of characters

Geisha

Memoirs of a Geisha, Arthur Golden (London, Vintage, Random House, 1997). A novel about geisha life before the war

Geisha, Lesley Downer (Headline, 2001). A non-fictional study of geisha life

Geisha, Liza Dalby (Vintage, 2000). Liza lived as a geisha in order to research this book

GLOSSARY

邦楽 **hōgaku**	*traditional music*
神楽 **kagura**	*Shinto dance*
伎楽 **gigaku**	*masked dance–drama*
雅楽 **gagaku**	*old Japanese court music*
舞楽 **bugaku**	*court dance and music*
琴 **koto**	*Japanese harp*
尺八 **shakuhachi**	*bamboo flute*
琵琶 **biwa**	*lute*
三味線 **shamisen**	*3-stringed Japanese guitar*
太鼓 **taiko**	*drum*
能 **noh**	
狂言 **kyōgen**	
舞台 **butai**	*stage*
能役者 **nōyakusha**	*noh actor*

仕手 **shi-te**	*main actor*
脇 **waki**	*supporting actor*
俳優 **haiyū**	*actor*
女形 **onnagata**	*male actor in female kabuki roles*
歌舞伎 **kabuki**	
文楽 **bunraku**	
落語 **rakugo**	*comic monologue*
踊り **odori**	*dance*
芸者 **geisha**	
舞子 **maiko**	*apprentice geisha*
カラオケ **karaoke**	
アイドル **aidoru**	*pop idol*
新劇 **shingeki**	*new theatre*
劇場 **gekijō**	*theatre*

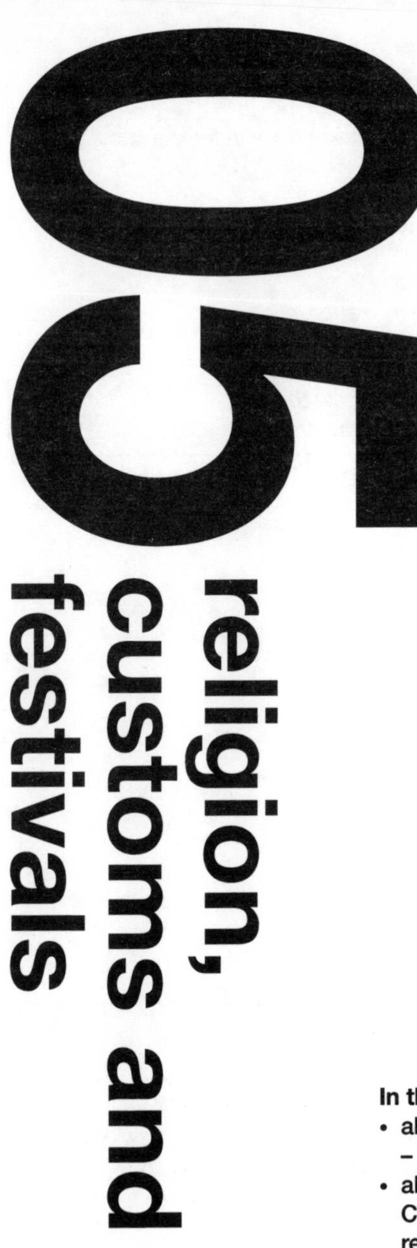

05 religion, customs and festivals

In this unit you will learn

- about Japan's main religions – Buddhism and Shinto
- about Confucianism, Christianity and new religions
- about annual events, festivals and holidays

Modern-day Japan has no state religion but its two main religions, Shinto and Buddhism, have influenced many aspects of Japanese spiritual, cultural, social and political life. This unit will also look at Christianity, Confucianism, new religions and the main annual festivals with their associated customs.

The coexistence of Shinto and Buddhism

The separate features of Shinto and Buddhism are discussed next but the two have been well integrated since the 8th century when Buddhist temples increasingly were built next to or within Shinto shrine grounds and Buddhist priests began to take Shinto services. At this time, two Buddhist priests, **Kūkai** and **Saichō**, devoted much time to identifying Shinto gods with their Buddhist equivalents. The simplicity of Shinto architecture also changed under the influence of the more ornamental and elaborate Buddhist styles. From the Meiji period (1868) until the end of World War II, the government separated Shinto from Buddhism and established Shinto as the state religion but in post-war Japan the two religions once more exist peacefully side by side.

Shinto (神道)

Shinto worship is native to Japan and can be traced back into ancient history and mythology. The kanji **shin** (also pronounced **kami**) means *gods* and the kanji **tō** means *path* or *way* – *Way of the Gods*. Shinto has no written doctrine and is concerned with ancestor and nature worship expressed through ceremony and ritual.

DID YOU KNOW?

The kanji 道 (**tō/dō**) meaning *way* or *path* is used in many of the traditional arts of Japan. Examples include: **sadō** (*Way of Tea* or tea ceremony), **bushidō** (*Way of the Warrior* or the warrior code), **kyūdō** (*Way of the Bow* or Japanese archery) and **jūdō** (*Way of Softness*). The word imbues these arts with a spiritual and mental dimension – they are not merely physical or leisure activities but are also concerned with the right state of mind, self-discipline and meditation.

What is Shinto?

At its simplest, Shinto religion is the veneration of natural objects such as mountains, trees and rocks. The belief is that **kami** (*gods*) are present everywhere and can be called on to protect and help humans. All **kami** have **tama** (this is like a soul or life force) which can be invoked at ceremonies to enter the venerated object. Humans also possess **tama** which leave them when they die but are invoked at Shinto ceremonies dedicated to ancestor worship.

Jinja (shrines 神社)

Shinto shrine Torii

Shinto worship is carried out at **jinja** (*shrines*). There are more than 85,000 **jinja** in Japan today and they range in size from small neighbourhood shrines to large nationally famous ones. The typical **jinja** is surrounded by a simple fence with a distinctive gateway known as a **torii**. This is made up of two vertical columns of wood with two horizontal ones across the top. The simplest and oldest **torii** are made from natural wood but dark orange-painted **torii** are very common. They symbolize the division between the outer everyday world and the sacred space of the shrine.

A tree-lined pathway normally leads from the **torii** to the **haiden** (*hall of worship*). There are steps leading up to this and at the entrance is a **saisen-bako** (*collection box*), normally of wood with a slatted top. Visitors to the shrine throw money into this as offerings to the **kami**. Hanging above this is a rope with a bell attached which is pulled to attract the attention of the gods.

Visitors also clap their hands twice to attract the gods and then pray. Near to the **haiden** is the **temizuya** which contains water and ladles so that people can purify themselves by washing their hands and mouths before visiting the **haiden**.

Behind the **haiden** is the most sacred building, the **honden**. Only Shinto priests are allowed here and it is in here that the **kami** and the associated venerated objects (**shintai**) are kept. Other features of the **jinja** are the two stone lions (**komainu**) which guard the entrance to the shrine and ward off evil. One lion has its mouth open and is called **a** (the first sound of the Japanese 'alphabet') and the other has its mouth closed and is called **un** (the last sound), and together they symbolize the first cry of a baby and the final breath before death.

Ritual objects and charms

Plaited straw ropes (**shimenawa**) which keep off plague and bad harvests are common in shrines and branches of the **sakaki** tree (a sacred tree) and are sometimes placed on Shinto altars. Purification rituals are important in Shinto worship and symbols of purification include folded zigzag paper strips tied to sacred trees, ropes and gateways, rice, sake (rice wine) and salt. Sumo wrestling has many Shinto rituals, for example, the wrestlers throw salt on the ring before fighting in order to purify the space and themselves. Shrines normally have an office selling prayer items and charms. **Ema** (*picture horse*) are small wooden plaques with a picture on one side of a horse or other divine object. People write prayers and wishes on them and attach them to a board within the shrine to be read by the **kami**. **Omikuji** are strips of paper with fortunes written on them which are rolled up inside bamboo sticks. You shake a stick from a box and read your fortune which can range from **daikichi** (*very good fortune*) all the way to **kyō** (*bad luck*). You then tie the strip of paper to the branches of a tree in the grounds of the shrine. **Omamori** are small cloth talismans which you can hang in your car or keep in your bag to ward off evil.

The Shinto priest (kannushi)

Kannushi and female assistants (**miko**) carry out the official duties at Shinto shrines and ceremonies. Priests wear a black headdress (**eboshi**), culotte-style trousers (**hakama**) and a robe with wide sleeves which is white for everyday wear and black for special ceremonies. They wear black wooden clogs and carry a wooden mace (**shaku**) as a symbol of office. The **miko** wear a red kimono with a white over-robe.

TWO FAMOUS SHRINES
Ise and Izumo

These are both national treasures and are the only shrines where Buddhist priests are not allowed to officiate at ceremonies. The **Ise** Shrine in the **Ise-shima** National Park (within easy reach of Nagoya) is believed to house the sacred mirror used by the sun goddess, **Amaterasu**, and, as **Amaterasu** is the central deity in Shinto religion, **Ise** is its central shrine. Legend tells how the daughter of an emperor was travelling through Japan looking for a place to house the sacred mirror when Amaterasu spoke to her and chose Ise. The Ise Shrine is rebuilt every 20 years in order to keep the site purified (traditionally, all shrines would have practised this ritual).

The **Izumo** Shrine in Shimane prefecture (north of Hiroshima) is the oldest shrine in Japan (founded 1,500 years ago) although last rebuilt in 1744. The god, **Okuninushi**, is said to have given the earth as a gift to Amaterasu's grandson and, as a way of thanking him, she built the **Izumo** Shrine in his honour. The shrine celebrates the **Kamiari Matsuri** from 11–17 October when it is believed that Shinto gods from all over Japan gather there. Small boxes are placed around the shrine grounds as houses for the gods and ceremonies are held to honour them. The traditional name for October was **kannazuki (kaminashi** in modern Japanese) meaning *month without gods* (referring to the rest of Japan).

The Yasukuni Shrine

This shrine in Tokyo is part of the tradition of national, state-sponsored Shinto which developed from 1868 until the end of World War II. During this period, the emperor was declared divine and Shinto religion was used to promote loyalty to the state and patriotism. In 1945, under the American occupation of Japan, the link between Shinto and government was broken and shrines were once more private organizations. Emperor Meiji ordered the building of the **Yasukuni** Shrine in 1869 to honour all those who had died fighting for Japan in the various wars since 1853. Although state support of shrines was banned after the war, this shrine is still surrounded by controversy, both by those who wish government support to be restored and those (particularly war veterans of the Allied forces, and countries who were occupied by Japan) who are strongly opposed to a shrine which honours, among others, men who were tried as war criminals. It only became public in 1976 that war criminals including the wartime Prime Minister, **Tōjo**, had been added to the list of wartime dead at the shrine, and in 1985 Prime Minister Nakasone caused massive international protests by visiting the shrine on the 40th anniversary of the end of the war. Other prime ministers have continued the annual visit amid objections which always make headline international news.

DID YOU KNOW?
Kamidana (Shinto family altars 神棚)

These are small wooden altars, often in the form of miniature shrines, which are placed in Japanese homes (usually in the room used to receive visitors) on a shelf above the door to honour the **kami** who are believed to be everywhere, including the home. Food and drink offerings such as **sake**, **mochi** (rice cakes) and satsumas, are placed in front of the altar, and a **shimenawa** (plaited rope) is hung above it. Other ritual items such as the zigzag paper strips are also hung there. In modern-day Japan, fewer homes have **kamidana**.

Buddhism (bukkyō 仏教)

Buddhism was started in India in the 5th century BC by an Indian Prince, **Gautama**, who decided to give up his privileged lifestyle when he saw a man dying so that he could discover the reason for suffering and the meaning of life. He became the first Buddha, a word which means 'one who understands the truth'. He spread his teachings to his followers so that all humans could achieve enlightenment (understanding of the truth of life and freedom from suffering) by rejecting worldly goods and desires, disciplining the mind and practising meditation. Buddhists believe that all beings are tied into a cycle of life, death and rebirth (reincarnation) because of attachment to worldly desires and that by freeing the mind of these, you can be freed from the cycle and achieve Buddhahood and nirvana (absolute peace and freedom).

One form of Buddhism which spread among commoners from the 3rd century BC was Mahayana Buddhism which emphasized that all people can achieve salvation. It also taught that, as well as buddhas (those who have reached enlightenment), there existed bodhisattvas (in Japanese known as **bosatsu**) who put off their own salvation until all humans have achieved theirs. This form of Buddhism spread to China in the 1st and 2nd centuries BC where it was modified to fit Chinese beliefs and culture. Added to it were Confucian ethics and more concrete ideas of the importance of loyalty, respect and good relationships with family, society and superiors. It was this form of Buddhism which reached Japan via Korea in the 6th century AD.

DID YOU KNOW?
Bodhisattvas or bosatsu

Bosatsu are still very popular in Japan because they can be called upon to help humans. The two most popular in Japan are **Kannon** who symbolizes compassion and **Jizō Bosatu**, the saviour of children. **Jizō** statues are found alongside roads, in ricefields and at village boundaries. They are often dressed in bibs and are usually depicted as monks with a jewel in one hand and a spear in the other. They have been assimilated with a native god, **dōsojin**, who is the guardian of roads and village boundaries. At Buddhist temples dedicated to lost (including aborted) children, the **Jizō** statues are clothed in red robes and worshippers adorn the temple complex with their own small statues in memory of their dead children.

Buddhism arrives in Japan

The historical document, the ***Nihon Shoki***, recounts how, in AD 552, a Korean king sent to the emperor of Japan a gift of a gold and copper Buddhist statue and a selection of Buddhist scriptures. The Japanese courtiers were divided over whether to accept this gift; some feared angering the native Japanese gods and the statue was twice thrown into the river only to be rescued again when plague and other disasters struck.

FAMOUS PEOPLE
Prince Shōtoku (AD 574–622)

Shōtoku Taishi, regent to the Empress **Suiko**, is credited with being the founder and first patron of Buddhism in Japan. He also put an end to the many wars between powerful families in the Nara area and established a centralized government. He made the spreading of Buddhism a central feature of government policy. Many legends around **Shōtoku** are reminiscent of the life of Christ. For example, he was said to have been born in front of a stable around which appeared a reddish-yellow light. These legends probably emerged when stories from the bible spread to Japan from China (see also p. 8).

Branches of Buddhism

During the Nara period (710–794) Buddhism became gradually established as the state religion and many great temples were built in and around Nara including the **Tōdaiji** temple (see p. 9). Since that time, a number of types of Buddhism have reached Japan and some of the main branches are now briefly examined.

Esoteric Buddhism (Mikkyō)

This spread from India via Asia to Japan in the Heian period (794–1192). It means *secret teachings* and its central belief was that the teachings of the Buddha were mystical and should be kept secret, to be studied only by those, such as priests, who were thought capable of understanding them. Followers were expected to live an austere life and to recite the teachings of the Buddha in order to gain enlightenment.

Pure Land Buddhism (Jōdokyō)

This came from China and was very popular in Japan, particularly in the 12th century. It taught that salvation was open to all but that you could not be saved through your own efforts. The Buddha **Amida** could be called upon to save you and guide you to the Pure Land (paradise) and Buddhahood. To be reborn into paradise you needed to chant the phrase **Namu Amida Butsu** (*I take my refuge in the Buddha Amida*). This chant is known as the **nembutsu** and needs to be recited repeatedly with sincerity and devotion. A key figure in these teachings was the priest **Shinran** (1173–1262), who founded **Jōdo Shin**, one of the leading Buddhists sects in Japan today, and sometimes referred to as Shin Buddhism in the West. Pure Land Buddhism was fiercely opposed by the more established Buddhist sects.

The Nichiren sect

This was founded by the priest, **Nichiren** (1222–82) and was responsible, together with Pure Land and Zen Buddhism, for the renewal of interest in Buddhism during the Kamakura period (1185–1333). Nichiren believed that only one book of the teachings of Buddha, the ***Hokekyō*** (the *Lotus Sutra*), was true and sacred and that only his sect could teach the way to salvation and enlightenment which he believed was attainable in this life. He suffered much persecution from other Buddhist schools and was exiled to **Sado** Island by the shogun. However, he predicted that Japan would be invaded if the shogunate did not believe in the **Nichiren** sect and, when his predictions came true with the Mongol Invasions of 1274 (see p. 13), the popularity of the sect increased hugely.

Zen Buddhism

This branch originated in India and came to Japan via China. Its teachings centre on the importance of meditation in order to experience enlightenment. The lotus position (**zazen**) is a feature of Zen meditation and originated in Indian yoga. The Zen emphasis on self-discipline, the emptying of the mind of worry and desire and the pursuit of beauty in simple and non-ostentatious forms made it very popular with the shogun and the military class from the Kamakura period (1185–1333) onwards. Zen Buddhism today has about 10 million followers in Japan and more than 20,000 temples.

Zen Buddhism had a great influence on cultural and artistic developments in Japan. Styles of painting developed such as black and white paintings (**suibokuga**) and landscape paintings (**sansuiga**) (see Unit 3) and such was the influence of Zen that a category of painting and calligraphy called **Zenga** was created and refers in particular to the works of Zen monks in the Edo period (1600–1868). Other art forms which developed and were influenced by Zen Buddhism were **ikebana** (flower arrangement), **teien** (gardens) and **sadō** (tea ceremony).

DID YOU KNOW?
Sadō (way of tea or tea ceremony 茶道)

The Chinese drank tea as a way of keeping the mind alert during meditation and this custom was brought over to Japan in the 8th century. By the 15th century the aristocratic class had developed tea drinking beyond meditation and religious ceremony, to a leisure activity in which ornate cups and teapots were used. The tea ceremony developed as a way of returning tea drinking to its Buddhist origins and making it into a simple and disciplined art. It was extremely popular among the shogun and the samurai class who held the principles of simplicity, austerity, self-discipline and meditation central to their philosophy of life.

The tea master **Murata Shukō** (1422–1502) was the first Buddhist monk to encourage a return to simplicity and Buddhist observance when drinking tea. He had been taught by the monk, **Ikkyū**, a key figure in the promotion of Zen Buddhism, that the drinking of tea in the right frame of mind was a way of reaching enlightenment. **Shukō** designed the first 4.5 mat tearoom (about

9 m²; rooms are measured by the number of mats), on which all modern tearooms are modelled. **Sen no Rikyū** (1522–91) completed the development of the tea ceremony and added its rituals and the Zen principles of **wabi** (simple elegance) and **sabi** (refinement) so that the ceremony represented the idea of true beauty in something which is simple and plain. Through the rituals of purification such as washing hands, mouth and utensils, the quiet contemplation of the hanging scroll, flower arrangement and teabowl (the beauty of the bowl is in its simplicity), and the actual etiquette involved in drinking the tea, participants can reach a meditative and harmonious state of mind.

The Buddhist temple complex (tera 寺)

Buddhist temple complex

There are about 78,000 Buddhist temples (**tera**) in Japan today. The layouts vary according to the sect and period, but there are certain general features and a visit to a Buddhist temple is an excellent way of learning more about classical Japanese architectural features.

The main buildings are the **hondō** (also called **kondō** or **butsuden,** *main hall*) and the pagoda. The **hondō** has an inner and outer sanctuary; worshippers gather in the outer part and pray facing the inner sanctuary where there are statues and other images of the Buddha. The pagoda normally has five storeys and it is here that the remains of the Buddha are kept. Large incense bowls are normally placed in front of the **hondō** and worshippers burn incense sticks and purify themselves by fanning the smoke over their bodies. Buddhist temples have a **bonshō** (large bronze or iron bell) which is rung to announce the beginning of a ceremony. On New Year's Eve it is rung 108 times to hail in the New Year and cast out the traditional 108 evils that humans are capable of according to Buddhist belief. The main temple gates are often looked over by a pair of guardian statues known as **nio**.

DID YOU KNOW?
Temple gardens (庭園)

Japanese gardens (**teien**) are famous and widely copied throughout the world. There are a number of types but the four main elements are green plants, rock, water and sand/gravel. Rocks are central to a Japanese garden and the priests who designed gardens were called 'rock-arranging monks'. Zen Buddhism had a great influence on garden design, in particular the **karesansui** (*dry mountain stream*) style in which water was symbolized by the sweep and patterning of the sand and gravel. A famous example is the **Ryōanji** Temple rock garden in Kyoto. The white sand symbolizes the ocean and the 15 rocks are the islands within it. Zen Buddhists believed, however, that by contemplating the garden and meditating you could find your own interpretation. Gardens may be representations of a natural landscape on a reduced scale (the rocks at **Ryōanji** get smaller towards the back to add perspective and make the space seem larger) or have symbolic meaning (a conical mound of gravel in the garden of the **Ginkakuji** (silver pavilion) in Kyoto represents Mount Fuji).

Shinto and Buddhism in Japan today

About 105 million people have some involvement with Shinto and 95 million with Buddhism in modern-day Japan out of a population of 127 million (many people participate in both religions). The two religions are well integrated and people use both for different purposes and events. The Shinto shrine is used for celebratory or agricultural events such as births, coming of age, weddings and rice planting whereas people turn to Buddhist ceremonies for solemn events such as funerals and memorial services. Japanese people will also consult Buddhist priests about a suitable name for their child or an auspicious day on which to get married and, although the majority of people marry in Shinto shrines, serious followers of Buddhism will have a Buddhist marriage ceremony. Nevertheless, although more than 80 per cent of Japanese people would describe themselves as Buddhist if asked for their religion, most would also say that they have no active or regular involvement in religious worship. The more recent surge in interest in new religious groups may indicate a search by some Japanese for spiritual meaning or explanation in modern-day life.

Buddhism in particular has become increasingly secularized in modern-day Japan and many Buddhist temples are perceived more as profit-making businesses than as religious centres. This change can be traced back to the Meiji period when a government edict allowed Buddhist priests to marry, have families, grow their hair, eat meat and only wear robes for services. As a result, entry to the priesthood has to a certain extent become hereditary, passing from father to son, particularly in the case of prosperous temples. Fees for Buddhist services can be very high, for example, the price of a single grave plot in Tokyo is about £10,000 ($20,000) and a gravestone is the same price again. Fees for funeral and memorial services are also high and if you wish to purchase a **kaimyo** (an afterdeath name given to Buddhist followers) for a dead relative, the longer the name the more you pay (longer names are thought to carry higher status). This is not to say that all Buddhist sects fit this description and there are still those which follow more austere and non-materialistic practices.

Confucianism (jukyō 儒教)

Confucius (or **Kong Qiu** as he is called in China) was a Chinese teacher and philosopher of the 3rd century BC. Confucianism is a philosophy or set of moral codes, not a religion but many of the ideas were transferred to Buddhism. Confucius believed that morality and social order should be taught by example from the political leaders of society and that the values of critical importance were loyalty to family, community and country, and filial piety (the respect of children for their parents, or to be precise, for their father as women had no social status). These ideas transferred to Japan with Buddhism from the 6th century. Confucianism enjoyed a revival in the Edo period in a new form called neo-Confucianism. This had a more intellectual flavour and was popular with the warrior class who had the leisure time to study it and were attracted by its moral codes and ethics.

During this time it was also used to promote obedience and inferiority of women to men which included an inequality in the rules of divorce: a man could divorce his wife if she talked too much; a woman could only divorce her husband if she became a nun for two years! Confucianism was given a nationalistic interpretation in the 1930s when it was used in national policy to promote social harmony, the merits of hard work and loyalty to the emperor as moral leader.

Christianity (kirisutokyō キリスト教)

Christianity was introduced to Japan from Portugal by the Jesuit, Francis Xavier, in 1549. Initially it was tolerated by the Japanese authorities but the military leader and unifier, **Toyotomi Hideyoshi** (1536–98), became increasingly suspicious of it and the Tokugawa shogunate banned it in 1612. Japanese Christians were forced to recant their belief or suffer death through burning or beheading. A particularly famous historical incident is that of the 26 martyrs, foreign and Japanese, who were crucified in Nagasaki in 1597. There is a monument to them in the Peace Park in Nagasaki. The ban on Christianity was finally lifted by the Meiji government in 1873 and in today's Japan there are an estimated 1.7 million Christians, about 1 per cent of the total population. Christianity is still considered 'foreign' in nature to most Japanese and at odds with traditional belief and ethics which are group led rather than individual.

New religions (shinkō shūkyō 新興宗教)

From the 19th century onwards, new religions have emerged, mainly taking their influences from Buddhism and Shinto. In the first half of the 20th century, the Japanese government controlled religious practice and made Shinto the official religion but after 1945 freedom of religion for all and the banning of state involvement in religion was written into the new constitution. As a result, many more new religions appeared, usually centred around a charismatic leader and often using the mass media to promote their teachings and recruit new members. The largest of these new religions with more than 8 million families as followers and more than 1 million members abroad is **Sōka Gakkai**. This religion is based on the teachings of the **Nichiren** sect of Buddhism and central to its belief are the acts of chanting, following Buddhist practices in one's everyday life and spreading the teachings of the religion to other people.

These new religions were well established and institutionalized by the 1970s but following in their wake was a group of new religions sometimes referred to as new new religions (**shinshin shūkyō**) to distinguish them from the more established ones. Some of these have centred around magical beliefs, others have gained notoriety by the control they have held over their members, in extreme cases this has resulted in mass suicide pacts. The most notorious of these groups in recent years has been **Aum Shinrikyō** whose leaders were arrested in 1995 after they had released sarin nerve gas on the Tokyo underground, causing the death of 11 people and injuries to 38,000 others. This was worldwide news and three of the leaders have already been served the death penalty of hanging (rarely used in Japan). The main leader, **Shoko Asahara,** is still undergoing trial and this is expected to last several years. **Aum Shinrikyō** called itself a new Buddhist sect and taught its members that the only way to find salvation was to let go of worldly desire by donating all personal wealth to the sect. **Shoko Asahara** had predicted the end of the world in 1999 by nuclear warfare unless 30,000 people achieved salvation. The group had been officially recognized as a religious organization by the City of Tokyo in 1989 and public outrage at the sarin attack and other related crimes brought about a new organization control law in 1999 which gave the government the powers to intervene when organizations were considered to be dangerous.

Annual events, festivals and public holidays

Japan has a huge variety of regional and national festivals on the themes of, among others, agriculture, ancestor remembrance, annual and lifecycles, historical and religious events. This section lists the main annual events of the Japanese calendar. There are many more regional and smaller events during the year including unusual ones such as mud-slinging festivals, **hiwatari** (walking barefoot across hot coals) and **gohan shiki** (a ceremony when people are forced to eat and drink huge quantities!). In total there are 15 public holidays in Japan. [**PH** = public holiday.]

Ō-misoka (*New Year's Eve*) and Shōgatsu (*New Year*) PH

This is the most important event in the Japanese calendar and almost all businesses are closed from 1–3 January. It is the Japanese equivalent of Christmas. Homes are decorated with traditional decorations such as **shimenawa** (straw rope), **kadomatsu** (pine and bamboo arrangement in front of the house) and **kagamimochi** (offerings of rice cakes to the gods). Most people spend New Year with family and New Year's Eve watching special programmes on TV. At midnight, temples all over Japan ring their bells 108 times in a ceremony known as **joya no kane**. People visit shrines and temples up until 7 January (a custom called **hatsumōde** – *the first visit*) to pray for good fortune in the new year. On New Year's Day (**ganjitsu**), special food is eaten called **osechi-ryōri** and relatives visit family homes, often wearing formal kimono to mark the special day. Children are given **otoshidama** (New Year pocket money) by parents and relatives. The Japanese send a total of about 4 billion New Year cards (the average family sends 100) called **nengajō** to work associates, family and friends. These are in the form of postcards with pictures of good luck objects or the animal of that year. They are sent to the post office in the weeks leading up to New Year and are then all delivered at the same time on New Year's Day.

Kurisumasu (Christmas)

This is not really celebrated in Japan and for most people is a normal working day. Many of the commercial aspects of Christmas are apparent, however, such as lights and illuminations, shop window displays and Father Christmas grottoes. Young children are usually given a special Christmas cake made of sponge and cream to eat at home. Couples go on special dates, usually booking an expensive restaurant weeks in advance.

3 February Setsubun (*Bean-throwing Ceremony*)

In homes and shrines, people throw **mame** (*soybeans*) while chanting **oni soto fuku uchi** meaning *devils out, good fortune in* in order to drive out sickness and bad luck. 3 February is the last day of winter on the Chinese calendar and so this is a type of spring cleaning ceremony.

3 March Hina Matsuri (*Girls' Day* or *Doll Festival*, also called Momo no Sekku)

This festival is for younger girls. On the day or some days before, families set out a tiered stand covered in red cloth and place dolls on it representing the imperial court of the Heian period with the prince and princess at the top. Tradition has it that if the dolls are not put away at the end of the day then the girls of the family will not get married.

8 April Hana Matsuri (*Flower Festival*, also known as the Buddha's Birthday)

On this day statues of the Buddha are anointed with hydrangea tea and flower festivals are held around the country.

5 May Kodomo no Hi (*Boys' Day*, also called Tango no Sekku) PH

Families with boys fly **koinobori** (long banners in the shape of colourful carp) from flagpoles outside their homes and display dolls in samurai costume. These symbolize the hope that the boys will grow up healthy and strong.

DID YOU KNOW?
Golden Week

Golden Week is the big holiday period in Japan, beginning with the public holiday on 29 April and ending with Boys' Day. There are four public holidays and most people take off the other days as well (many businesses close during this period). With virtually the whole of the country on holiday, roads, train stations and airports become very congested and some people opt to stay at home, away from the crowds.

7 July Tanabata (*Star Festival*)

Tanabata is the celebration of the legend of two lovers, the Weaver Princess and the Cowherd, who are represented by two stars in the sky, separated by the Milky Way. On this night they are allowed to cross the Milky Way and meet. Children write wishes on strips of paper and tie them to bamboo branches which they place in the garden.

15 August Obon (*Ancestor Remembrance Festival*)

Bon or **Obon** is another very important festival and holiday. In Buddhist belief, this is when the spirits of the dead return home and so many Japanese people return to their family homes, clean the family graves and give offerings of special food to the dead. During August there are also many firework displays and **matsuri** (*festivals*) with **bon odori** (*dancing*) which varies from region to region. Flights, trains and roads are very busy and booked up at this time of year.

15 November Shichi-Go-San (*7–5–3 Festival for Children*)

This ceremony is a celebration for girls aged 3 and 7 and boys aged 5 years old. Children dress up in colourful kimono or their best Western clothes and visit the shrines with their families to pray for good health and fortune. They are given a long bag of traditional sweets sold at the shrine called **chitose-ame** which means '*thousand-year candy*' and is a symbol of long life.

Other key dates include:

2nd Monday in January **Seijin no Hi** (*Coming of Age Day*) PH
11 February **Kenkoku Kinenbi** (*National Founding Day*) PH
21 March **Shunbun no Hi** (*Vernal Equinox Day*) PH
29 April **Midori no Hi** (*Green Day* – appreciation of nature) PH
3 May **Kenpō Kinenbi** (*Constitution Memorial Day*) PH
4 May **Kokumin no Kyūjitsu** (*Citizens' Day*) PH
20 July **Umi no Hi** (*Day of the Sea*) PH
Mid-September **Tsukimi** (*Moon Viewing Festival*)
15 September **Keirō no Hi** (*Respect for the Elderly Day*) PH
23 September **Shūbun no Hi** (*Autumn Equinox Day*) PH
2nd Monday in October **Taiiku no Hi** (*Sports Day*) PH
3 November **Bunka no Hi** (*Culture Day*) PH
23 November **Kinrō Kansha no Hi** (*Labour Thanksgiving Day*) PH
23 December **Tennō Tanjōbi** (*Emperor's Birthday*) PH

And finally . . .

Japan has many other interesting gods, supernatural creatures, good luck talisman, folk traditions and folk tales. You can find out more about these from the suggested reading and sources in Taking it further.

Taking it further

Books

JTB guides: *A Look into Japan* and *Japanese Festivals* (Japan, JTB, 1990)

Hyōten (*Freezing Point*) Miura Ayako, examines Christianity in a Japanese context and won the *Asashi* newspaper prize. Available in original and Japanese through OMF books, ISBN 9971 972–23–9

Chimmoku (*Silence*), Endō Shūsaku (Tokyo, Sophia University and Tuttle, 1969) about the persecution of Christians in 17th-century Japan

Japanese Mythology, Juliet Piggott (Newnes Books, Hamlyn, 1982)

Buddhism: Japan's Cultural Identity, Stuart Picken (Tokyo and New York, Kodansha International, 1982)

A Zen Forest: Sayings of the Masters, Sōiku Shigematsu (New York and Tokyo, Weatherhill, 1981)

A Japanese Touch for your Garden, Kiyoshi Seike *et al.* (Tokyo and New York, Kodansha International, 1980)

Information

Japan Information Network website (see Unit 1), select **Japan Atlas** for information on festivals.

GLOSSARY

宗教 **shūkyō**	*religion*
神道 **Shintō**	
仏教 **Bukkyō**	*Buddhism*
神 **kami**	*gods*
魂 **tama**	*soul, life force*
神社 **jinja**	*shrine*
鳥居 **torii**	*shrine gateway*
神主 **kannushi**	*Shinto priest*
神棚 **kamidana**	*family altar*
菩薩 **bosatsu**	*bodhisattva*
禅 **Zen**	*Zen (Buddhism)*
茶道 **sadō**	*tea ceremony*
寺 **tera**	*temple*
庭園 **teien**	*garden*
儒教 **jukyō**	*Confucianism*
キリスト教 **kirisutokyō**	*Christianity*
新興宗教 **shinkōshūkyō**	*new religions*
祭 **matsuri**	*festival*
お正月 **oshōgatsu**	*New Year*
元日 **ganjitsu**	*New Year's Day*

09 food and fashion

In this unit you will learn

- about different types of food and drink
- about a selection of classic dishes
- how to eat out successfully in Japan
- about Japanese fashions and designers, past and present

Japanese food (washoku 和食) and cookery (ryōri 料理)

Japanese food has become hugely popular outside Japan in recent years and restaurants specializing in certain types of Japanese cuisine have sprung up in most major cities across the world. A visit to Japan, however, will reveal an even greater range of dishes and an enormous regional variety.

Rice (kome 米)

Rice is the staple of the Japanese diet. It was introduced from China and Korea during the Yayoi period (300 BC–AD 300) and is grown using wet rice cultivation which needs good irrigation and is highly labour intensive. It is thought that the Japanese extended family system developed because of these labour demands. Under the feudal system in Japan, farmers were required to give more than half of their rice production in taxes and often could not afford to eat rice themselves, eating barley, millet and wheat instead. During World War II, with most of the population engaged in the war effort, very little rice was produced and there were huge food shortages. After the war, land was redistributed in small plots to farming families who received subsidies from the government in order to accelerate the production of rice. Today the government continues to subsidize farmers by buying rice at high prices and selling it to the consumer at a more realistic price but people are eating less rice and farmers are being offered bonus payments to change to other crops. However, the profits are not as lucrative as rice growing and Japan continues to rely heavily on imports for other foodstuffs.

Some facts about Japanese rice

- When rice is growing or uncooked it is called **kome** whereas in its cooked state it is called **gohan** or **meshi**.
- The word **gohan** also means *meal* and the words for breakfast, lunch and dinner (**asagohan**, **hirugohan**, **bangohan/yorugohan**) literally mean *morning*, *midday and evening rice*, showing the importance of rice as the cornerstone of the meal.
- In the last 30 years, rice consumption has decreased by 40 per cent, largely due to foods introduced from the West such as bread, meat and milk.
- Japanese rice is shorter grained and more glutinous (sticky) than the Indian and Chinese rice consumed in Western countries.

- Almost 100 per cent of rice consumed is produced in Japan and it is the only food in which Japan is self-sufficient.
- Only about 16 per cent of land is cultivable due to Japan's mountainous and forested terrain of which about one-third is used for rice growing.
- Farms are small scale (averaging about 1.6 hectares of land) requiring intensive farming to achieve maximum production. Traditionally, the labour was by hand but today small-scale machinery is used for much of the work.

DID YOU KNOW?
A healthy diet

The benefits of a traditional Japanese diet are widely recognized nowadays both in Japan and abroad. Traditional Japanese dishes are low in fat and calories and high in protein (from soybeans and fish). The basic components of a Japanese meal are boiled rice, **miso** (*bean paste*) soup and three other dishes such as fish, pickles, vegetables and seaweed. Seaweed is high in beneficial iodine and all are low in fat. High salt content, however, is provided by products such as **shōyu** (*soy sauce*) and **tsukemono** (*pickles*). This is thought to explain the high incidence of stomach cancer in Japan. And in recent years, younger generations have eaten increasing amounts of meat and dairy products which are high in fats and cholesterol and there has been a corresponding increase in obesity and heart disease. At the same time, Japanese people born after the war are much taller and stockier in build than their parents and grandparents.

Five classic dishes

This section is an introduction to only a small fraction of Japanese cuisine. Taking it further (p. 124) will offer sources of information to explore this topic in more detail and try out some Japanese food for yourself and there are three recipes in Appendix 2 for you to try. The following five dishes are available in restaurants outside Japan.

Sushi (寿司)

Sushi means literally *vinegared rice* and is not, as is often thought, raw fish (see **sashimi** below). Sushi rice is made by seasoning cooked rice with rice vinegar (**su**), sugar and salt. Particular restaurants have their own secret method for preparing sushi rice which they guard carefully and professional sushi chefs take up to ten years to become fully qualified. There are different types of sushi, the original being **edomaezushi**, meaning *in front of the city Edo*, because in the Edo period the fish used to top the rice was caught fresh in the bay in front of the city. This style of sushi is now called **nigirizushi** (**nigiri** means *squeezed* because the chef squeezes the rice in his hand) and is the classic sushi consisting of ovals of sushi rice with toppings such as raw fish, seafood and omelette-style egg and a dab of **wasabi** (hot green mustard) in between. Other types of sushi include **makizushi** (**maki** means *rolled*) which is made by spreading sushi rice on squares of **nori** (*dried seaweed*), placing seafood, vegetables or pickles on top, rolling it up in its **nori** covering and cutting it into segments.

Sushi-ya (sushi restaurants) range from small bars to high-class restaurants. If you sit at the counter, you can point to the fresh ingredients displayed behind the glass window and order what you want. Each order will come as a pair of **nigirizushi**. You can also order sets which come in three price brackets: **nami** (regular), **jō** (special) and **tokujō** (extra special). Green tea is normally provided with the sushi (but beer or sake make good accompaniments, too) and you dip your sushi into soy sauce mixed with **wasabi** and eat pickled ginger (**gari**) to refresh the palate.

Ten popular types of sushi are: **maguro** (*tuna*), **ikura** (*salmon roe*), **tamago** (*egg*), **toro** (*tuna belly*), **ebi** (*shrimp*), **hototegai** (*scallop*), **uni** (*sea urchin*), **tako** (*octopus*), **tai** (*sea bream*) and **ika** (*squid*).

DID YOU KNOW?
Seaweed

The idea of seaweed is often repellent to people unaccustomed to Japanese food who have an image of the slimy, smelly seaweed found on beaches. A more accurate word would be sea plants and there are many varieties of these, all of which add distinct flavours and seasonings to Japanese dishes. **Wakame** seaweed is used in **miso** soup and salads and **nori** seaweed in thin, crisp green sheets is eaten with rice at breakfast or wrapped around **sushi** and **onigiri** (*rice balls*).

Sashimi (raw fish 刺身)

Sashimi is raw, very fresh, sliced fish of which there are many varieties. The skill is in the cutting of the fish and the presentation of the dish together with garnishes such as shredded **daikon** (*Japanese radish*), **shiso** (green leaf with a distinctive flavour) and **wasabi** (*hot green mustard*). Popular cuts of fish are **tai** (*sea bream*), **maguro** (*tuna*), **ika** (*squid*) and **awabi** (*abalone*). The delight of eating sashimi is in its texture – it almost melts in the mouth like smoked salmon and does not have the slimy texture or strong smell that many Westerners associate with uncooked fish.

Tempura (天ぷら)

Tempura owes its origins to Portuguese traders in 16th-century Japan but has developed into a uniquely Japanese cuisine, popular both inside and outside Japan. It consists of seafood, fish and vegetables deep fried in a very light, crisp and succulent batter and dipped into a **dashi**-based sauce called **tentsuyu. Dashi** is a fish stock made from **kombu** (*kelp*) and **katsuobushi** (*dried bonito fish flakes*). Essential to good tempura is the right consistency of batter and the right temperature for frying.

Sukiyaki (すき焼き)

Sukiyaki is one of a number of Japanese dishes which are cooked in hotpot (**nabemono**) style, at the table. **Yaki** means *grilled* or *fried* and **suki** is the word for a spade, suggesting that sukiyaki was originally cooked outside using a spade as the cooking 'pot'. The raw ingredients are very thinly sliced top-quality beef, **tofu** (*bean curd*) cut in cubes, sliced **negi** (*thin leeks*), Chinese leaf, **shiitake** mushrooms and **shirataki** noodles (thin, jelly-like noodles made from **konnyaku** – a root translated as *devil's tongue*). The meat is browned in a cast-iron pot at the table then a soy sauce-based broth is added along with the other ingredients. As the sukiyaki cooks, you pick out items with chopsticks and before eating dip them into beaten raw egg which cooks slightly from the heat of the food. (See Appendix 2 for recipe.)

Other **nabemono** dishes include **shabu-shabu** (thinly sliced beef and vegetables dipped in boiling stock) and **chanko-nabe** which is the protein-rich food of sumo wrestlers, eaten by them to build up their size.

Yakitori (焼き鳥)

Yakitori means *grilled bird* and traditionally was pieces of various parts of chicken, dipped in either a sweet-sour soy sauce or in salt and grilled on bamboo skewers over charcoal. Nowadays, grilled pieces of vegetables, beef and pork are also cooked yakitori style. (See Appendix 2 for recipe.)

FAMOUS FOOD
Unusual fare

Every country has its unusual food dishes, often highly exotic and even repellent to the outsider. Japan has its fair share of these and here are a few to whet your appetite!

Ikizukuru (called *dancing fish* in English) is a type of sashimi where the whole fish is cut so skilfully that the fish appears to be alive and its tail and backbone continue to twitch when it is served. **Fugu** is the highly prized (and priced!) blowfish which has extremely poisonous parts including the liver. Incorrect preparation of the fish has led to a number of deaths and nowadays only specially licensed chefs are allowed to serve **fugu**. Even so, deaths from **fugu** poisoning do occasionally occur and a recent one led the chef to commit suicide. Most ordinary Japanese people have never tasted it but connoisseurs say that the poison in small and safe quantities causes a pleasant numbing of the lips and tongue! **Dojō-nabe** (*loach hotpot*) is a dish of live loach, tofu and stock cooked over a flame at table. As the stock heats up, the loach swim into the tofu for coolness where they die and are then eaten. **Basashi** is raw horsemeat, only the best cuts marbled with fat are used. Finally, snake (**hebi**) centres exist in small numbers in Japan where people can go and drink fresh snake's blood which is believed to have aphrodisiac and vitality properties.

Eating out in Japan

Japanese restaurants outside Japan tend to offer a range of Japanese dishes whereas those within Japan normally specialize in one type of food. For example, **sushi-ya** sell **sushi, sukiyaki-ya** sell **sukiyaki, soba-ya** serve noodles and **tonkatsu-ya** specialize in pork cutlets. **Noren** (short, split curtains, normally navy blue) are hung outside Japanese-style restaurants to advertise their speciality dish and show that they are open. At the cheapest end of the restaurant trade are the red lantern establishments (so called because a red lantern – **akachōchin** – hangs outside, usually with the main speciality written on it) which are small drinking places (**izakaya**), specializing in 'home cooking' such as **yakitori**, grilled fish and pickles.

At the other end of the scale, **ryōtei** are restaurants specializing in high-class cuisine known as **kaiseki ryōri** which has its origins in the tea ceremony. Like the tea ceremony, it is simple but artistic, and there is a special etiquette for both serving and receiving **kaiseki ryōri. Ryōtei** restaurants are set out in traditional style with **tatami** mat rooms and views overlooking Japanese-style gardens. They don't normally have large signs outside and trade on a discreet but highly chic image. They can also be very expensive.

As well as traditional cuisine, Japan has a wide range of restaurants specializing in all sorts of European, Asian and American cooking including curry houses, Chinese restaurants and many, many fast food places. The first McDonald's opened in the Ginza shopping area of Tokyo in 1975 and since then all the well-known names have appeared everywhere in Japan. However, Japan has its own brand fast food restaurants as well with fascinating 'foreign' names such as Dom-Dom Burger, Love Burger and the somewhat offputting Moss Burger! So-called family restaurants are also big business in Japan and sell a range of Western and Japanese food. It is also possible to order food from sushi, noodle and other restaurants and have it delivered to your home in the proper dishes. This service is called **demae** and delivered by people on mopeds or motor bikes with special carriers containing the food on the back. When you have finished the meal you leave the dishes outside and these are picked up later.

DID YOU KNOW?
Yatai (street food 屋台)

Yatai are street stalls which cook and sell various snacks and drinks. They are also found in parks, fairgrounds and the grounds of shrines on festival days. Food items include **yakitori**, grilled **ika** (*squid*), **takoyaki** (octopus pieces cooked in a pancake-like dough), **yakisoba** (stir-fried noodles) and sweet potatoes.

Five useful tips for eating out in Japan

1. Many Japanese restaurants display the food they serve in the form of plastic models in the window. If you are unsure of the name of a dish, take the waiter outside, point to the item and say **Are o kudasai** (*That one, please*).
2. When you enter a restaurant, you are greeted with the word **Irasshaimase** meaning '*Welcome, we are ready to serve you*'.
3. Traditional restaurants may have both Western-style table and chairs and tatami mat areas with low tables. You remove your shoes before stepping onto a tatami-matted area.
4. Once you have made your order, a copy is placed on your table. At the end of the meal, you take this to the counter by the door to pay.
5. To show your appreciation of the meal, say **Gochisōsama deshita** (lit. *that was a feast!*) as you leave the restaurant.

Noodles (menrui 麺類)

There are three main types of noodles in Japan: **udon** (flat or round, white noodles made from wheat flour), **soba** (thin, brown noodles made from buckwheat flour) and **rāmen** (Chinese noodles, yellowish in colour). All are served in a variety of ways and **soba** and **udon** can be eaten hot or cold. Noodles make a fairly inexpensive meal, particularly **rāmen** which is sold at street stalls and around stations and served in huge bowls with a variety of toppings and broths. **Toshikoshi-soba** is eaten on New Year's Eve and the long noodles are symbolic of long life. The Japanese film ***Tampopo*** gives wonderfully visual and amusing accounts of the skills of noodle serving and the competition between restaurants (see Taking it further). At the other end of the scale, instant noodles (**kappu-men**) were invented in Japan and are hugely popular.

DID YOU KNOW?
Buddhist cuisine

Meat was not widely eaten until the Meiji period because of Buddhist beliefs. **Shōjin ryōri** is the name of the vegetarian food eaten by Buddhist priests from the 6th century AD which became particularly popular with Zen Buddhists from the 13th century onwards. It is simple, plain fare and doesn't use meat, fish or eggs. Kyoto has many restaurants serving this type of food. One well-known dish is **yudofu**, which is tofu (made from soybean curd) cooked in a simple broth and dipped in soy sauce with chopped spring onions and grated ginger.

Home cooking

The emphasis on careful preparation and presentation of food extends into the home and traditional preparation of food is very time consuming. Japanese housewives tend to shop every day or so in order to buy fresh ingredients rather than doing a weekly shop. It is striking going round a Japanese supermarket and noticing the large proportion of fresh rather than frozen or microwave food. Times are changing, however, and many Japanese women have part- or full-time jobs so the demand for ready meals is growing. Also, although traditionally the Japanese wife would rise before the family in order to cook the rice and prepare the breakfast of **miso** soup, pickles and fish, nowadays people are as likely to eat toast, eggs and coffee, or to eat *en route* to work.

FAMOUS FOOD
Obentō (お弁当) and ekiben (駅弁)

Obentō are boxed lunches which can be prepared at home to take to work or school or bought from special **obentō** shops. The box has different compartments which contain rice, pickles and, depending on the type of **obentō**, fish, meat, tempura, sushi, sashimi and so forth. **Ekiben** (station **obentō**) are sold in trains and stations all over Japan. Specific stations sell their own specialities and variations.

Drinking in Japan

The main alcoholic drinks are **sake** (*rice wine*) and **bīru** (*beer*). Sake is sold in three grades, **tokkyū** (special grade), **ikkyū** (first grade) and **nikyū** (second grade). **Tokkyū** can be double the price of **nikyū**. It is drunk warm in winter, served in a **tokkuri** (sake flask) which is placed in hot water to warm it up, and cold in summer, when it is called **reishū** and is often served in small glasses. On special occasions such as a festival or New Year, **komokaburi** (large wooden sake casks covered in rush matting) are blessed, broken open and drunk. Sake has an alcoholic content of about 20 per cent.

Beer making has been dominated for many years by four breweries, Kirin, Sapporo, Asahi and Suntory, which all produce lager beer of a fairly similar taste. Since 1994, however, government regulations on alcohol production have been relaxed and smaller microbreweries (called **ji-bīru** – *regional beer*) have begun producing a much wider variety of types and tastes. Vineyards have also appeared, particularly in Yamanashi prefecture in the area around Mt Fuji and, as the price of imported wine has come down in recent years, the popularity of wine drinking has increased hugely.

Shōchu is a colourless spirit, not unlike vodka, made from potato, rice and grain. It is drunk straight or as **chūhai** when it is mixed with flavoured syrups. The Japanese are also very keen **uisukī** (whisky) drinkers and sometimes have a whole bottle of whisky put on one side for them at their local bar which they drink each time they go there. There are many **nomiya** (*drinking places*) in Japan, frequented by men after work but increasingly by young people of both sexes.

Green tea

The traditional non-alcoholic drink is **nihoncha** or **sencha** (green tea – referred to as **cha** in everyday speech). There are various grades and qualities with some of the best green tea grown in the Uji region near Kyoto. Tea leaves are processed with steam and then dried. It is drunk without milk or sugar in round bowls without handles. **Matcha** is a powdered form of green tea used in the tea ceremony. Nowadays, the Japanese also like to drink coffee and the full range of soft drinks. Drink machines selling both hot and cold canned drinks are ubiquitous in Japan – there is even one on the top of Mt Fuji!

Fashion and clothing

Traditional clothes

The kimono is the traditional dress of Japan and was worn by both men and women on a daily basis (as well as simpler robes and **hakama** trousers) up until the Meiji period. From 1868, men began to wear Western-style clothes, sometimes combined with traditional Japanese clothing such as bowler hats with kimono. A Meiji government decree made it compulsory for male civil servants to wear Western-style suits and clothing. Women did not really stop wearing kimono on a daily basis until after World War II. Nowadays, people only wear kimono for special or formal occasions such as weddings, funerals and New Year although you do still see older generations of

Men's and women's kimonos with accessories

Japanese, particularly women, wearing plainer style kimono for everyday wear.

DID YOU KNOW?
Aristocratic dress of the imperial court

Various styles and fashions emerged over the centuries which included the **karuginumo** in the Heian period (794–1185). This was a many-layered silk kimono worn by women. Each layer was a different colour and longer than the one over it so that the edge of each could be seen, creating a beautiful array of colours. Women grew their hair very long and it hung down their back with shorter lengths framing their face. Pictures of women dressed in this style are a very popular subject for postcards and other souvenirs in Japan. Men wore a ceremonial outfit called **sokutai** which was a many-layered upper garment with loose trousers underneath.

Women's kimono

A woman's kimono consists of a long undergarment (**nagajuban**), an over-robe made of silk and an **obi** (long, wide sash) which is tied in an elegant knot at the back (there are various styles). The **obi** is held in place by a cord called the **obijime**. Women wear white socks called **tabi** (split toe) and footwear called **zōri** which resemble thick-soled flip-flops covered in leather or cloth. There are two types of women's formal kimono, the **furisode** worn by unmarried women which has long sleeves and is more colourful and the **tomesode** worn by married women which has normal length sleeves and is usually in darker colours. The patterns and designs of kimono give each one its individuality. Formal kimono are made of silk whereas the everyday type may be made of wool, cotton or synthetic materials. The **yukata** is a cotton kimono which women wear for summer festivals, usually with a plain coloured cotton **obi**.

The obi

The **obi** is often considered more important than the kimono for formal wear and may cost substantially more. It is 3–4 metres in length and 30 cm wide. It is usually woven in silk and the patterns are ornate and very beautiful, with repeated motifs often of plants, animals or flowers. For formal occasions, a professional kimono fitter is employed to dress the woman in a kimono, tie the **obi** correctly and style the hair.

Men's kimono

For formal occasions men wear a black silk kimono with a half-coat (**haori** or **montsuki**) over the top half and **hakama** (culotte-style trousers) over the lower half. The **haori** is decorated with round motifs which are the family crest (known as **mon**). Men also wear an obi called **kakuobi** which is 9 cm wide and tied in a half bow at the back, **tabi** socks and **setta** (footwear similar to **zōri**). On less ceremonial occasions they wear the kimono without the **hakama** trousers. At summer festivals they may wear cotton **yukata** or **happi** coats (cotton jackets with baggy sleeves) and shorts. At hot spring hotels, both men and women may wear cotton **yukata** (normally blue and white) provided by the hotel and tied with a thin belt. **Geta** are also worn on these occasions – these are wooden sandals with high supports which tip forward as you walk.

DID YOU KNOW?
Wedding kimono

At modern-day weddings, brides may wear up to three outfits. The traditional wedding kimono is made of heavy and very fine-quality white silk, woven with good luck symbols such as cranes which symbolize long life. These kimono are so expensive (about £20,000) that people rarely buy them but hire them instead. The bride wears the white kimono at the Shinto ceremony with a white headdress called **tsunokakashi** (*hiding the horns*) which is symbolic of the 'horns of female jealousy', while the groom wears a black kimono and **hakama** trousers. At the wedding reception the bride will often change into a red silk kimono with gold brocade then, after the meal and speeches, both bride and groom may go out to change into Western-style white dress and morning coat. The guests wear formal black kimono and unmarried girls may wear more colourful ones.

Fashion in modern Japan

The Japanese today are among the biggest consumers of up-to-date fashionable and designer clothes in the world. A stroll through any large Japanese city will reveal a wealth of fashions and outfits from conventional business suits through classic women's outfits to the more outrageous and daring get-ups of the younger generation. Designer labels are big business – the Japanese love them and, for those travelling abroad, a shopping stop at major cities and fashion houses is a must. And despite the much talked about economic recession, Japanese people's hunger for shopping has not yet shown any signs of abating. For the younger generation, anything goes and one fashion is quickly abandoned for another: perms, body piercing, blond hair dyeing, platform shoes, all black to shocking pink clothes, **rusu-sokkusu** (baggy white socks fixed to the legs with sock glue!) – the list is endless and is seen as a rebellion and statement against the group ethic and conformity which has been so much a part of Japanese society and upbringing.

Nevertheless, uniform and 'accepted' dress still rank high in Japanese society but, even in these cases, quality is paramount. Businessmen and women dress in suits of muted colours but well-cut classic styles, department store assistants wear elaborate and 'super-smart' outfits, even groups of hikers appear uniformly dressed in all the latest walking gear. Secondary school uniforms are still very strict and formal: girls may wear sailor-style outfits and boys are all in black with black caps to match (p. 165). However, Japanese society has been rapidly changing in the past 20 years or so and fashion is one indicator of the conflicts arising between older and younger generations, of conformity versus individuality, and traditional versus new.

DID YOU KNOW?
Beyond the designer label

Recent tastes for fashion in Japan have shown a move away from obvious labelled wear to more personalized dressing and statements. This can be demonstrated by the rapid growth of two chain stores, **Muji** and **Uni-qlo**, which have become big business in Japan and abroad. **Muji** means *no label* and is exactly this – a range of clothes and household accessories which are 'brandless', simple in style and plain in colour. Of course, this very simplicity and plainness 'labels' the goods with the **Muji** name. **Uni-qlo** is a chain of stores selling cheap but high-quality clothes (**uni** is short for *unique* and **qlo** for *clothing*), the brainchild of a Japanese businessman, **Yanai Tadashi**. It began in 1997 and there are now almost 500 stores across Japan which in 2000 sold more than 300 million items of clothing. Stores are also opening worldwide. The popularity of **Uni-qlo** is put down to the fact that it sells everyday basics such as trousers, sweaters and fleeces in stylish cuts and colours which can be combined with classier designer labels.

Four Japanese designers at the forefront of international fashion

Modern-day Japanese fashion designers have had a huge influence on the international fashion scene. Originally dismissed as imitators of European designs or grouped together as 'Asian designers', four individuals have very much come to the forefront in recent years. **Miyake Issei** (born 1938, famous as **Issey Miyake** in the West) first came to the attention of an international audience with fashion shows in New York (1971) then Paris (1973) where he exhibited a 'non-gender specific' range of clothes. He applies traditional textile designs to modern materials and folds rather than cuts his materials following the tradition of Japanese tailors who believed in wasting as little material as possible. His designs are unconventional and often described as body sculptures because of the lightweight materials he uses. He has used models as old as 80 in his shows. **Mori Hanae** (born 1926) set up her own design company in 1963 and was the first Asian to be awarded the much coveted Chambre Syndicale de la Haute Couture in 1977. She gives an oriental look to her designs and has specific motifs such as her trademark butterflies. She has used traditional dyeing techniques in her materials and creates close-fitting, feminine clothes in classic styles.

In the 1980s, two other Japanese designers came to prominence. **Kawakubo Rei** (born 1942, famous as **Rei Kawakubo** in the West) is the founder of 'Comme des Garçons'. She exhibited in Paris in 1981 and her anti-fashion style was described by some as the 'bag lady look'. She experiments with many different fabrics, textures and dyes and believes that the importance of clothes is in the shape and feel of the cloth, not the showing of the body. Her designs are loose fitting, a recent range was described as the 'Swiss cheese' look because of many and random holes – the wearer chooses where to put head and arms. Her principle colours are black, dark grey and white – her models normally wear combat boots. **Yamamoto Yōji** (born 1943, famous as **Yohji Yamamoto** in the West) is known for his sparse, understated and functional designs. His cuts are often asymmetrical and designed to conceal rather than show the body. His Y collection shown in Paris in 1981 was described as 'the end of the world' look. He uses mostly black, navy blue and white, and is fond of 'black on black' looks. His company, Y's, has its headquarters in Paris. The designs and styles of these designers have influenced the direction of international fashion. For example, they have made black fashionable rather than dowdy and introduced the concept of one-size garments.

Taking it further

Tokyo Food Pages **http://www.bento.com** for information on eating and drinking in Tokyo, speciality cuisine, recipes and reviews

Tampopo, film directed by Itami Jūzo for an irreverent and funny look at Japanese food customs

At the Japanese Table, Lesley Downer (Chronicle Books, 1996). An excellent collection of recipes and where to find ingredients

Sake: A Drinker's Guide, Hiroshi Kondō (Tokyo and New York, Kodansha International, 1980)

A Taste of Japan, Donald Richie (Tokyo and New York, Kodansha International, 1985). Essays on different types of Japanese cuisine

Contact the JICC of the Japanese embassy (Unit 1) for details of Japanese restaurants in your country. The city guides available in major cities across the world will also have a list of Japanese restaurants.

At Japan Information Network (Unit 1) select **Trends in Japan** for up-to-date information on fashion and **Nipponia** for articles on recent trends.

GLOSSARY

食べ物 **tabemono**	*food*
飲み物 **nomimono**	*drink*
和食 **washoku**	*Japanese cuisine*
料理 **ryōri**	*cookery*
米 **kome**	*uncooked rice*
ご飯 **gohan**	*cooked rice, meal*
飯 **meshi**	*cooked rice, meal*
朝ご飯 **asagohan**	*breakfast*
昼ご飯 **hirugohan**	*lunch*
晩ご飯 **bangohan**	*dinner*
夜ご飯 **yorugohan**	*dinner*
醤油 **shōyu**	*soy sauce*
寿司 **sushi**	
刺身 **sashimi**	
天ぷら **tempura**	
すき焼き **sukiyaki**	
焼き鳥 **yakitori**	
レストラン **resutoran**	*restaurant*
飲み屋 **nomiya**	*drinking place*
居酒屋 **izakaya**	*eating and drinking place*
会席料理 **kaiseki ryōri**	*high-class cuisine*
屋台 **yatai**	*street food*
麺類 **menrui**	*noodles*
そば **soba**	*buckwheat noodles*
うどん **udon**	*round, white noodles*
ラーメン **rāmen**	*Chinese noodles*
酒 **sake**	*rice wine*
ビール **bīru**	*beer*
ワイン **wain**	*wine*
ウイスキー **uisukī**	*whisky*
着物 **kimono**	
帯 **obi**	
ファション **fashon**	*fashion*

07 creativity and achievements in modern Japan

In this unit you will learn

- **about science and technology, including Japan's greatest inventions**
- **about cinema history and ten great Japanese films**
- **about TV, radio, newspapers and comic books**
- **about the mobile phone boom and the internet in Japan**

This unit looks at Japan in the past 100 years in the areas of science, technology and mass media (to include cinema; TV and radio; newspaper, magazines and cartoon books; and telecommunications and the internet).

Science and technology (科学と技術)

It hardly needs stating that Japan is a world leader in the area of technology and it has built a worldwide reputation second to none in the development of cameras, clocks and watches, cars, audio-visual equipment, household electrical appliances, robots, computers and semiconductors. In science also it has its important names and discoveries, mainly within the last 100 years, and there have been nine Nobel Prizes awarded to Japanese scientists, the latest two awarded for chemistry and physics in 2002 to **Tanaka Koichi** and **Koshiba Masatoshi**. A small number of the main inventions and discoveries of the last 100 years or so are listed in the following box.

1897	Power loom designed by Toyoda Sakichi, 'father' of Toyota Motor Corporation
1889–90	Kitasato Shibasaburō grows tetanus bacterium in pure culture and develops serum treatment for tetanus (studying under Dr Robert Koch in Germany)
1903	Cherry Camera, Japan's first camera, produced by predecessor of Konica
1904	Japan's first automatic vehicle – a steam-powered bus
1908	**Ajinomoto** (monosodium glutamate) discovered by Ikeda Kikunae from **kombu** (type of seaweed)
1908	Mikimoto Kokichi develops cultivation method for cultured pearls
1911	Discovery of vitamin B1 in rice bran by Suzuki Umetaro
1917	KS magnetic steel developed by Honda Kōtaro
1926	**Yagi-Uda** antenna, now the world's most popular TV antenna, invented by Yagi Hidetsuyu and Uda Shintaro
1927	Invention of Japan's first robot, using Western technology
1929	Kyota Sugimoto invents typewriter for Japanese language
1931	Japan's first passenger car is produced by Datsun (now Nissan)
1946	Masaru Ibuka and Akio Morita (co-founders of Sony) invent automatic rice cooker

1949	Yukawa Hideki receives Japan's first Nobel Prize for physics
1955	Sony produce the world's first transistor radio
1963	Japan develops its first nuclear power reactor
1964	Seiko clock technology used at Tokyo Olympic Games
1969	Japan develops world's first quartz crystal watch using Swiss technology
1970	Launch of Japan's first satellite
1976	JVC develop VHS video recorder system
1979	Sony launch the world's first Walkman
1982	Sony develop the first CD player
1983	Nintendo launch **Famicom** (family computer)
1989	Nintendo launch **Gameboy**, invented by Gunpei Yokoi
1992	Mamoru Mori is Japan's first astronaut on the US space shuttle, *Endeavour*
1997	Takao Doi is the first Japanese to walk in space
1999	Sony launch the minidisc Walkman and **Aibo** (robotic dog)
2001	Sanyo launch the soap-free washing machine

Up until the 1980s, Japan carried out most R&D (research and development) by purchasing technology and patents from Western countries then refining and adapting them, and using them for new purposes. For example, the inventor of the magnetic tape which made the Walkman viable was an American, Jerome H. Lemelson (he also invented the VCR). Sony bought the patent and went on to develop the Walkman. Japan's success in the field of technology has been credited to the high level of private investment and the innovative use of foreign technologies. A science and technology basic policy law was passed in 1995 to encourage creativity of R&D within Japan.

Robot technology

Japan is the world leader in artificial intelligence R&D and produces half the world's robots. Many of these are industrial robots such as those that work on production lines. Other examples of industrial robots are microrobots used in medicine to detect abnormalities, landmine detectors, nursing care robots and fire fighters. Japanese scientists also have a fascination with the development of humanoid robots which can interact with humans. Sony launched their robotic pet dog, known as **Aibo**, in

1999 (**Aibo** is short for Artificial Intelligence roBOt but **aibo** also means *pal* in Japanese and **ai** means *love*). The first 3,000 were sold over the net in 20 minutes at a cost of £1,500 or $2,500 each. It has a virtual mind of its own with six emotions and four yearnings, and responds both to being loved or neglected. Its behaviour changes depending on how it is treated and there is no 'return to the start'. A badly treated dog will even leave puddles around the house! And plans for the future include a personal robot which will greet its owner at the door, have conversations, switch on the TV and pass messages on to people. It is 1.5 m (5 feet) high, has video cameras for eyes and microphones for ears. It will even do the shopping, getting items off the shelves according to the order.

Aibo, the robot dog, leaving a puddle

DID YOU KNOW?
The Japanese and gadgets

The Japanese love gadgets and there is a constant turnover of new ideas and items, many of which never reach Western markets. Miniaturization of electronic goods is also big business in Japan; a recent invention is the Casio watch which is also a digital camera and can store images with names and phone numbers too. These can be viewed on screen, printed on a PC or sent down the phone line. And Japan is the world leader in fuzzy engineering, a process which simulates human thought and was originally invented in the USA. (The word 'fuzzy' implies the unpredictability of human thought.) There is a wealth of household gadgets stamped with the trade name 'fuzzy logic' such as irons which automatically change temperature by sensing the type of material to be ironed and washing machines which calculate the load, the amount of washing powder and the length of the wash. And finally, a somewhat crazy inventor called Kenji Kawakami has taken the Japanese fascination with gadgets to new heights with his **chindogu** idea which means *unuseless inventions*. He pokes fun at his nation's obsession with gadgets through inventions such as a shoe-powered hairdryer (bellows attached to the shoes send air through tubes into a plastic cap so you can dry your hair on the way to work!) and the baby mop (mops attached to the front of baby-grows mean babies can be put to use polishing the floor as they crawl around!).

Mass media (masukomi マスコミ)

Masu means *mass* and **komi** is short for *communication*.

Japanese cinema (日本の映画)

The film industry began in Japan in the late 19th century, not long after it was established in the USA and Europe. The golden age of Japanese cinema was the 1950s when Japan received international acclaim for films such as Kurosawa Akira's ***Rashomon*** (1950; set in medieval Japan) which won the Venice Film Festival Golden Lion Prize and Kinugasa Teinosuke's ***Jigokumon*** (*Gate of Hell*, 1953; the first successful Japanese film in colour) which won the Cannes Film Festival Grand Prix. During this period, the war and reflections on Japan's role in World War II were recurrent themes in many films, such as Ichikawa Kon's ***Biruma no tategoto*** (*Harp of Burma*, 1956; Ichikawa remade this film in 1985) and Kobayashi Masaki's six-part film, ***Ningen no Jōken*** (*The Human Condition*, 1959–61; the story of a soldier in World War II).

The advent of television in the late 1950s had a hugely detrimental effect on cinema attendance and quality of films (with some notable exceptions) and saw the rise of gangster films and **pinku** (*pink* – soft porn) movies. American and British films (with subtitles) have tended to be more popular than home-grown ones but the 1980s and 1990s have seen a revival of interest in Japanese films and a number have received prestigious international prizes. These include Kurosawa Akira's ***Kagemusha*** (*The Shadow Warrior*, 1980; an epic war film set in 15th-century Japan) which won the Cannes Film Festival Grand Prix, Kitano Takeshi's ***Hanabi*** (*Fireworks*, 1997; a violent disillusioned cop story also starring the director who is better known as Beat Takeshi in Japan) which won the Venice Film Festival Golden Lion Prize and Imamura Shohei's ***Unagi*** (*The Eel*, 1997; a man, who has served eight years in prison for the passion killing of his wife, begins a new life as a barber) which won the Cannes Film Festival Palme d'Or.

Ten great Japanese films

This selection is in addition to the films mentioned elsewhere in this book, all of which are classics of Japanese cinema and, when put together, give a comprehensive selection of some of the very best movies and directors. All are subtitled and the range of subjects offers a unique insight into Japanese society and thinking. The list is made up of two films from each decade (1950s–90s). The director's name is given after the date.

Tokyo Monogatari (*Tokyo Story*, 1953), Ozu Yasujirō. An exploration of post-war Japanese society and of the changes in family life, it tells the story of an elderly couple who visit their children in Tokyo and experience loneliness and isolation. It starred Hara Setsuko, one of Japan's most famous actresses.

Shichinin no Samurai (*Seven Samurai*, 1954), Kurosawa Akira. Famous for its spectacular battle scenes, the story is of seven samurai who protect a village from bandits. The American Western, *The Magnificent Seven* (1960) was an adaptation of this film.

Yōjimbō (1961), Kurosawa Akira. Set in the Edo period, it tells the story of a masterless samurai who saves a town from the fighting between two rival gangs. This is Clint Eastwood's favourite film and he based his spaghetti Western character '*the man with no name*' on it.

Suna no Onna (*Woman of the Dunes*, 1964), Teshigahara Hiroshi. Based on the novel of Abe Kōbe, it tells the story of a schoolteacher who becomes trapped in a sandpit where he is forced to take the place of a woman's husband and is a satirical comment on the entrapments of urban living.

Ai no Korida (*In the Realm of the Senses*, 1976), Oshima Nagisa. Telling the true story of the sado-masochistic relationship between a prostitute and her lover whom she strangled to death, this film enjoyed great box office success, particularly in France, amid criticisms of its highly pornographic content.

Tora-san (series of films throughout 1970s and 1980s), Yamada Yōji. These highly popular films follow the life of a carefree man who tries to help others but often finds himself in trouble. They are a humorous statement on the pitfalls of modern-day living.

Kazoku Gēmu (*The Family Game*, 1983), Morita Yoshimitsu. This black comedy takes a satirical look at family life in modern Japan and the obsessions of the **kyōiku mama** (competitive mothers who push their children to greatest possible success at school).

Osōshiki (*The Funeral*, 1984), Itami Jūzo. Another satirical comedy, this time poking fun at the conventions of the Japanese funeral.

Yume (*Dreams*, 1990), Kurosawa Akira. Kurosawa created this sumptuously colourful and often frightening film from eight of his dreams, many of them containing references to Japanese folk and ghost tales. In 1990, he received an honorary Oscar for his lifetime achievement in the cinema.

Shall We Dance? (1996), Suo Masayuki. This film enjoyed massive box office success in the USA and is a wonderful and modern portrayal of the 'new man' in Japan, sweeping away the many stereotypical images of Japanese family life and Japanese males.

Anime (animation films アニメ)

Japanese animated films have won worldwide acclaim because of the sophistication of the animation techniques and the detailed artwork. The first animated film was produced by the navy in 1943. Called ***Momotarō no Umiwashi*** (*Momotaro and the Sea Eagles*) it was an account of the attack on Pearl Harbor. The comic strip artist, Tezuka Osamu, moved animation on to new creative heights in 1963 with the adaptation of his long-running comic story, ***Tetsuwan Atomu*** (*Astro Boy*) for television. This was hugely popular and was later dubbed into many languages. Another animated film which won much critical acclaim was ***Akira*** (1988) by Ōtomo Katsuhiro, a futuristic story set in Tokyo in 2019 and translated into many languages. Maybe the best-known animator of recent times is the director, Miyazaki Hayao, whose high-quality films have won him international fame. He created ***Tonari no Totoro*** (*My Neighbour Totoro*) in 1988, a gentle film about a ghostlike creature who can only be seen by children and which also carried a message about environmental protection. He also produced ***Mononoke Hime*** (*Princess Mononoke*) in 1997 which was a huge success in the USA in 1999 as was *Pokemon: The First Movie* by Yuyama Kunihiko in the same year.

TV (テレビ) and radio (ラジオ)

The first TV channel, NHK (**Nippon Hōsō Kyōkai** or Japanese Broadcasting Corporation) began broadcasting in 1953 and the popularity of TV grew rapidly, helped by the televising of the emperor and empress's wedding in 1959 and the Tokyo Olympic Games in 1964. In the early days of black and white TV, viewing was very much a family affair (as it was in many other countries) and programmes with themes common to all the family, such as **hōmu dorama** (*home dramas* or *soaps*) were very popular. By the mid-1970s, everyone had a colour TV and many homes had more than one set and so programmes aimed at different age groups became more common. In 1999 there were 127 terrestrial commercial TV companies, many of which are regional. NHK is the only publicly run corporation, paid for by licence fees (it is not compulsory to pay these but 98 per cent of Japanese people do) and has two terrestrial channels, a general and an educational one. As far as screening of programme content is concerned, this is left largely to the discretion of the broadcasters. Late night viewing in Japan can often reveal programmes of a fairly high sexual or violent content and, although full frontal nudity is not allowed on TV or in film, programmes which could be classed as 'soft porn' are not uncommon and hotels normally have a number of paying pornography channels. NHK also has two MW and one FM radio stations plus a shortwave overseas service called Radio Japan. In addition, there are about 100 commercial radio stations including foreign-languages stations such as FEN (Far Eastern Network) broadcast by and for the American forces based in Japan.

Japanese viewers' favourite programmes

A survey carried out in March 2000 in Japan revealed that the average viewer watches 3.5 hours of TV per day (compared with 4 hours in the USA, 3.5 in Britain and 3.25 in Australia), an increase of half an hour compared to 15 years ago. The favourite types of programme are:

1 news
2 weather
3 dramas
4 sport
5 music
6 culture (history, nature, travel)
7 variety shows
8 documentaries (political, economical, social affairs)
9 daytime talk shows
10 movies

Terebi dorama (TV dramas テレビドラマ)

TV dramas have enjoyed great success in Japan since their introduction in the 1950s. They are Japan's equivalent of soap dramas but cover a much wider range of topics including historical and 'whodunnit' plots. The longest running drama is ***Tōshiba Nichiyō Gekijō*** (*Toshiba Sunday Theatre* – a series of family dramas), which began broadcasting in 1956 and is still on air. One of the most popular dramas is TBS's ***Mito Kōmon*** (*Counsellor Mito*), which has been running since 1969 and is a samurai 'putting wrongs to rights' story set in the Edo period. Recent dramas have moved away from the **hōmu dorama** (*home drama* or *soap*) setting and looked at the interests of young people such as the issues of single life in a big city, a good example being Fuji TV's ***Tokyo Rabu Sutōrī*** (*Tokyo Love Story*). **Anime** cartoon series often explore **hōmu dorama** themes such as the highly popular ***Sazae-san***, running since 1969 and taking a light-hearted look at life in a three-generation household.

DID YOU KNOW?
The Endurance Game

This particular show has sprung to international notice in recent years with its 'on the edge of endurance'-style challenges, such as contestants buried to their necks in ice and being forced to eat huge quantities of noodles! This has presented Japanese TV to the outside world as being rather bizarre and crazy but, of course, it needs to be seen in the context of the full variety of TV programmes broadcast in Japan. *The Endurance Game* is something of a 'one-off' programme, shown at special times such as New Year, but there are many quiz and game shows on TV. One of the more popular ones, ***Naruhodo Za Wārudo*** (*That's the World!*), looks at bizarre happenings and customs in other countries and quizzes the celebrity contestants about them.

Future of television

Satellite broadcasting has an increasing number of subscribers in Japan (nearly 14 million in total in March 1999) and NHK broadcasts a 24-hour news service from across the world including the USA, UK, France and China, with simultaneous translation. Commercial channels offer specific types of programmes such as foreign movies, sports, pop music and Japanese theatre which have to be paid for separately. Satellite broadcasting has been available in digital format since 1996 and cable TV is becoming more widely available with some companies supplying internet access through cable. Finally, Hi-Vision TV, the Japanese equivalent of high-definition TV, began development in the 1960s and has been broadcast experimentally since 1985. NHK have developed a system with sound and picture quality equivalent or better than 35 mm motion pictures and a screen 3–4 times the size of conventional TV but it is still very expensive with limited broadcasting.

Newspapers (新聞), magazines (雑誌) and comic books (漫画)

Japan has the highest readership of newspapers in the world followed by Korea and the UK. This is partly due to the very high literacy rate in Japan (almost 100 per cent and second only to Iceland). More than 90 per cent of newspapers published every day are delivered to home subscribers, and Japan is one of the few countries where there are both morning and evening editions (evening editions tend to be tabloid style, with gossip and scandal ranking high). Japan's ***Yomiuri Shimbun*** has the highest circulation of all the major world newspapers. There are four English-language newspapers, the *Japan Times*, and the ***Yomiuri***, ***Asahi*** and ***Mainichi Shimbun***, and over half their readership is made up of Japanese people. There is also a large number of regional and specialist papers such as sports and economics. Japanese newspapers tend to be light on investigative journalism and to present factual news with little comment. The major newspapers do not represent specific or opposing political views and journalists all belong to press clubs which are closely associated with government and other public organizations and so present these viewpoints. Nevertheless, under the Japanese constitution, there is no media censorship.

Magazines and **manga** (*comic books*) enjoy huge popularity in Japan across all the age groups and in some ways are the equivalent of tabloid-style newspapers. Weekly photo magazines in particular, such as *Focus* and *Friday*, are full of **sukandaru** (*scandal*) about famous personalities and political figures and are sometimes on the edge of good taste, for example, when they printed photos of a teenage pop idol after she had committed suicide by jumping from a high-rise building or of a business tycoon shot to death by a yakuza gang outside his home (this was also shown on TV). Women's magazines are very popular and include Japanese-language versions of *Cosmopolitan*, *Vogue* and *More*.

Foreign visitors to Japan are often surprised to see adults engrossed in comic books, which are regarded as children's reading material in Western countries. However, **manga** comics are written with themes for all age groups, including stories on politics, economics and law. Two of the most popular comics are written for boys and sell 4 million copies each per volume. **Manga** are books rather than magazines, averaging 150–200 pages per volume (see Taking it further, p. 138).

DID YOU KNOW?
Manga (comic strips)

Manga are big business in Japan and the sophisticated and high-quality artwork is admired across the world. Examples of comic drawings can be traced back to ancient times and comic pictures were produced in ever increasing numbers from the Edo period onwards. Some of the **ukiyoe** painters (see Unit 3) such as **Hokusai** made humorous and erotic woodblock prints but **manga** found its real popularity in the 1950s and 1960s and has been growing ever since. The narratives are character oriented (mortal heroes rather than superheroes) with themes which can have a violent and/or sexual content (including violence against women in some men's **manga**). The characters are normally drawn with oversized 'Western-style' eyes and, particularly in the case of girls' **manga**, are very **kawaii** (*cute*). One recent trend has been educational **manga** aimed at both children and adults. Another (1990s) trend has been horror **manga**, the best of which have left the reader both fascinated and terrified. Inuki Kanako is a female artist who has been dubbed the Queen of Horror because of her spooky **manga** based on old Japanese ghost and folk tales and urban myths. And Ito Junji has produced a massively popular series called ***Tomie*** in which a beautiful girl is continually being reborn from pieces of flesh and blood and drives people to kill each other.

'Typical' manga character

Telecommunications and the internet

Mobile phones (keitai denwa 携帯電話)

The mobile phone industry has boomed in Japan with well over half the total population (75 million) owning one in 2001 and the number growing all the time. This means that there are now more mobiles than there are fixed phones in homes and offices. The latest phones are fitted with I-modes which make it possible to browse the web and send e-mails from the phone. There is even a phone with an attachment for a digital camera making it possible to take photos and send them by phone or print them out on a small printer. The future looks mobile with Japanese electronic designers currently experimenting with 'bluetooth modules' which can be fitted into mobile phones to control all the electronic gadgets in the home even when you're out of the house. They have earned the name '*Electronic Swiss army knives*' because potentially they can do everything!

DID YOU KNOW?
PHS (personal handyphone system)

This is a very cheap mobile phone system which has enjoyed great popularity in Japan, particularly among young people (although numbers are beginning to decline since the onslaught of cellular phones). Rather than working on a cellular network, the phones receive signals from local antennae which can work up to distances of 500 metres and can even be used on the underground! PHS phones are very small and come in a wide variety of exciting designs and colours – some even take the form of large rings on the finger! They are used both as a cordless phone in the home and a mobile phone outside – one number fits both. Japanese people use this phone system to have text conversations and nowadays it is quite a familiar sight to see young Japanese people texting away in silence and at top speed on the underground. They even have a name – **oya yubi toku**, which means 'the finger-thumb tribe'!

The internet

Although Japan is the global leader in wireless internet use, the number of domestic users has been lower than in other industrial countries such as Iceland, Finland and the USA. Use is spreading rapidly, however, and the Japanese government has made a pledge that every Japanese home will have access to high-speed internet by 2005. It is possible to e-mail using Japanese characters but on an international scale there are still some problems with the technology between different systems and messages tend to be sent across the world using rōmaji (Japanese written using the romanized alphabet).

Taking it further

Websites

Japan Patent Homepage – list of inventions by Japanese **http://www.jpo.go.jp**

Chindogu – 101 useless but useful inventions by Kenji Kawakami (Harper Collins, London, 1997)

TV Programmes: **http://www.nhk.or.jp** The user can choose English or Japanese, look up specific programmes and read summaries of them

Japan Information Network (see Unit 1) has information on science and technology, including advanced technology under the headings **Japan Atlas, Trends in Japan** and **The Japan of Today**.

Books and magazines

Mangajin, a magazine of selections of Japanese manga, with English explanations and grammar notes. Available from specialist Japan bookshops

Japanese language versions of *Cosmopolitan*, *Vogue* and *More* are both interesting and challenging reading practice

Japanese Cinema: An Introduction, Donald Richie (Hong Kong, Oxford, New York: Oxford University Press, 1990)

Places

Mainstream and arts cinemas have regular Japan seasons and screenings so keep a look out for these – there is usually quite a variety of film type and theme. It is also a good opportunity to listen to spoken Japanese (the films all have subtitles).

In Tokyo, it is possible to visit the NHK Broadcasting Centre (JR Yamanote line, 10 minutes south-west of Harajuku station), to see actual filming and a broadcasting science museum. There is also the National Science Museum in Ueno, Tokyo which is packed full of historic, present and futuristic technology.

GLOSSARY

科学と技術 **kagaku to gijutsu**	*science and technology*
マスコミ **masukomi**	*mass media*
映画 **eiga**	*films, movies*
アニメ **anime**	*animation*
テレビ **terebi**	*TV*
ラジオ **rajio**	*radio*
新聞 **shinbun**	*newspaper*
雑誌 **zasshi**	*magazine*
漫画 **manga**	*comic book*
携帯電話 **keitai denwa**	*mobile phone*

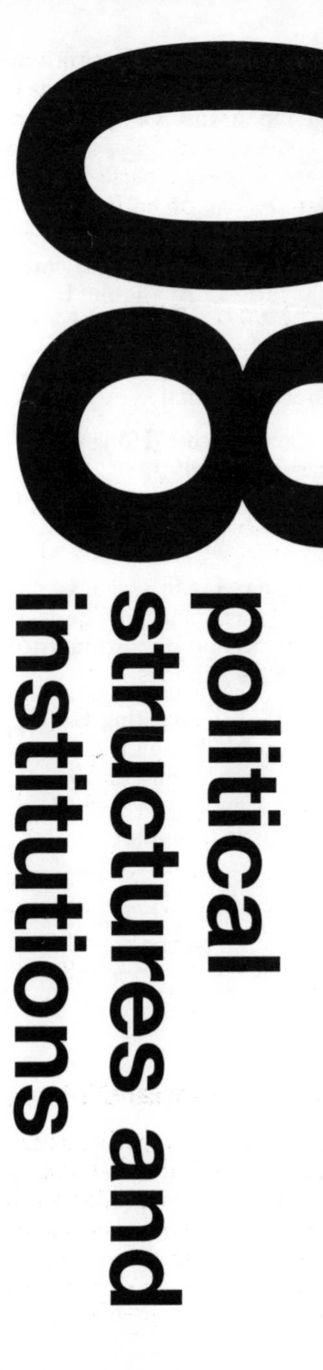

In this unit you will learn

- about politics before and during the war
- about post-war democracy and the Constitution of Japan
- about government and politics today
- about political scandals and reforms
- about the Japanese emperor

The political system which exists now in Japan was implemented by the USA during its seven-year occupation of Japan following World War II. However, it was as a result of the Meiji restoration in 1868 that Japan moved from a feudal government system under a shogun ruler to a parliamentary government based on the German model of constitutional monarchy and its modern political history begins here.

The Meiji restoration (1868) and political reform

As explained in Unit 1, Japan made rapid moves towards modernization during the Meiji period and chose Western models from Europe and the USA to achieve this. With the restoration of the emperor as the head of state, Japan looked to the German empire as a political model with its 'iron chancellor' Bismarck, although this was to result in a government which was highly authoritarian.

The Iwakura Mission, 1871–3

The purpose of this 18-month mission was for leading members of the newly formed Meiji government to study Western learning and systems through a series of goodwill and fact-finding visits to the USA and Europe. The mission was headed by Iwakura Tomomi and included Itō Hirobumi who brought about many of the important political reforms of the time and is considered to be one of the great statesmen of the Meiji period. Itō returned to Europe in 1882 to study various forms of constitutional government and in particular that of Germany. He became Japan's first prime minister in 1885 and, under the guidance of Iwakura, endorsed Japan's first constitution, the **Meiji Constitution**, in 1889.

The Meiji Constitution and the Imperial Diet

Japan was the first country in Asia to establish a parliamentary style of government when it created the **Teikoku Gikai** or imperial diet in 1890 (diet is the word used for parliament in Japan and is the law-making branch of the government). However, Japan was not yet a true democracy because the emperor held sovereignty over the Japanese people and the diet. Moreover, the upper house of the diet was only open to those in the privileged class. In addition, only about 1.5 per cent of the population held the right to vote; universal male suffrage was introduced in 1925 but women had to wait until 1945 and the US occupation to achieve their right to vote.

There existed an uneasy balance between parliamentary government (the diet) and the sovereignty of the emperor from the outset, as illustrated in the following diagram.

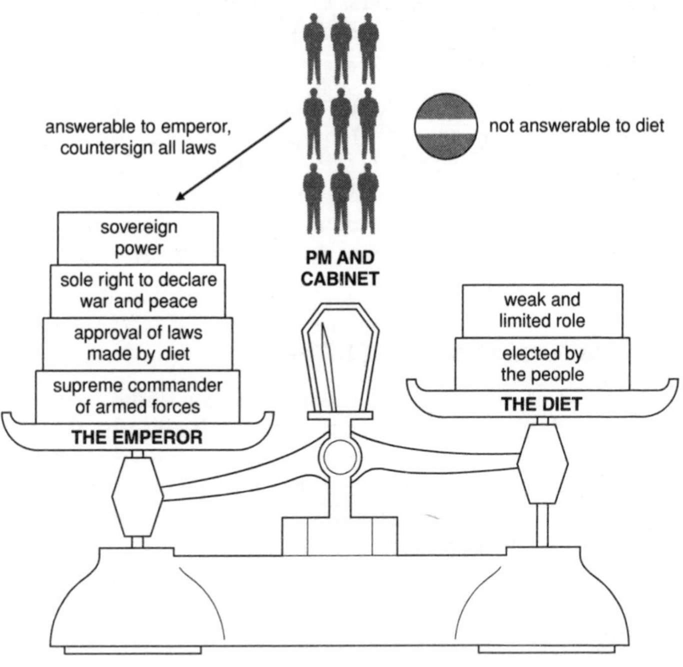

Balance between parliamentary government and the emperor

The situation worsened with an imperial ordinance of 1900 which rewarded the leaders of the newly formed navy and army with the powerful positions of ministers of state for the armed forces. The mechanisms for Japan's move into militarism and World War II were now firmly in place (see Unit 1 for more details).

Democratic government in post-war Japan

With Japan's surrender to the Allied forces and its signing of the Potsdam Declaration, authority over Japan was handed to the Supreme Commander for the Allied Powers (SCAP), General Douglas MacArthur. His role was to bring about the democratization of Japan and to dismantle the empire and the armed forces. This included a complete reform of the political system and the removal of supreme power from the emperor to the Japanese people. The model finally chosen was a British-style parliamentary government headed by the prime minister and cabinet, with the emperor (like the British monarch) becoming the symbol of the Japanese people and state with no decision-making powers.

The Constitution of Japan, 1946

This replaced the Meiji Constitution of 1889 and was put forward by the staff of General MacArthur after difficult consultations with the Japanese cabinet. It was intended as a completely democratic document and was based on American and British models. It contains nine chapters and 103 articles dealing with the role of the emperor, human rights (including freedom of speech and sexual equality), the separation of religion from the state and the establishment of the diet as '*the highest organ of state power*' (article 41). Another key feature was article 9 which declared that '*the Japanese people forever renounce war as a sovereign right of the nation and the threat or use of force as a means of settling international disputes*' and that '*land, sea, and air forces, as well as other war potential, will never be maintained*'. (See Unit 12, p. 225 for more about Japan's self-defence forces.)

Present system of government

There are three branches of government each with separate powers. These are the legislative branch headed by the national diet (**kokkai**); the executive and administrative branch headed by the prime minister and his/her cabinet (although as yet there has not been a woman prime minister in Japan); and the judicial branch headed by the supreme court.

The diet (kokkai 国会)

Under the new constitution, the diet became the most important branch of government: it makes political decisions and laws on behalf of the people; it approves the appointment of prime minister and ministers of state to the cabinet; and its lower house has the power to pass motions of no confidence in the cabinet. The diet has two houses, the lower house called the House of Representatives (**Shūgiin**) and the upper house known as the House of Councillors (**Sangiin**). Members of both houses are elected by the people in national elections. The ruling political party has to have a majority in both houses or form coalitions with other parties (this has happened often in recent years, see p. 151). The House of Representatives has the casting vote over the House of Councillors in areas of disagreement such as the selection of a new prime minister or the passing of a bill.

Following electoral reforms in 1994 and 2000 (see pp. 151–3) there are now 480 seats in the House of Representatives, all voted for by the public in national elections held normally every four years. There are 252 seats in the House of Councillors and councillors stand for six-year terms with elections for half the seats taking place every three years. Candidates standing to be elected to the House of Representatives must be over 25 years old and those for the House of Councillors over 30 years old.

The prime minister and cabinet (shushō to naikaku 首相と内閣)

The prime minister has the power to appoint and remove cabinet ministers and can also dissolve the diet and call a general election. Following any general election, a new prime minister is elected and a new cabinet formed. The prime minister is elected by majority vote in both houses and this is then 'rubber stamped' by the emperor. The prime minister and his cabinet are responsible to the diet and the majority of cabinet ministers must be members of the diet, elected by the people. In theory, cabinet ministers should head the drafting of legislation in consultation with the bureaucrats and civil servants who work in the government ministries and agencies. These bills are then presented for approval to the diet with ministers available for questioning as necessary. In practice, however, the system has been quite different.

The bureaucrats (kanryō 官僚)

It has been the chief bureaucrats within the ministries who have written and presented new legislation to the diet and cabinet ministers have rarely been available for questioning or even been acquainted with the content of proposals. This has meant in effect that the day-to-day running of government and making of policy has been controlled by a group of powerful bureaucrats not appointed through popular election. As the Japanese people have become more impatient with their political system and its inability to solve the recent economic and financial problems, various shakeups of government have taken place and this has included a new law which makes it compulsory for cabinet ministers to attend diet sessions in order to answer questions.

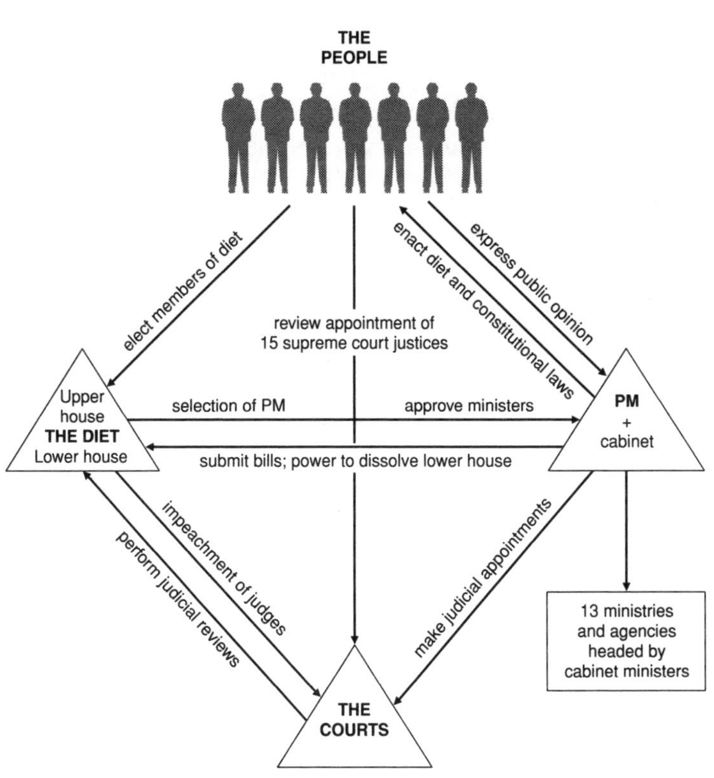

Key functions of government in Japan

In an attempt to curb the powers and privileges of bureaucrats, electoral reforms were put into effect from January 2001. As a result, the system of Prime Minister's Office has been reorganized into a cabinet office which has greater powers and functions, and the 23 ministries streamlined into one office and 12 ministries. The cabinet office is now made up of the prime minister and a maximum of 17 ministers, some of whom head the 13 ministries and agencies and some of whom have no specific portfolio. Also within the new cabinet office system are four councils (including the Council for Fiscal and Economic Policy) which provide support for the prime minister and direct new national strategies. The creation of the fiscal council is in response to Japan's recent financial and economic crises and the need to take away some of the power of the Ministry of Finance (see p. 150).

The diagram on the previous page illustrates the key functions of government in Japan.

THE MAIN POLITICAL PARTIES

The changing political and economic climate in the 1990s brought about a number of changes in party names and also the creation of new parties, mainly in order to present viable options to the long-term dominant party, the LDP. The main parties as they stood in 2000 are listed here.

LDP (Jiyū Minshu Tō/Liberal Democratic Party)

Founded in 1955, it has dominated post-war Japanese politics as a one-party system although in the 1990s has increasingly had to enter into coalitions (most recently with the Liberal Party and **Komeitō**) to achieve a majority. It is essentially a conservative party.

DPJ (Minshu Tō/Democratic Party of Japan)

Founded in 1996, this is a progressive, centre democratic party which has campaigned hard for electoral reform and is currently the main opposition party.

SDP (Shakai Minshu Tō/Social Democratic Party of Japan)

Founded in 1945 and changing its name in 1991 from JSP (Japan Socialist Party), this was the first party to have a female leader, Doi Takako. In 1994 it joined a coalition with the LDP to achieve a majority. To qualify as a ruling party, it had to reject its long-term stance against Japan's self-defence forces. For many years it was the main opposition party to the LDP.

Liberal Party (Jiyū Tō)
This party joined forces with the LDP in 1999 to achieve a majority. It withdrew its support in 2000 causing a split in the party and more than half its members left to form the **New Conservative Party** which remained in alliance with the LDP.

JNP (Japan New Party)
Founded in 1992 it led the non-LDP coalition in 1993 and its leader, Hosokawa Morihiro, became the first non-LDP prime minister in 38 years and brought into law a new electoral system. It is now defunct and its members have split three ways to become part of the DPJ, the Liberals or New Komeitō.

JCP (Nihon Kyōsan Tō/Japanese Communist Party)
Founded in 1922, it was declared illegal during the 1930s and was treated with suspicion by the US occupation forces. It disassociated itself from the Russian and Chinese Communist Parties in the 1960s and in recent years has campaigned for the return of the Russian-held islands to the north of Japan (see Unit 12, p. 226).

New Komeitō (New Clean Government Party)
The original **Komeitō** Party was founded in 1965 with the backing of **Sōka Gakkai**, a new Buddhist group (see Unit 5, p. 102). It reorganized into a new party in 1998 and joined the LDP–Liberal Party coalition in 1999.

Sakigake (Pioneers)
This is a small progressive conservative party, established in 1998, which is also concerned with environmental issues.

Political and financial scandals

In the 1990s Japan saw its economy take a spectacular nose dive in what is frequently described as the bursting of the 1980s' bubble economy (see Units 10 and 12). The mismanagement by the Japanese government of its plummeting economy has had far-reaching effects on the political system. The problem has been that the political system stagnated once the post-war targets of resurrecting an economy which had hit rock bottom in 1945 had been achieved. Politicians began to be out of step with the demands of modern-day conditions and the increasingly global economy. Both the Japanese and the international community looked to the Japanese government to solve the problems of the 1990s recession and the ever rising unemployment rate (currently 4.8 per cent) but the government appeared to be incapable of making the changes necessary and found itself under increasing scrutiny and criticism. This resulted in a flurry of political resignations and at least ten changes of prime minister.

The main issues can be categorized as follows.

Complacency of the LDP and its resistance to change

Many people now see the problems of ineffective government to be the result of a ruling party which has been dominant for too many years. In the period 1955–93, the LDP was the only ruling party and people saw no particular reason to vote for any other party while the economy was buoyant and people enjoyed a good standard of living. The Japanese political system has been essentially a one-party system, with factions within the LDP competing with each other for majority control. There are three or four factions headed by a powerful leader and, with any cabinet reshuffle, each of these factions is assured of several cabinet posts. Although the diet elects the prime minister, it has been almost impossible to become prime minister unless you are the leader of a faction. As if that were not bad enough, many LDP diet members have virtually inherited their seats from fathers or grandfathers, and companies have been able to give large cash donations to diet members and factions. This has created a government which is not open and accountable and diet members (not only those of the LDP) whose primary aim has been to ensure a good cashflow back to their constituencies. A final twist was that, before 1994, there could be several seats (up to six) in one constituency, particularly in rural areas where the LDP has enjoyed strong support, which frequently meant that the LDP would win seats for different factions in one constituency, guaranteeing the return of a majority.

Mistresses

Japan's reaction to the attempted impeachment of President Clinton following allegations of an illicit affair was that it was '*so American*'. It has been generally accepted in Japan that politicians may have mistresses or extra-marital affairs and, at the very most, this might result in questions being asked in a diet session, but would not be grounds for impeachment. An example of this is the case of Hashimoto Ryūtaro (Prime Minister 1996–8) who, following accusations of an affair with a Chinese spy, admitted in the diet that there had been a relationship in the 1980s and the issue was then dropped.

However, female politicians and voters have become more powerful and vocal in recent years and are becoming less tolerant of politicians' illicit affairs. There have been two cases recently of prime ministers' affairs becoming headlines and influencing public opinion. The first case was Uno Sosuke, Prime Minister in 1989, who was forced to resign after three months because of his patronage of a geisha. The reason for his resignation, however, was not because of the relationship itself but because it came to light that he had tried to pay the woman off cheaply to keep quiet. This was felt to be both dishonourable and miserly.

The second case was that of Prime Minister Obuchi Keizo, when it came to light in 1998 that he had been paying large amounts of money to his mistress. Again, the concern was not about the mistress, but about the alleged illegal source of the money. He was also embroiled in allegations of using public office for private gain by improperly acquiring stock in two telecommunications companies and making $64 million from an initial investment of $55,000. The purchases were in the names of his secretary and brother but it was widely held that this was simply a concealment of his own ownership. He died of a heart attack before he could be brought to account.

No pan shabu shabu ('no pants shabu shabu' or 'hotpot without panties!')

An intriguing phrase which has come to epitomize the financial corruption that has debilitated Japan's economy and the disgust that Japanese people have begun to feel towards the behaviour of their politicians and financial leaders. The expression refers to hostess bars, particularly in Tokyo, where the waitresses take off their underwear and sit on a businessman's knee in return for a payment, usually 10,000 yen (about $85 or £60). The scandal which shook Japan involved the Ministry of Finance's chief inspector of banks. While police were investigating an entirely separate case, it came to light that the chief inspector had been accepting bribes from four major banks (mainly by leaking to them the date of inspections so that they could put their books in order) in return for the payment of lavish entertainment, famously of the **no pan shabu shabu** variety! He became the first financial bureaucrat to be arrested, the finance minister was forced to resign and three of the inspector's colleagues committed suicide.

This is only one of many examples of the bribery and corruption which have been a feature of Japanese post-war politics. One politician, Sato Eisaku, involved in the 1954 shipbuilding scandal went on to be Prime Minister (1964–72) and to win a Nobel Peace Prize! The difference now, however, is that people are worried about the state of the economy and have much greater expectations of their politicians and bureaucrats. They are no longer prepared to tolerate the use of public office for private gain while the rest of the country suffers the effects of a prolonged recession and they expect their politicians to be more culpable and accountable.

Bailing out the banks

The 1990s saw the toppling of some of Japan's biggest banks and financial institutions and revelations that many had lied about the extent of their debts and had not been challenged or sufficiently investigated by the Ministry of Finance. Examples include the Hyogo Bank which collapsed in 1995 with 25 times greater bad loans than it had reported. Other banks and financial institutions followed and the government kept on borrowing large sums of money in order to bail them out. Opposition parties voiced concerns that there was too close a relationship between the government and financial institutions.

Process for political reform begins

From the early 1990s the pressure for electoral and political reform in the wake of increasing financial scandals began to mount and two LDP prime ministers tried to submit bills for a fairer electoral system based on single-seat constituencies and proportional representation. They both met with huge resistance from both the LDP and opposition parties; Prime Minister Kaifu was forced to resign and Miyazawa to call a general election in 1993.

The LDP falls from favour

The 1993 election was fought over the issues of political reform and the breaking of the LDP stronghold. It was highly successful, leaving the LDP short of a majority for the first time in 38 years and creating a non-LDP coalition. This enabled a law to be finally enacted in 1994, creating a new electoral system based on a combination of single-seat constituencies and proportional representation. It was hailed as a new beginning for Japanese politics although, in the 1994 election, the LDP gained a majority by creating a coalition and have remained in power since. There is still resistance to change but the LDP has had to deal with an increasingly critical electorate and to rely on coalitions to secure majorities. When Prime Minister Hashimoto in 1997 failed in his attempts to reduce the power of the Ministry of Finance and the economy took a further downfall, the LDP were unable to secure a majority in the 1998 upper house elections and he had to resign.

Present situation

Since electoral and political reforms began, changes have happened which may never have been possible previously. Whereas under previous LDP governments, corruption had been treated as the problem of individual politicians and 'business as usual' was swiftly re-established, under the coalition cabinets of the 1990s, corruption scandals have been addressed and discussed in the public forum and used to bring about much needed political reform and a restructuring of the political system. The LDP themselves have had to put their house in order and in 2000 changed the way that the party leader was chosen so that now the whole membership, including the local branches, has the right to vote (before it was LDP diet members only). And so, in April 2001, for the first time in LDP history, Koizumi Junichiro, who was neither the leader of a faction nor aligned to one, was elected prime minister.

FAMOUS PEOPLE
Three movers and shakers

Koizumi Junichiro (born 1942) was elected in April 2001 and, as the man with 'the wild hair' and a love for the highly popular glam rock band X, he has already made his mark. He has stated categorically that he is going to address proactively the problems of a ten-year economic slowdown, government mismanagement and corruption, and rising unemployment. He has said that he is going to abolish LDP factions, force banks to sort out their own bad loans without the government to bail them out, revise the constitution and look into privatizing the Post Office bank. (This is one of the biggest banks in the world and has been used by the government to borrow money and boost the budget.) These are brave proposals and he can expect to meet much opposition but Koizumi is enjoying huge popular support for his proposals and has been hailed as a maverick who will give the system the shakeup it needs. Nepotism within the LDP is still alive, however – Koizumi's father was an LDP minister and his grandfather a prime minister!

Kan Naoto (born 1946) has achieved huge popularity in Japan because of the stance he has made over the HIV-infected blood scandal. In the early 1980s, the Japanese Health Ministry was warned that blood needed to be screened because of the probability of infected blood but nothing was done about this for several years. As a result, thousands of people became infected with HIV through blood transfusions. Groups had been lobbying for years but the government had refused to accept responsibility and ministers had hidden behind powerful civil servants in the Health Ministry who were the real policy and decision makers. Kan was appointed as Minister of Health and ordered the bureaucrats to investigate the infected blood issue. He then admitted liability on behalf of the government and promised that compensation would be paid to victims. He was also one of the founders in 1996 of the **Minshu Tō** (Democratic Party of Japan) which is now the second most powerful party in Japan (after the LDP).

Makiko Tanaka (born 1944) is one of only a few female ministers and Japan's first female Foreign Minister. She has a reputation for being very outspoken (she said in a recent interview 'I usually like to say what's on my mind. I think that's what diplomacy is about' and told Prime Minister Yoshiro Mori that the best way he could help Japan would be to place a large adhesive bandage over his mouth). She is famous, first, because of her connections – her father, Kakuei Tanaka, was Prime Minister 1972–4 but resigned over the Lockheed scandal in which he agreed with President Nixon to buy aircraft from the USA in return for huge payments from the manufacturers, Lockheed. However, as member of the SDP (Social Democratic Party of Japan) she has made her own name because she was the first foreign minister to demand to be involved in the appointment of diplomats and ambassadors (done previously by senior civil servants). Her determined stance against bureaucratic corruption has won her massive public support and the endearing nickname 'Maki-chan'. She has even been tipped by some to become Japan's first female prime minister!

Local government

Local government is independent of the national administration and its leaders are chosen through local elections. The role of elected members is to supervise the work of local government employees and administer local matters such as education, social welfare and environmental issues. In addition, every prefecture, city, town and village has its own assembly and mayor, also chosen by local election. These assemblies approve annual budgets, enact local laws and authorize expenditures.

Justice and the courts

The judiciary is completely independent of the other branches of government and consists of the supreme court, eight high courts, 50 prefectural district courts, 438 summary courts and 50 family courts. The diet also has a court of impeachment for hearing cases for dismissal of judges. All judges act independently of government, are bound only by the articles of the constitution and must retire at an age set by law.

The supreme court is the court of final resort for deciding the constitutionality of laws, and regulations. There are 15 justices including a chief justice who is appointed by the emperor following cabinet selection. **Summary courts** try relatively simple civil and criminal cases whereas **district courts** initially try the more complex cases which can then be referred on to the **high court. Family courts** are for hearing domestic complaints such as divorce and juvenile cases (under 20 years old in Japan).

Trials must be conducted publicly, except where the judges decide unanimously that this would be dangerous to public order or morals. There is a death sentence (hanging) although the number has been steadily declining and many are reduced on appeal. Seven death sentences were handed out in 1998. The most recent notorious case has been the salin gas attack on the Tokyo underground (see Unit 5, p. 103).

Japanese pressure groups and Amnesty International have been campaigning for some years against the current practice of detaining suspects awaiting judgement in police station cells rather than prisons. The concern is that placing detainees under the custody of police who are involved in investigation of crime is a violation of the suspects' rights.

The emperor (tennō 天皇)

The imperial system was retained by the Americans in the drawing up of the new constitution despite fierce debate about Emperor Hirohito's part in the war. His powers as ruler were taken away and he became the symbol and figurehead of the state and people. The issue remains controversial with a small number of Japanese people believing that Japan cannot be a true democracy while it retains a monarch, and another small but very vocal group of extreme right-wing activists organized by the yakuza (Japan's mafia, see Unit 11, p. 211) who believe that the emperor is divine and should be reinstated as sovereign. These extremists gather in Tokyo on Sundays, playing the national anthem and waving the rising sun flag while making their views known through loudspeakers. A recent prime minister, Mori Yoshiro, saw his popularity plummet when he referred to Japan in public as a '*divine nation centred upon the emperor*'. Outside Japan, war veteran groups from the USA, Britain and the Commonwealth countries are still calling for an official apology from the emperor and government for war crimes (see Unit 12, p. 228). The 1999 visit of Emperor Akihito and his wife to Britain was met with strong opinions expressed in the media and, during a procession through London, a group of veterans made their feelings known by turning their back on them.

The majority of Japanese, however, have no strong opinion and the current emperor and family enjoy a great deal of favourable press. The coronation of Emperor Akihito in January 1989 sparked a huge amount of publicity and media coverage and he made a statement, well received by the Japanese public, that his role was as a symbol of the people and no more. In general, the imperial family make relatively few public appearances compared with, for example, the British royal family but in recent years there has been an increasing amount of speculation and curiosity about their lives.

Emperor Akihito and Empress Michiko have two sons and one daughter. Both sons attended Oxford University and the second son, Prince Fumihito, was the first to marry in 1990. The press followed the romance in great detail starting with their meeting in a Tokyo coffee shop and the Japanese public couldn't get enough of the photographs and stories which mushroomed in all the tabloid papers and magazines. Speculation then grew about the marriageability of the Crown Prince Naruhito, who was considered the less handsome of the brothers. His subsequent choice of bride in 1993 succeeded in eclipsing the huge interest in Princess Diana in the Japanese media. Owada Masako was not only good looking, she was clever, too, and had worked for several years in the Ministry of Foreign Affairs. As time passed, however, and Prince Fumihito had two daughters, speculation again grew, this time over whether the Crown Prince and Masako were ever going to produce children and, more importantly, a male heir. At last, the couple had their first baby on 1 December 2001, a girl named Princess Aiko. This has reignited the debate about changing the male-only inheritance law.

National flag (kokki 国旗)

Japan's national flag is called the **hinomaru**, meaning *sun disc*, and is a red circle symbolizing the sun on a white background. This is in keeping with the word for Japan, **Nihon** meaning '*land of the rising sun*'. It is thought to date back to the 13th century and became the official flag in 1870. During the war, the rising sun flag was used which has 16 black rays rising from it. This is still used by the self-defence forces at sea and also by extreme right-wing groups in Japan campaigning for the restoration of the emperor as sovereign.

National anthem (kokka 国歌)

The name of the national anthem is **Kimigayo** meaning '*His Majesty's Reign*'. The words are from a **waka** poem of the 10th century and were put to music in 1880. Along with the national flag, the anthem was only given national status in August 1999 and over the post-war years has attracted controversy with some schools refusing to sing it at official ceremonies such as graduation or to raise the Japanese flag, seeing these acts as unwanted reminders of Japan's military past and as the glorification of the emperor as divine. (See also the section on the emperor on p. 154.)

Translation of national anthem

> *Thousands of years of happy reign be thine; Rule on, my lord, till what are pebbles now; By age united to mighty rocks shall grow; Whose venerable sides the moss doth line.*

(Written in the traditional Japanese scale)

DID YOU KNOW?
Election time in Japan

Both local and national elections in Japan create a lot of activity for the candidates who become very public figures, their faces appearing in posters all over the constituency and in local newspapers as they attend weddings, funerals and shop openings of residents. Noise pollution increases, too, as candidates and party supporters travel through towns and cities in cars and vans, using megaphones and tannoy systems to call on voters to vote for them. Nevertheless, voters' disillusionment with politics recently has resulted in low turnout for Japan – it was 65 per cent in the April 2000 election.

Taking it further

Books and magazines

Years of Trial: Japan in the 1990s (Japan Echo Inc., 2000). A series of essays looking at the changes in Japan over the past decade

There are also two English-language magazines on Japanese current affairs, *The Japan Echo* and *Insight Japan* which you can subscribe to by contacting the JICC of your Japanese embassy (see Unit 1).

Websites

Keep up with current affairs in Japan by using the *JapanTimes* website: **http://www.japantimes.co.jp/** You can also find out specific information on Japanese politicians and politics on the site: **http://www.japanesepoliticians.com/**

Other sites which regularly update information about politics and government include: **http://www.geocities.com/~watanabe_ken/** for information on politics (look up the links on politics) and the *Japan Digest* site: **http://www.japandigest.com/** which has recent and past news headlines (and you can subscribe to buy more in-depth articles).

Finally, *Japan Information Network* (see Unit 1) has information about current affairs under the links **the Japan of Today** and **Japan Directory**.

The Imperial House has two websites: **http://www.kunaicho.go.jp/** (in Japanese) and **http://www.joseijiho.co.jp/** (in English – click on **English** on the home page)

GLOSSARY

政治 **seiji**	*politics*
政党 **seitō**	*political party*
政府 **seifu**	*government*
民主 **minshu**	*democratic*
国会 **kokkai**	*diet*
内閣 **naikaku**	*cabinet*
投票 **tōhyō**	*voting, poll*
首相 **shushō**	*prime minister*
総理 **sōri**	*prime minister, premier*
政治家 **seijika**	*politician*
経済 **keizai**	*economy*
大臣 **daijin**	*cabinet minister*
衆議院 **shūgiin**	*House of Representatives*
参議院 **sangiin**	*House of Councillors*
皇居 **kōkyo**	*Imperial House*
天皇 **tennō**	*emperor*
官僚 **kanryō**	*bureaucrats*
自由民主党 **jiyūminshutō**	*LDP*
民主党 **minshutō**	*DPJ*
社会民主党 **shakai minshu tō**	*SDP*
自由党 **jiyūtō**	*Liberal Party*
共産党 **kyōsantō**	*Communist Party*

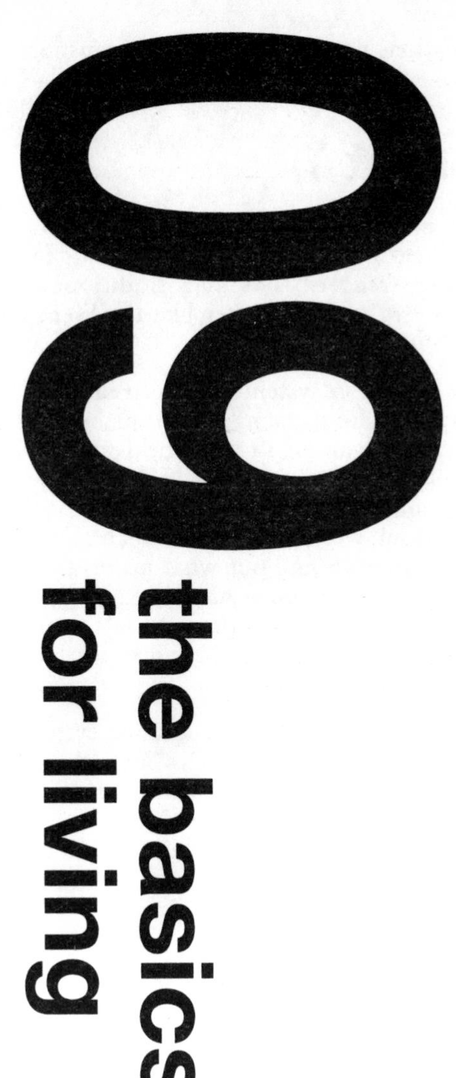

09 the basics for living

In this unit you will learn

- about the highs and lows of the education system
- about illness, mortality and healthcare in Japan
- about features of Japanese homes and the cost of living
- about transport

This unit looks at education, health, housing and transport issues in Japan.

Education (kyōiku 教育)

Education in Japan, as in many other Asian countries, is highly valued and parents have very high expectations and goals for their children. The **sensei** (*teacher*) has also traditionally been given revered status and respect, rather like the French *professeur*.

In recent times, Japan's education system has received much press coverage overseas ranging from claims that its method for teaching maths is the most advanced in the world to more negative articles on school bullying, rising rates of school-aged suicides and the pressures and 'examination hell' of the school system. While educators from Western countries such as the USA and UK have visited Japan to find out what makes their education system successful, the Japanese have been looking towards European and American education models amid concerns that the Japanese system is too rigid and suppresses creativity.

Since the 1980s, Japan has been reviewing its education system and has already made some significant changes including a wider choice of optional subjects for school students and a five-day week (students no longer have to attend school on Saturday mornings). Research is currently looking into how education can become more liberal and creative. The buzz phrase is **kokoro no kyōiku** (*education of the mind*).

If you were to walk into a secondary school at present in Japan, however, the system might still appear rigid compared to countries such as the UK and USA. Students sit in rows and the teachers deliver lecture-style classes with little or no interactive learning. Students take notes and traditionally the emphasis has been on rote learning rather than discussion or in-depth 'investigation'. To prepare for the English section of a university entrance examination, for example, students have been expected to learn long lists of difficult words and their definitions without having to be able to pronounce them or use them in context. There may be 40 or more in a class and students are generally taught to the average ability without allowances for more or less able pupils.

The 6-3-3-4 education system

The 1946 Constitution proclaimed that '*All people have the right to receive an equal education correspondent to their ability, as provided by law . . . (and) compulsory education shall be free*' (article 26). During the occupation the Americans established the 6-3-3-4 schooling system.

Type of school	Age	Number of years
Shōgakkō (elementary or primary)	6–12	6
Chūgakkō (middle or junior high)	12–15	3
Kōkō (high or senior high)	15–18	3
Daigaku (university)	18–22	4

In addition, parents normally pay for their children to attend nursery school (**hoikuen**) from as young as three months and kindergarten (**yōchien**) from about three years old. There is competition to get into those kindergarten considered to give the best pre-school education and ones offering English and maths are very popular (Japanese children don't begin learning English normally until junior high school).

Gimu kyōiku (compulsory education) lasts nine years (ages 6–15) and Japan has one of the world's highest rates of progression to non-compulsory high school education at 96.8 per cent. The school attendance rate has been impressive too, at 99.98 per cent in 1998. Nevertheless, the number of long-term school refusers (pupils who don't attend school for more than 30 days) has increased twofold since the beginning of the 1990s. The reasons given for not attending school (not including illness) are '*anxiety, emotional and behavioural problems, juvenile delinquency, apathy and social problems*' (from *Monbukagakushō* report, December 2000).

Examination hell (shiken jigoku 試験地獄)

All public education from ages 6–15 is free and the Constitution requires '*equal education, correspondent to . . . ability*'. There is also a private school system which parents pay for but, whether public or private, there is fierce competition in Japan to get into the best schools and families will even move house in order to be in the catchment area of the top-ranking elementary and junior high schools. Senior high schools and universities hold entrance examinations (**nyūgaku shiken**) and use the results to select the best students. Getting into the most prestigious schools, particularly senior high schools, ensures progression to the top universities and the widest choice of career. **Shiken jigoku** is a phrase coined by the media to describe the huge pressure Japanese students are under to pass these entrance examinations, with many attending **juku** (cram school) at the end of each school day for extra tuition and working long hours into the night. Figures of attendance for **juku** have been decreasing in recent years. Junior high school students preparing for the senior high school entrance exams make up the biggest number with more than half attending **juku**.

Kyōiku mama (教育ママ)

The education mother phenomenon describes the over-ambitious mother who pushes her children to the extremes of study in order to succeed at school and is also soft (**amai**) on discipline. She will register her children's names at birth for the best nursery school, drive them to and from **juku** and after-school clubs as necessary, and take hot drinks and snacks up to their bedrooms as they work late into the night. This pressure to succeed at school is thought to have contributed to the educational problems of school non-attendance, bullying, apathy and other emotional and social problems which have increased in recent years. It is also thought that fathers' long working hours have put too much pressure on mothers to take sole responsibility in bringing up their children and this has exacerbated the **kyōiku mama** problem. Schoolteachers are also reporting that discipline problems in school are increasing and that the image of the hallowed and highly respected **sensei** is being eroded. The extent to which these problems are being taken seriously can be seen by the gradual decrease of the working and school week from six to five days and a 1990s' televised campaign by the government to encourage fathers to spend more time at home with the family.

Bullying (ijime 苛め) and suicide (jisatsu 自殺)

Ijime in schools has been a serious concern in Japan since the 1970s and the main reason behind a rise in school-aged suicides. It has taken the forms of physical violence, verbal abuse and the ostracizing of particular students. One theory put forward has been that because Japanese education emphasizes the importance of group identity and cooperation rather than individuality, students who stand out in some way become easy targets for bullying. In a number of cases too, teachers have been compliant in the bullying by turning a blind eye or worse. In one notorious case in the late 1980s, a bullied student who committed suicide named his teacher as one of his tormentors in his final suicide note.

School violence (**kōnai bōryoku**) has also been a problem in secondary schools, both towards other students and teachers. It became a particular problem in the late 1980s when one-third of all cases at junior high schools were serious enough to involve police arrests or the juvenile courts. The problem has not yet gone away and it has been suggested both that teachers lack the strictness to cope with unruly and gang mentality behaviour and also that in many cases they are overstrict and have used excessive corporal punishment towards students, resulting in students copying and reacting to it. There are also concerns about the rise in juvenile crime which include a few shocking murders such as the 14 year old who beheaded an 11 year old and placed the head at the school gates with a note in the mouth which read '*I can't help myself – I love killing*'.

Educators in Japan in recent years have visited the USA and European countries to look at policies on bullying and discipline. Some Japanese critics fear that Japanese education is in danger of becoming too liberal and 'un-Japanese' and the whole issue continues to be fiercely debated in the media.

Monbukagakushō (Ministry of Education, Culture, Sports, Science and Technology) and local administration

Monbukagakushō (previously called **Monbushō**) has an advisory role in education with the local boards of education taking the main administrative role and schools having relatively little independence. For example, teachers do not apply for advertised jobs but are moved on to another school, usually within a five-year period, at the decision of the board of education. They may be offered a choice of school, but cannot choose when they change jobs. **Monbukagakushō** issues guidelines on school courses and approves school textbooks. Recent reforms mean that the system is no longer so rigid that a student in Hokkaido would be studying exactly the same page of a textbook as a student of the same grade in Kyushu but there is a national curriculum which all schools must follow.

The history book debate

Concerns that Japan has not yet faced up to its responsibility and behaviour in the first half of the 20th century are no better illustrated than by the cases of the history textbooks. **Monbukagakushō** reviews all textbooks and has the power to modify or reject them. China and Korea launched their first official protest in 1982 over the presentation of war and empire building in Japanese school textbooks and this continues to be a contentious issue. The textbooks describe Japan's wars with China and the annexation of Korea as expansion rather than invasion and give scanty descriptions of war scenes and brutal behaviour.

A textbook writer, **Ienaga Saburō** took **monbukagakushō** to court several times in the 1960s, 1970s and 1980s in cases known as **Ienaga Soshō** (the **Ienaga** textbook lawsuits). When his ***Shin Nihonshi*** (*New History of Japan*) was rejected by **monbukagakushō** he was initially successful in proving that this was a violation of his freedom of speech but the supreme court overruled the decision. In another lawsuit he claimed that **monbukagakushō** were overstepping their authority when they asked him to downplay his descriptions of the brutal behaviour of Japanese soldiers in World War II. The court agreed on the point of authority but **monbukagakushō** have retained the right to review and reject textbooks.

Recent educational reforms

Reforms implemented in 1992 have led to wide-ranging changes particularly in the areas of information technology (Japan was surprisingly slow to introduce computer courses to the school curriculum but most schools now have internet access), English, social studies (including history) and moral education. English courses, for example, have moved from an overemphasis on reading and writing skills to greater emphasis on speaking skills. This is partly being achieved by the huge increase in foreign English teachers through the JET (Japanese English Teachers) programme. Over 5,000 teachers are recruited annually from eight countries including the USA, Canada, Australia and the UK. There has also been a move towards more student-centred learning.

School life (gakkō no seikatsu 学校の生活)

The school year begins in April and there are three terms with six weeks' holiday in summer and two weeks' holiday in spring and New Year. The school day is usually from 8.30 a.m. to 3.00 p.m. followed by many after-school clubs, including baseball, soccer, martial arts and music. Lunch is eaten either in the classroom or a canteen and at elementary school the pupils serve lunch and eat in the classroom with their teacher. **Seifuku** (*school uniform*) is compulsory at secondary school and tends to be quite formal. The traditional uniform is navy blue pleated skirts and sailor-style blouses for girls and black or navy blue trousers and jackets with brass buttons and stand-up collar and cap for boys. Recently jacket and tie for girls and boys has become more popular. Elementary school pupils wear more casual clothes but first years wear yellow hats for road safety purposes and pupils normally have leather satchels called **randoseru**. These are often bought by grandparents when children start school. An interesting fact about uniform is that in June and October every year, there is an event called **koromagae** (*change of clothing*) when all schoolchildren (and business people too) change between winter and summer clothes.

Children in traditional school uniform

DID YOU KNOW?
Cleaning the school

Japanese students have to clean their own school! At the end of every day, they form well-organized groups led by teachers and student monitors and proceed to clean classroom, corridors and toilets. The image of ten Japanese students, running on all fours while pushing a polishing cloth in front of them, is not easily forgotten! Students also remove outdoor shoes at the school entrance and wear indoor shoes or slippers in school.

University education (daigaku no kyōiku 大学の教育)

There are both public (national, prefectural and municipal) and private universities in Japan. The most prestigious tend to be the public and in particular the national universities. In general the standard of universities varies hugely and the famous ones are very competitive to enter. The equivalent of the UK Oxbridge or the USA Harvard/Yale universities are Tokyo University (public) and Waseda and Keio Universities (private). Currently about 48 per cent of 18 year olds go on to four-year university compared with 47 per cent in the USA and 65.5 per cent in the UK. A further 24 per cent attend **tanki daigaku** (two-year junior colleges, the vast majority here are girls), correspondence schools or technical colleges. Parents pay the full tuition fees which are about $2,500 a year at public universities and almost double this at private ones. Getting into university involves a lot of hard work but university life itself is notoriously easy and seen as a four-year 'break' before beginning working life. The large majority of students pass final examinations and traditionally have found work very easily. Rising unemployment has had some effect on this and also an increasing number of young people are choosing to put their career on hold so that they can travel and see the world (see also Unit 10).

Health (kenkō 健康)

Japanese people currently have the longest life expectancy in the world. Look at the table.

Average life expectancy

	Japan	Australia	UK	USA
Men	76.8	75.5	74.5	73.4
Women	82.9	81.1	79.8	80.1

Some of the oldest people in the world are Japanese including the oldest twins, Kin and Gin, who were household names in Japan (Kin lived to 107 and Gin died aged 108 in 2001). Japan's oldest person at 120 was Shigechiyo Izumi (died 1986).

The reasons given for such long life expectancy are, first, the traditional diet which is low in fats and, second, improved healthcare and better public hygiene leading to a sharp decrease in infant mortality rates and fatal diseases such as tuberculosis.

The post-war healthcare system costs patients 10–30 per cent of the full cost and everyone is part of the national insurance scheme and can also take out health insurance through work. Health checks are carried out at schools and workplaces which include a regular chest X-ray for tuberculosis, a throwback to the 1930s and 1940s when it was the biggest killer in Japan. It has been on the decrease ever since although recent statistics show that there are still twice as many cases per year as in the USA and seven times more than in the UK.

Main causes of death

These are cancer (**gan**), heart disease (**shinzōbyō**) and strokes (**nōkōsoku**). The four most common cancers are stomach, lung, liver and pancreas. The Japanese diet has a high salt content and this is seen as a major contributor to stomach ulcers and cancer and to heart disease. Heavy drinking is a major reason for high incidences of liver cirrhosis and cancer and alcohol consumption continues to rise. On a worldwide scale, however, Japan is only 25th, just behind the USA, UK, Australia and New Zealand (the top three alcohol consumers are Luxembourg, France and Portugal).

Smoking in Japan

Japan is in the world's top ten when it comes to smoking. Since the mid-1990s the rate has been decreasing slightly and in 2002 49.1 per cent of men and 14 per cent of women smoke (compare this with 40 per cent of men and 27 per cent of women in France or 28 per cent of men and 26 per cent of women in the UK). Recent tobacco advertising has been targeted at women although as yet seems to have met with little success. However, information about links between smoking and lung cancer is poor and cigarette packets don't carry health warnings.

DID YOU KNOW?
The tobacco industry

Japanese smokers spend a grand total of about $25 billion per year on cigarettes. **Nihon Tabako Sangyō** (Japan Tobacco, Inc.) holds the monopoly on tobacco production (it also has the monopoly on salt sales) and most Japanese cigarettes are made from tobacco grown in Japan, with some imported tobacco added for extra flavour.

Jisatsu

Jisatsu (suicide) is the sixth biggest cause of death in Japan (fourth and fifth are pneumonia and accidents). It used to rank behind old age but has now overtaken it. A main reason for this is the increase in suicides among old people. As the elderly population increases, a common reason given for suicide is '*not wanting to be a burden on family or society*'. This may explain why there are higher rates of suicide among old people living with children and grandchildren than those who live separately.

Increased costs of healthcare

The increasing elderly population and more expensive medication have caused a rapid rise in national healthcare costs in recent years and this is a major political and social issue for Japan. In 1996 the costs per person had doubled from ten years previously.

Japanese attitudes to health

Japanese people are very conscious of their state of health and it can be quite disconcerting as a foreigner to find that one sneeze will cause Japanese friends or colleagues to enquire **kaze desu ka** (*is it a cold?*) followed by putting a thermometer under the armpit to check if you have **netsu** (*fever* or *temperature*). And the onset of winter sees the appearance, strange at first to outsiders, of white cloth masks worn over the mouth and nose. Japanese people wear these at work and in public places mainly if they have a cold and don't want to spread germs but also sometimes to prevent catching colds from other people. The masks are only really effective for an hour or so until the antiseptic in them has worn off but people wear them for much longer. You can even buy them in different colours nowadays!

Attitudes to AIDS (eizu エイズ)

The first isolated cases of AIDS became headline news in the mid-1980s and the attitude then (not unlike other countries) was that it was a foreign disease and not directly a threat to Japanese people. Critics inside and out of Japan have expressed concern over the lack of public information about the disease and the long delay before blood transfusions were screened. Since 1989 doctors by law have to tell the prefectural governor the name and address of any patient who tests positive and how s/he contracted the virus. This has been seen by critics as a violation of human rights and doctor–patient confidentiality. Reported cases of AIDS have risen fivefold since 1992, HIV cases have doubled and both continue to rise. The majority have been victims of infected blood transfusions.

DID YOU KNOW?
Chinese medicine (kanpō 漢方)

Chinese medicine has been practised in Japan since the 6th century AD and is still popular today. **Kanpōyaku** are herbal drugs which are said to have no side-effects and can be bought at most pharmacists. **Hari** (acupuncture) is the stimulation of **tsubo** (pressure points on the body) with hair-thin needles in order to activate specific internal organs and the natural healing powers of the body. **Shiatsu** is a type of Japanese massage which stimulates the **tsubo** using finger pressure and is especially good for relieving tiredness or stress. You often see Japanese people practising a simple form of **shiatsu** called **katatataki** on each other by pounding the shoulders. You can relieve tiredness by stimulating the **tsubo** in the soles of the feet – lie on your front and get someone to stand on the soles of your feet or tread on a curved piece of wood (a piece of split bamboo is ideal) every day for a few minutes.

Calling the emergency services

Ambulances (**kyūkyūsha**) and fire engines (**shōbōsha**) are called by dialling 119. The police (**keisatsu**) emergency number is 110. There are small police stations, called **kōban** (police box) on city street corners which house community police officers on duty. In rural areas they are called **chūzaisho** and the police officer, known as **omawarisan**, lives there. **Kōban**-based police visit every home in their area twice a year to pass on crime prevention information and to listen to complaints and other information. The nosey neighbour takes on a new meaning in rural Japan where it is said that if you want to know the latest gossip, ask a police officer!

DID YOU KNOW?
Fire and earthquake drills

Earthquakes (**jishin**) occur somewhere in Japan every day though the majority are slight tremors, often not detectable. All schoolchildren practise earthquake drills at school and all Japanese people are trained to know that you should shelter under a solid object such as a table or doorframe until the tremors decrease and then, if necessary, make your way to designated meeting points in the neighbourhood. Fire is the greatest danger following an earthquake and is also one of the hazards of living in houses made mainly of wood. Voluntary fire fighters, particularly in rural areas, will even patrol streets to remind people to switch off gas and paraffin appliances and many local authorities hold disaster prevention days to inform people of emergency plans.

Housing (jūtaku 住宅)

Although for most people in Japan, income and standard of living are on a par with other industrialized countries, they still lag behind in quality of housing. The average living space per household in 1997 was 93 m^2 which was almost half the area of the average American home. And facilities do not always compare favourably either – it is still not unusual for homes to have 'pit' toilets which are not connected to the mains sewerage system (although the number declines year on year) and most homes do not have central heating systems. For much of the year heating is not necessary but winters can be very cold and people rely on a combination of paraffin heaters and electrical devices which seems surprisingly old fashioned to visitors of Japan.

The price of a home

Land is a valuable and limited commodity in Japan. Sixty-six per cent of the land is mountainous and lightly populated whereas the majority of the population is concentrated on urban conurbations in coastal areas, the three main ones being Tokyo, Osaka and Nagoya (see map on p. 3). Limited land space means high demand and prices, and currently Tokyo is a close second only to Hong Kong in terms of land and house prices. According to 1996 figures, residential land in Tokyo was eight times as expensive as London and Sydney, and 30 times as expensive as

New York. House prices in Tokyo were similar to Hong Kong but four times more expensive than New York, three times more than Sydney and double those in London. A major contributor to the bubble economy of the late 1980s was the rocketing of land prices in Tokyo, Osaka and Nagoya although, following a government clampdown, these have stabilized and, with the recession, have begun to fall slightly. Currently, the average price of a starter home is almost five times the annual average income and about 61 per cent of Japanese people own their own home (compared to 60 per cent in the USA and 66 per cent in the UK).

Types of housing

For many Japanese, the ultimate dream is to own a two-storey detached house (**nikaiya** or **ikkodate**) but for about 50 per cent of the population, this remains a dream and of those who do live in such a house, 20 per cent rent rather than own it. The rest of the population live in some type of multi-unit known generally as **apāto** (*apartment*). These may be in large high-rise buildings called **danchi** which are publicly subsidized or in smaller more exclusive buildings called **manshon** (from *mansion* but with a changed meaning). There are also semi- or multi-detached single-storey houses. In the countryside there are a greater number of detached one- or two-storey buildings. Traditionally, because houses are made of wood and so do not have a long lifespan, a home is dismantled and rebuilt with new wood after about 20 years. Nowadays, modern materials such as concrete, aluminium and steel as well as wood are used to build houses. Houses for rent or sale are described as DK (dining–kitchen area) or LDK (L = living room) plus a number in front to indicate additional rooms. 3LDK is a house with three rooms plus living–dining–kitchen area. Size of rooms are measured by the number of **tatami** mats which are about 2 × 1 metres (but smaller in Tokyo and Osaka).

A traditional Japanese home

Look at the pictures of a 'typical' traditional Japanese home on the next page. Modern homes contain some or many of these features. For example, every home whether a detached two-storey house or an apartment in a **danchi** has an area for removing shoes before entering the main home. Modern homes usually incorporate a mix of Western and traditional features, such as a formal **tatami**-matted living room alongside the more modern practice of separate bedrooms for parents and children (where space permits). Only the ground floor is illustrated here. Two-storey houses typically have a combination of carpeted and **tatami** bedrooms on the upper floor. (Numbers relate to diagram.)

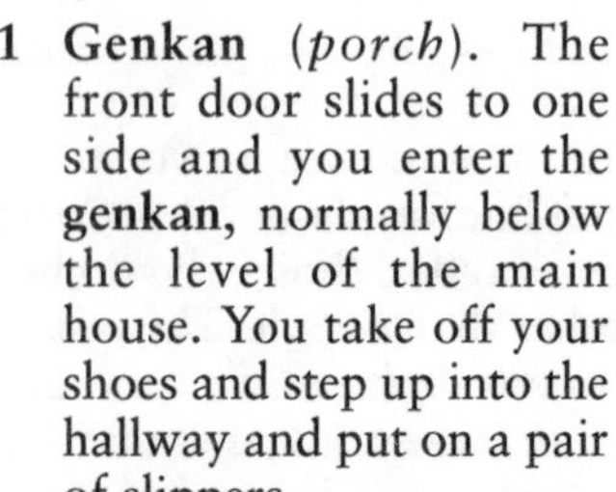

1 **Genkan** (*porch*). The front door slides to one side and you enter the **genkan**, normally below the level of the main house. You take off your shoes and step up into the hallway and put on a pair of slippers.
2 **Washitsu** (**tatami** room). All rooms apart from the kitchen were traditionally **tatami** rooms and were used as living space during the day and sleeping space at night. In smaller homes children and parents would use the same room. Nowadays, depending on space, they are used as living rooms (the family sit on the floor around a low table to eat and watch TV) and may also be used by parents or grandparents as bedrooms.

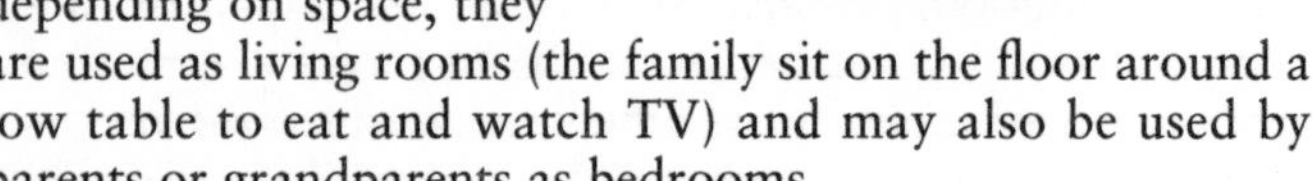

3 **Yōshitsu/ima** (*Western-style room/living room*). In post-war Japan, having a Western-style living room with carpet, sofa, chairs and maybe piano was a sign that you had really made it! It tended to be used for the formal receiving of guests although nowadays it might also be used as a family room. A Western-style dining room with table and chairs is another recent addition in larger homes.
4 **Ofuro to otearai** (*bathroom and toilet*). These are always in separate rooms (the Japanese think that the Western one-room arrangement is most unhygienic). More affluent

Japanese have another toilet upstairs. **Ofuro** (*baths*) are deeper and shorter than Western ones and are either filled with mains hot water or heated by a gas device under the bath. Japanese people clean themselves outside the bath using a shower or water in a basin and then soak themselves up to their neck in hot, clean water. The whole family share the same bath water and people tend to bathe every day. Before the war, many homes did not have a bathroom and people went to the **sentō** (*public bathhouse*) every day to bath and chat with neighbours. Over 90 per cent of Japanese homes now have a bathroom and the tradition of **sentō** is dying.

5 **Oshiire** (*closet*). The main function is to store **futon** (*bedding*) which is aired every day from the balcony then put away and laid out again at night.

6 **Tokonoma** (alcove). This is used to display precious items such as a hanging scroll, a precious vase and **ikebana** (flower arrangements). Ninety per cent of new homes have **tokonoma.**

7 **Engawa** (*veranda*). Traditionally, a narrow wooden feature around the house, nowadays it is often within the house, outside a **tatami** room. Apartments usually have balconies from which futon and washing can be hung. The washing machine is often kept here. Most houses have only a small **niwa** (garden) or yard if at all. Cars are usually parked on the street and in Tokyo you are not allowed to own a car unless there is somewhere to park it.

Shōji (sliding paper screens) and fusuma (room dividers)

A common Western misconception used to be that Japanese homes were made from paper. This probably arose because of the use of **shōji** and **fusuma** in the home to create privacy and divide up space. **Shōji** are wooden lattice frames covered with thin white paper and are used to divide **tatami** rooms off from corridors. The paper allows the diffusion of natural light and ventilation while stopping draughts. **Fusuma** are doors with wooden frames, covered in thick layers of paper which are used between rooms to create less or more space.

Cost of living

Japan's standard of living is high and compares well with other industrialized countries but the cost of living is also high. For example, although the Japanese average wage is higher than the American (2,276 yen per hour compared to 2,097 yen equivalent in USA), the Japanese spending power is about two-thirds of the American. Rice bought in Tokyo costs double that bought in New York or London; petrol is twice the USA price although still about 25 per cent cheaper than the UK; and a round of golf is four or five times more expensive than in the USA or UK at 16,900 yen ($129 or £78) per person in Tokyo. However, it is cheaper to buy camera films, video recorders and tissues in Japan (a box of tissues is more than twice the price in the USA and eight times more expensive in the UK!), and nearly 70 per cent of Japanese say that they are satisfied with their lifestyle.

Transport

Railways

In Japan almost one-third (30 per cent) of annual passenger travel is done by train. This is a very high percentage and Japan stands out when compared to other countries with well-developed rail systems such as the UK (5 per cent), France (8 per cent) and Switzerland (13 per cent). The three main reasons for this is that the rail system in Japan is highly efficient, travel by car can be very slow and the distances between major cities are relatively long. For example, the rail distance from Tokyo to Osaka is 515 km (309 miles) and from Tokyo to the northern tip of Kyūshū is 1,069 km (641 miles).

The railway system is run by the now privatized **JR** (Japan Railways) plus a number of other private companies. Many of these companies run other businesses such as department stores and baseball teams from which they get most of their profits. There are a range of local, express, limited express and fast trains, the pride and joy of which is the JR-owned **shinkansen** (new trunk line), better known outside Japan as the bullet train because of its shape and speed. It was once the fastest train in the world and is now second to France's TGV, but it still manages a top speed of 275 km/hour (165 mph) and JR are aiming at a future top speed of 300 km/hour (180 mph). At present the journey from Tokyo to Osaka takes 2 hours 30 minutes and a **shinkansen** runs every seven minutes! The **shinkansen** has an excellent record for safety and punctuality and is fitted with ATC (automatic train control) which ensures safe distances between trains. The system will cause trains to stop automatically if it detects earth tremors and to brake if it exceeds the speed limit.

The railway network was started in the 1880s with the help of British engineers. It is for this reason that Japan's trains run on the left, following British practice, and consequently that cars are also driven on the left side of the road. The **shinkansen** railroad system, begun in the 1960s, is admired around the world and influenced the development of other high-speed trains and railways such as the French TGV and the British HST (high-speed train). Some of the most advanced technology in the world has been used to develop, for example, the **Seiken** Tunnel (1985) built under the sea between the islands of Honshu and Hokkaido (see map on p. 3). At 54 km (33.5 miles) it is the longest railway tunnel in the world and the technology was used to build the Channel Tunnel (31 miles) between England and France. The most recent feat of rail and road technology is the series of 17 suspension bridges linking Honshu with Shikoku and smaller islands on the inland sea (see map on p. 3), begun in 1975 and finally completed in 1999. There are two levels with roads on the upper and rail lines on the lower. They form the longest suspension span in the world and make a spectacular sight.

The future looks exciting for rail travel, too, as Japan makes headway with the development of the linear motor train or *maglev* (magnetically levitated train) begun in 1979. In tests taken in 1999 the *maglev* reached a speed of 552 km/hour (331 mph), the fastest ever speed for a manned train. This would reduce the travel time between Tokyo and Osaka to just one hour!

Driving in Japan

There were 48 million cars registered for private use in Japan in 1997 making an average of one car per household and putting Japan behind only the USA and Canada for the number of cars per person. New cars are fairly cheap in Japan (you can buy a small 'run-around' 600 cc for about $3,000 or £2,000) but roads tend to be narrow and fairly crowded and so traffic moves quite slowly, particularly in built-up areas. As a result, the percentage of passenger travel by car is relatively low (62 per cent) when compared to other developed countries such as Switzerland (80 per cent), UK (89 per cent) and the USA (93 per cent). Other problems are the cost of fuel and lack of parking. The Japanese have come up with an ingenious 'space-saving' car park system in larger cities which is not unlike a large indoor ferris wheel. You drive your car into a compartment at ground level and when you return the 'wheel' is turned until your car is once more at ground level.

The number of traffic accidents is high with about 10,000 people killed on the road each year. As a result, speed restrictions are imposed strictly and police often set up speed traps, nicknamed **nezumi-tori** (*rat catching*!). Speed limits are quite low; in cities it is 40 km/hour (24 mph) and people frequently exceed this. The top speed limit is 100 km/hour (60 mph) and cars are often fitted with an alarm which rings if you go over that speed (but you can switch it off!). Drink driving rules are very strict – you are not allowed to drink at all and drive, and police spot checks are frequent, especially late at night. Police initially talk with the driver and smell the breath then take a breathalyser test if there is any doubt. If the test is positive, you lose your licence, incur a heavy fine and can be jailed.

Pollution caused by car exhaust fumes has been a big problem in Japan and cities like Tokyo and Osaka have suffered badly from smog. It used to be possible, for example, to see Mt Fuji from Tokyo but this is rarely so anymore. In recent years a number of laws have been enacted to curb exhaust emissions and air pollution has been reduced.

Other forms of transport

Boats

Japan is made up of islands and so ship and ferry travel still exists although the most common form nowadays is sightseeing boats, sometimes in the shape of swans, dragons or traditional ships.

Buses

Cities, towns and rural areas all have bus networks although these are not simple for foreign visitors to use because the destinations are written only in Japanese script. Coaches are used for sightseeing tours and as a cheaper alternative to trains for long-distance travel.

Underground trains

There are underground systems, called subways, in all the major cities including Tokyo, Osaka and Kyoto. These are very simple for foreigners to use because every station has signs (in romanized script as well as Japanese) with its own name plus the previous and next stations, so that you can be ready for your stop.

Taxis

There are plenty of taxis in Japan, identified by a sign on the roof and also a small sign inside the windscreen on the passenger side which lights up red if the taxi is for hire and green if it is taken. Two striking features of Japanese taxis are that the door opens and closes automatically (this catches many foreigners out!) and the taxi drivers wear white gloves. Taxi drivers rarely speak English and are often reluctant to pick up foreigners, especially if it is late at night. You need to be confident about giving directions in Japanese or have your destination written down. Fares are quite high but there is no need to tip.

Aeroplanes

There are three national airlines, JAL (Japan Air Lines), ANA (All Nippon Airlines) and JAS (Japan Air System). Forty-six million passengers arrive in and depart from Japan every year and, as in many other countries, airports have had to expand to deal with the increased air traffic. Narita International Airport serves Tokyo and had a new terminal building in 1992. Discussions with local farmers are still taking place to purchase land for another runway. Osaka now has a second international airport (Kansai International) which has been built on an artificial island and has suffered some land movement and subsidence since it opened in 1994. A further offshore airport is currently under way in Nagoya, due to open in 2005.

Taking it further

Websites

Japan Information Network (see Unit 1) has lots of interesting statistics on all the topics covered in this chapter (click on **Statistics** in the menu) and can also keep you up to date with recent trends in education and society (click on **Trends in Japan**).

An interesting book on Japanese education is *The Japanese Educational Challenge: A Commitment to Children*, Merry White (New York, Free Press; London, Collier Macmillan, 1987)

GLOSSARY

教育 **kyōiku**	*education*
先生 **sensei**	*teacher*
自殺 **jisatsu**	*suicide*
苛め **ijime**	*bullying*
文部科学省 **Monbukagakushō**	*Ministry of Education, Sports, Science and Technology*
学校 **gakkō**	*school*
大学 **daigaku**	*university*
小学校 **shōgakkō**	*primary/elementary school*
中学校 **chūgakkō**	*junior high/middle school*
高校 **kōkō**	*senior high school*
勉強する **benkyōsuru**	*to study*
健康 **kenkō**	*health*
医者 **isha**	*doctor*
歯医者 **haisha**	*dentist*
病院 **byōin**	*hospital*
看護婦 **kangofu**	*nurse*
タバコ **tabako**	*cigarettes*
住宅 **jūtaku**	*housing*
家 **ie, uchi**	*house, home*
家族 **kazoku**	*family*
アパート **apāto**	*apartment, flat*
和室 **washitsu**	*Japanese-style room*
洋室 **yōshitsu**	*Western-style room*
新幹線 **shinkansen**	*bullet train*
車 **kuruma**	*car*
バス **basu**	*bus*
電車 **densha**	*train*
乗る **noru**	*to get on, ride*

Japan at work and play

In this unit you will learn

- about the ups and downs of post-war Japan's economy
- about the main industries, names and products
- about work life in Japan for men and women
- how the Japanese relax and spend leisure time

Hatarakukoto wa bitoku de aru

Work is a virtue (Japanese saying)

The economy (keizai 経済)

At the end of World War II, Japan was a bankrupt country, its economy in tatters. It was given the status of a less-developed country and the allied forces put in motion a number of policies aimed at restarting the economy. The rapidity with which this was achieved was seen as an economic miracle – in 1952 Japan's consumption per person was one-fifth of the USA but by 1968 it had overtaken West Germany to become the second largest economy in the world. The average annual growth of the economy until 1975 was an astonishing 8 per cent (reaching 11.8 per cent in the 1960s) and even when it slowed down following the oil crises of the 1970s (for Japan, like other industrialized countries, had switched from coal to oil-based energy), it still maintained higher growth than other countries. The event which is seen by many as the pinnacle of this incredible achievement was the Olympic Games held in Tokyo in 1964 which focused the world's eyes on a country which had overcome the shame of the war and worked tirelessly to rebuild itself.

The main reasons for the success of the Japanese economy were, first, that most of Japan's factories were destroyed during the war and so had to be completely rebuilt and updated. The high level of personal savings by Japanese people also played an important role because it gave the banks the finances necessary

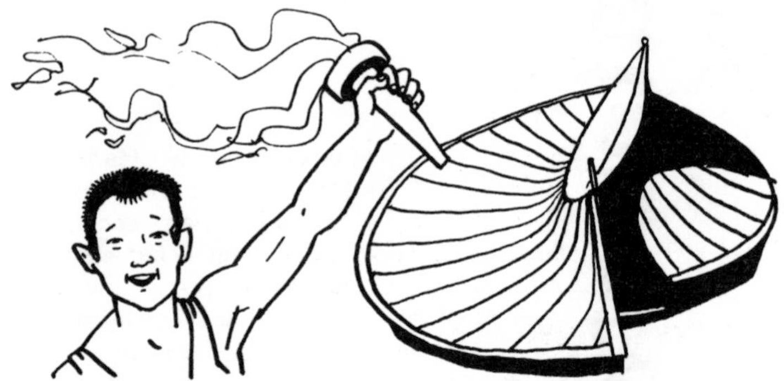

Japanese athlete running in front of Yoyogi stadium carrying Olympic flame

to lend to companies so that they could invest in new equipment, technologies and R&D (research and development). Then there was a major shift from the primary industries of agriculture and fishing to heavy industries such as steel and iron, shipbuilding, cars and electrical goods, the last in response to the huge surge in demand for consumer goods which began in the 1950s. The oil crises in the 1970s saw a slowdown in heavy industries such as shipbuilding and Japan shifted to the production of microelectronic items using the new 'microchip' technology and to the development of service and information industries such as banking, tourism and computers.

The bubble bursts

'Bubble economy' was used to describe the quick but fragile growth of the Japanese economy in the 1980s. Japan was increasingly criticized for its overreliance on exports (see Unit 12) and in 1984 a yen–dollar agreement was made with the Reagan administration to create a strong yen. Japanese industries responded by moving from reliance on manufacturing and exports to massive investments in land and stock while Japanese people continued to 'spend, spend, spend' and purchase home-produced goods. At the beginning of 1990, the Tokyo Stock Market began to slide and land prices to fall, causing consumers and companies to tighten their belts and growth to slow right down. By 1991, the bubble had burst and in 1997 Japan suffered its worst economic crisis ever, as one financial institution after another went bankrupt, stock and land prices fell even further, companies' profits plummeted and unemployment rose to a then all-time high of 4.9 per cent. Japan was officially in recession and the world markets had lost confidence in the Japanese government's ability to address the issues (see Unit 8). At the time of writing, the economy has become calmer, companies are restructuring and the government is implementing new measures. The world's markets are still waiting to see if Japan is able to put its house in order and how the new climate following 11 September 2001 ('9/11') will affect this.

Industry (sangyō 産業)

Japan had a relatively late 'industrial revolution' (**sangyō kakumei**), at the beginning of the Meiji period (1868–1912) when it began exporting raw silk and tea in exchange for income to set up a cotton and weaving industry. It built up its post-war economy on heavy industries such as steel and shipbuilding and since then Japanese products and manufacturers have been household names all over the world. Here is a quick breakdown of the main industries, names and products.

Electronics

This is one of Japan's most important industries, producing more than 30 trillion yen worth of goods each year (about 25 per cent of all manufacturing). It is made up of domestic goods (TVs, washing machines, VCRs, DVD players), industrial goods (telecommunications equipment and computers), and electronic parts such as semiconductors. Household names include Sony, Hitachi, Toshiba, Mitsubishi, Sanyo, Sharp, NEC and Fujitsu. The industry has used advances in digital technology to develop audio-visual goods such as DVD players, digital video cameras and mobile phones and generally to expand the whole area of broadcasting and telecommunications.

Robots and machine tools

These are an important part of Japan's machine industry, accounting for about 1.4 trillion yen of production a year. Japan leads the world in robot technology and 58 per cent of the world's industrial robots are made in Japan.

Cars

The automobile industry is one of Japan's big post-war success stories, with names such as Honda, Toyota, Nissan, Mitsubishi, Mazda and Isuzu known worldwide. This was despite critics who initially said it would be better to import from the USA than invest money in domestic production of cars. Indeed, by 1980, Japan had overtaken the USA to be the world's number one automobile producer and trade frictions were beginning to develop. For this reason and a slump in export profits, Japanese car manufacturers began to establish factories abroad in the USA, Canada, South-east Asia and Europe. The recent recession has hit the car industry badly with sales falling by over 12 per cent in 1998, resulting in job losses and the closing of some factories. The companies have begun massive restructuring such as the 1999 merger of Nissan with Renault, Mitsubishi's 'truck alliance' with Volvo and, in the case of Toyota (Japan's biggest car producer), the strengthening of its ties with other Japanese companies such as Daihatsu.

Other merchandise

Japan is one of the world's main producers of watches, clocks and cameras. Who hasn't heard of Japanese manufacturers such as Seiko, Casio, Canon, Pentax, Konica, Nikon, Minolta and Olympus? These manufacturers have led the development of digital watches, SLR (single-lens reflex) (about 80 per cent of world production is Japanese), compact and disposable cameras, to name but a few.

Steel and aluminium

Japan's steel is world renowned for its quality, although nowadays it is competing with countries such as Korea and Brazil. Despite a slowdown following the 'bursting of the bubble', Japanese aluminium is still in high demand in, for example, car parts and beer cans.

Agriculture, fishing and forestry

As in many other industrialized countries, these industries are in decline in Japan. In 1960, 30 per cent of the workforce was employed in agriculture and it accounted for about 40 per cent of the GDP (gross domestic product). Today less than 5 per cent of Japanese are farmers and 65 per cent are aged 60 or over. Together with fishing and forestry, it accounts for only 1.7 per cent of GDP. Japan is still almost 100 per cent self-sufficient in rice but imports large percentages of other foods such as meat (44 per cent) and fruit (47 per cent). The Japanese eat one-sixth of all the world's fish but overfishing in their own seas has led to the decline of small family-run fishing fleets and an increase in imports (currently over 40 per cent). Japan has also had difficult negotiations with countries around the Pacific and Atlantic to use their fishing grounds following the worldwide implementation of the 321-km (200-mile) fishing zones in the 1970s. Two-thirds of Japan is forested but the number of people working in this industry is declining and 83 per cent are aged 50 or over. Japan uses huge amounts of wood for paper and housing (see also p. 230) and currently imports about 80 per cent of it from the USA, Russia, South-east Asia and New Zealand.

DID YOU KNOW?
The most expensive apples in the world!

Japan has become increasingly reliant on imports of foods such as fruit and vegetables. Items such as cucumbers, aubergines, tomatoes, mandarin oranges, Japanese pears (**nashi**) and persimmons are still grown in Japan. In fact, mandarin oranges are the most widely consumed fruit. The price of imported fruit, however, can be extremely high because of tax and distribution costs and it is not unusual to see single large apples or speciality melons for sale for as much as 10,000 yen (about $85 or £60)! These fruits are usually wrapped in presentation boxes to be bought as gifts and it is possible to buy cheaper fruit but, in general, fruit prices are high compared to other countries.

Services

These include retailing, catering, finance, insurance, administration and social services and employ over 60 per cent of the entire workforce. The retail industry alone employs nearly 11 per cent of the working population and in 1997 its annual sales totalled 148 trillion yen. Visitors to Japan frequently comment on the excellent service and presentation of goods in department stores, supermarkets and even small shops, and other countries have looked to Japan to improve their own customer services. Here are some examples of customer care in the retail industry:

- As you enter a store, the shop assistants will call out **Irasshaimase** (*Welcome/How can I help you?*).
- When you purchase a gift, it will be carefully and beautifully wrapped for you.
- In department stores, the attendants all wear a uniform usually complete with hat and white gloves.
- A female attendant is employed in large stores to wipe the escalator handrail and others to work the lifts and tell customers what is on each floor, all accompanied with a deep bow to show respect to the **okyakusan** (*honourable customer*).

Interestingly, fewer than 1 per cent of retail outlets are large stores with 50+ employees whereas small shops of four or fewer employees make up about 75 per cent of the total. Also, although supermarket chains have been the leaders of the retail industry, their slice of the total retail sales is only 6.7 per cent, lower than many other industrialized countries, and the specialized and local shop (often 24-hour convenience stores such as 7–11) is still very much in evidence. All retailers, however, have suffered losses with the recent recession and consumers have begun to be more demanding of high-quality goods at lower prices. Accompanying this change in consumer demand, has been the growth of second-hand shops and DIY stores (it used to be considered 'poor form' to buy second hand and people were more likely to throw away and purchase a more up-to-date model).

Once the recession is over and as free time increases, other service industries which look set to grow include software and information industries, leisure, health and fitness and educational facilities.

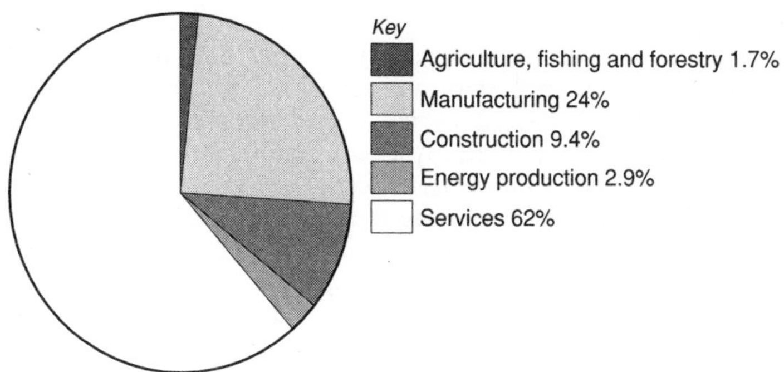

The composition of Japan's GDP (2000)

Small and medium enterprises (chūshō kigyō 中小企業)

It may come as a surprise to learn that the majority of Japanese companies and factories are small to medium sized, especially as many people's experience of a Japanese factory is based on those built overseas by large companies such as Toyota, Nissan and Sony. In fact, 99 per cent of all Japanese companies are small or medium enterprises (defined as having 300 or fewer employees; and smaller numbers of 100 for wholesale and 50 for retail). The majority are family-run or small businesses of under four employees and about two-thirds are subcontactors of larger firms. For example, the manufacturing industry consists of large numbers of small factories employing around ten workers which are subcontracted by the larger factories in order to cut costs and keep quality. These small businesses thrived during the 1960s in response to the consumer goods boom and continued to hold their heads well above water even during various economic crises. The government's support of these businesses, including finance and guidance, is one of the most wide ranging in the world.

The employment and pay structure

There are three main types of employees in the Japanese workplace: regular employees, taken on immediately after university graduation who normally work for the same company until retirement; temporary employees who make up 20 per cent of the workforce (mainly women), have less secure conditions of service and are paid about half the wages of regular workers; and employees working for subcontractors who have fixed periods of work and poorer conditions of service. In addition, employees of smaller companies have fewer perks than those in larger companies and their wages are lower (about 70 per cent). Regular workers used to be offered **shūshin koyō** (*job security for life*) and could expect to progress financially through the **nenkō joretsu** (*seniority system*) which linked salary with age and years of work. Promotion also depends on educational background with those attending the best universities progressing faster. However, the pattern is beginning to change with some companies offering promotion based on merit and many no longer able to offer 'a job for life'.

DID YOU KNOW?
Bonus (shōyo 賞与)

Bonuses are paid twice a year (June and December) to regular employees in most workplaces and can amount to the equivalent of several months' wages in larger companies. Bonus day is usually marked with great celebrations and a large number of inebriated workers waiting on stations for very late trains home! Temporary and part-time workers are not usually entitled to bonuses and, as bonuses are calculated according to companies' annual profits, they have fallen in recent years.

Labour unions (rōdō kumiai 労働組合)

About 20 per cent of Japanese workers are in unions (compared to 15.5 per cent in the USA and 39 per cent in the UK) although this number has been decreasing in recent years. Unions are usually organized on a company basis with both white- and blue-collar workers belonging to the same one. About two-thirds of all workers belong to unions which are part of **Rengo** (Japanese Trade Union Confederation) and there is a high degree of worker–management cooperation. An example is **shuntō** (the spring wage offensive) when annual wage increases are negotiated across all the industries. These have been very low in recent years (2.2 per cent in 1998) with both workers and management agreeing not to 'rock the boat' during the recession.

Women at work

Although Japan's Constitution stated that all people were equal under the law and that there should be no gender discrimination, in reality women in post-war Japan have been treated very differently in the workplace. After graduation from university or two-year college, women who were taken on by companies were expected to work only a few years before marriage (some companies even required women to resign after marriage or having children) and so were given lower paid work than their male peers and were not given promotion. Many women were taken on as the official or unofficial OL, short for 'office lady' – the person who made the tea for her male colleagues and clients. Promotion is traditionally given according to years of service, not merit (known as **nenkōjoretsu** or seniority system) which discriminates against women who do not have enough continuous service to qualify. And at the bottom of it all was (and still is) an entrenched belief that women are less able than men and their role is as homemaker and supporter of the man as main breadwinner.

Some of these facts and perceptions have gradually eroded and changed in recent years but others remain. The number of women going on to higher education had overtaken men in 1997 (but was 48.7 per cent of women and 49.8 per cent of men in 2001), and women are marrying later and having fewer children. As a result, more women are seeking longer term careers and the number of women in managerial positions, although still low when compared to other industrialized countries, has risen to 9.5 per cent of all managers. (In 1990, only 1 per cent of women had people working under them.) The high cost of living and the large 'consumer appetite' of Japanese society has also led to an increase in married women returning to work, usually part time. In 2001, over 64 per cent of women aged 15–64 were in work and over half worked part time. However, women are still only paid an average wage of about 60 per cent of men's and of Japan's total workforce of 65 million, 26.7 million (41 per cent) are women although this number continues to rise.

There is still a long way to go for Japanese women before they achieve true equality in the workplace both in conditions of service and perceptions but the government has introduced a range of legislation in recent years to address some of the issues. The revised 1999 Sex Discrimination Law designed to stop discriminatory practice in the hiring and promotion of women has finally made it obligatory for companies to implement measures. Two other recent laws on child and family care have allowed male and female employees with children under the age of one to take full- or part-time leave from their jobs and to take up to three months off to look after a sick or elderly family member.

A day in the life of a Japanese worker

The working day of a typical Japanese man has become almost a cliché: the long commute to work in a crowded train, long hours in the office followed by compulsory 'socializing' after work with the boss, then a late return home after the children have gone to bed. He may work a six-day week and even spend Sunday playing golf with boss and clients. The Japanese used to work longer hours than workers in other industrialized countries and take fewer holidays, normally only about half of those to which they were entitled. The government in the last decade has been taking steps to reduce working hours to 40 hours per week (from 48 hours in 1988). The average working week in the manufacturing industry, for example, is now 38.8 hours compared to 42.8 (USA) and 43.7 (UK). Nearly 90 per cent of companies now have a five-day week and younger men (and women) are wanting to spend longer with their family. Nevertheless, and particularly in smaller, family-run companies, people are still working long hours and not taking their full holiday entitlement.

DID YOU KNOW?
Absent fathers (tanshin funin 単身赴任)

This term is used to describe male workers who are transferred to other companies in Japan or abroad and go without their wives and families. This can be for a number of months or years and has often been very detrimental to family relationships. The transfer is seen as part of the promotion path and so few would dare to refuse but it has been difficult for families to transfer as well, mainly because of concerns over the children's education. In recent years, a growing number of families have transferred together and positions in English-speaking countries are particularly popular because they are seen as an opportunity for children to become good English speakers (see Unit 12).

Unemployment

Japan has suffered its highest unemployment rate ever, reaching 5 per cent in 2001. This is low compared to other countries but has had a massive impact on Japanese workers, particularly graduates who can no longer assume that they will find regular or permanent employment and older workers who are the first to be made redundant following restructuring. Many companies have a retirement age of 55 even though pension entitlement doesn't begin until 60. This is leaving an increasing number of men in their late 50s with no job prospects and there has been an increase in the rate of suicide for men in this age group. Middle-aged men have committed suicide or simply never returned home rather than suffer the shame of telling their family that they have been made redundant. It is thought that a significant number of homeless people living in the 'cardboard cities' of large cities come from this group.

Japan at play

The '*work hard, play hard*' maxim is nowhere more applicable than in Japan. Although the Japanese take relatively few holidays and may work long hours during the week, leisure and sporting activities are an integral part of society, beginning with the multitude of clubs at school and ending with membership of a local 'pensioner-friendly' **gētobōru** club (*gateball* is a type of croquet). Group identity and working as a team are two important principles in Japanese society and so the Japanese tend to be keen participators in a range of group leisure activities. The recession has seen a reduction in spending on leisure activities but, as both free time and the ageing population increase, this aspect of Japanese life can only increase too.

Free time

If you ask a Japanese person what they do in their free or spare time, the answer may often be **rirakkusu** (*relax*) or even **nemasu** (*sleep*)! Actually, most people participate in organized activities and/or leisure activities with the family. However, long hours at work or school often mean that time for sleeping or simply relaxing is limited and grasped at when there is chance. Visitors to Japan often comment with amazement on Japanese people's ability to sleep on a crowded train (sometimes standing up!) and still wake up in time for their stop. Reading is also a national pastime in a nation where 99.8 per cent are literate. Walk into a bookshop at the end of a working day and you will see large numbers of Japanese people leafing through the latest **zasshi** (*magazines*), **shōsetsu** (*novels*) and **manga** (*comic books*). On trains, too, it is notable how many Japanese people of all ages have their noses stuck in a book of some kind although young people nowadays prefer to send text messages on their mobile phones.

The average daily amount of leisure time is on the increase (6 hours and 26 minutes in 2001). Here is how Japanese people spend some of that time.

Activity	Hours and minutes spent
Watching TV, listening to the radio, reading	2.34
Rest and relaxation	1.19
Hobbies and amusement	0.42
Sports	0.11

Source: Statistics Bureau and Statistics Centre

In addition, the average nightly sleep amounts to 7 hours and 42 minutes!

The Japanese, who love statistics and **ankēto** (*market research*), have produced these figures for their top ten chart of favourite free time activities (in 2001).

Rank	Activity	Millions of participants (approx.)
1	Eating out at restaurants	78
2	Travelling within Japan	64
3	Going for drives	60
4	Karaoke	51
5	Watching videos	47
6=	Listening to music	44
6=	Visiting zoos, gardens, aquaria, museums	44
8	Using personal computers	41
9	Gardening	40
10	Going to the cinema	40

Source: White Paper for Leisure Activities

Teenagers are great fans of video and computer games such as Nintendo and play-stations and board games such as Monopoly are popular family games. Cinema has always been popular in Japan and has been enjoying a boom with all-time record box office takings of 194 million yen ($1.6 million) in 1998 although the recession has seen lower takings since. Finally, shopping does not appear in the top ten above but continues to be a highly popular activity, particularly with younger people, despite the recession (see Unit 6) and Japanese people name France, Hong Kong and Italy as their top three shopping destinations.

Holidays and travel

Compared to other industrialized countries, the Japanese do not have many holidays. Including weekends and the 14 national holidays, the average allocation in 2001 was 112.7 days per year. Compare this with 138 days in France, 136 in the UK and 132 in the USA. In addition, although on average a Japanese worker can take almost 20 paid days' leave per year, s/he actually only takes nine of these and does not receive pay in place of the unclaimed leave. This is a practice which has been in place for years; it simply isn't done to take your full leave entitlement! Most of those claimed days are taken together during the summer when children are on holiday and during **obon** in August (see p. 106), when the whole of Japan seems to be on the move! The other popular holiday time is Golden

Week in April/May when a cluster of national holidays means that many companies close down completely and the roads, train stations and airports are full of Japanese people taking advantage of the extended break.

Many people use holiday time to travel within Japan. During the winter people go to the mountains at weekends to ski or travel to the many hot spring resorts to relax in naturally hot and healing waters, eat good food and pamper themselves. Many of the hot springs are outside, some (but in decreasing numbers) are mixed and there are some in more remote places which are even frequented by bears and monkeys! In the summer time, people like to escape the humidity of the cities to cooler places either in the mountains, in the northern areas of Japan, or the seaside. In contrast, the more temperate climate of the spring and autumn takes people to famous sightseeing places such as Kyoto. Of course, this is a generalization, but it is certainly true that during the popular holiday seasons, the more famous sightseeing and tourist spots are extremely busy.

The Japanese abroad

Travel abroad has been on the increase but is still relatively low when compared to other countries. In 2001 about 16 million Japanese travelled abroad on holiday (about 12.5 per cent, compared with 35 per cent of Britons and 50 per cent of Germans). Traditionally, the two main groups of travellers have been honeymooners and older couples, who have travelled in organized groups for relatively short (4–7 days) 'whistle-stop' tours of the USA, Asia, Australasia or Europe. Most people's image of the Japanese abroad is of a group of people following a guide bearing a flag or umbrella to a famous tourist spot where they take some quick snaps or video shots before returning to the coach for the next leg of the tour! However, for many Japanese people, the expense incurred in taking a trip abroad and the lack of long holidays has meant that they may have only one opportunity and so need to squeeze as much as possible into the schedule. Increasingly, Japanese people are prioritizing leisure over work and in the early 1990s an increasing number of families made the big trip abroad. Another fairly recent trend has been the independent traveller, usually Japanese university graduates who want to put careers on hold and travel or work abroad for a year or longer. It is often parents who foot the bill!

The ten most visited countries in 2000 can be seen in the following table.

Rank	Country	Millions of visitors
1	United States	4.3
2	South Korea	2.1
3	China	1
4	Thailand	0.7
5	Australia	0.6
6	Hong Kong	0.58
7	Taiwan	0.55
8	Singapore	0.46
9	Italy	0.4
10	Indonesia	0.39

Source: Judicial System and Research Department

It is unclear what the long-term effect of 11 September 2001 ('9/11') will be on travel abroad but in the immediate aftermath many Japanese cancelled their planned trips overseas.

Sports

Whether as participators or spectators, the Japanese love sports. The top three spectator sports are **sakkā** (*football/soccer*), **yakyū** (*baseball*) and **sumō**. Baseball has the status of national sport in Japan but has recently been overtaken in popularity by football, especially among the young. Other popular team sports are **basukettobōru** (*basketball*) and **barēbōru** (*volleyball*), the latter especially popular with women. The most popular participation sports in Japan are gymnastics, bowling and jogging. The main professional sports are baseball, football, **sumō**, volleyball, figure skating, golf and tennis. At the 2000 Sydney Olympics, Japan won five gold, eight silver and five bronze medals in swimming, judo, the marathon, wrestling, taekwondo and softball. Sixty per cent of the population switched on to watch Takahashi Naoko win the marathon, knocking 1 minute 38 seconds off the Olympic record and becoming Japan's first ever gold medallist in the women's track and field. In fact, 13 of Japan's 18 medals were won by women and Japan set up a Sports Promotion Policy after the Olympics aimed at doubling the number of medals over a ten-year period.

DID YOU KNOW?

Three Olympic Games have been held in Japan: the 1964 Tokyo Summer Olympics, the 1972 Winter Olympics in Sapporo and the 1998 Winter Olympics in Nagano.

Some facts about yakyū (baseball)

Yakyū began as a professional sport in Japan in 1936 and there are currently two leagues, Central and Pacific, and 12 teams, all based in the main cities and funded by large regional companies. For example, Japan's first professional baseball team, the Yomiuri Giants who are supported by one-third of all baseball fans, have a stadium in Tokyo and are financed by the *Yomiuri Newspaper*. Others include the Tōyō Carp in Hiroshima, the Hanshin Tigers in Osaka and the Yokohama Bay Stars. Twenty-two million Japanese a year attend baseball games and many millions more watch it on TV. The teams include a number of foreign players, primarily from the USA, including Cecil Fielder of the New York Yankees and Joe Crawford of the New York Mets. The Japanese player, Nomo Hideo, became the first Japanese to play for American major league baseball when he joined the LA Dodgers in 1995. The main professional baseball event of the year is the Japan Series when the winners of the two leagues fight it out to be overall winner over seven games. Another major event is the High School Baseball Tournament held biannually in spring and summer at the Hanshin Tigers' Koshien Stadium (Japan's first baseball stadium, built in 1924). The tournament is watched avidly every day by millions of Japanese and is a highly prestigious event for the high schools across Japan who qualify to play.

Some facts about sakkā (football/soccer)

Sakkā has been played on an amateur level, especially in schools, since 1873 but has become very popular since the professional J-League was established in 1993. There are 26 teams, and a number of foreign players, including England's Gary Linneker, Brazil's Zico and Germany's Pierre Littbarski, have played in Japan. There are also non-Japanese managers including Frenchman Philippe Troussier who has coached the national team. In 1998 Japan, for the first time ever, qualified for the World Cup in France and football's popularity soared even higher. Japan's joint hosting of the 2002 World Cup with South Korea marked the first time that the event had been held in Asia. The demand for the 1.35 million tickets available to

Japan was huge with people forming long queues at post offices for application forms and the internet site receiving 10 million hits per day. Japan has begun to export its players too such as Inamoto Junichi from **Ganba Osaka** who was signed by the English team, Arsenal, in 2001 and Nakata Hidetoshi who has played for the Italian teams AC Perugia and AS Roma.

Sumō

Sumō, with its huge, powerful male wrestlers in **mawashi** (*loincloth belts*) and ancient ceremonial rites dating back 2,000 years, is popular both inside and outside Japan. There are six main **basho** (*tournaments*) each year held in Tokyo (three times), Osaka, Nagoya and Fukuoka. Each **basho** lasts 15 days and at other times of the year, **sumō** wrestlers travel around Japan giving demonstrations. The basic aim of **sumō** is to overcome the opponent by pushing him to the ground or outside the **dohyō** (*hard clay ring*). There are officially 70 winning techniques but about 25 are used regularly. Before each bout, the wrestlers scatter salt on the ring to purify it. The two opponents may spend several minutes trying to psych each other out by squatting and glaring at each other, raising their legs and stamping or scattering more salt. The actual bout may only last a few seconds and, to move upwards in the divisions, a wrestler

Sumō moves

must win more bouts than he loses over the 15 days. There are six ranks of wrestler (**rikishi**), the two highest being **ōzeki** and **yokozuna**. These are the only two ranks who are allowed to wear their long hair in the special 'ginko-leaf' topknot style during tournaments and who receive a regular salary (**yokozuna** can earn as much as 2.74 million yen, about $24,000 or £16,000 per month!). Their sporting life lasts only about 15 years, however, and it is essential that they lose weight after they stop competing. There have been some foreign-born wrestlers and the Hawaiian-born Taro Akebono was the first foreigner to become a **yokozuna**. He was extremely popular and retired in 2001 after a 13-year career with a retirement payment of 100 million yen ($900,000 or £590,000).

Budō (martial arts)

Many of the best-known martial arts originate in Japan such as **karate** (meaning '*empty hand*' because no weapons are used), **jūdō** (which came from **jūjutsu**), **kendō** (fencing with bamboo swords), **aikidō** (called '*Zen in motion*' because of the spiritual emphasis) and **kyūdō** (*Japanese archery*). Posture and body movement are central to martial arts but so also is the correct mental attitude and the training is both of body and mind. A school of martial arts is called a **dōjō** and it is still a popular leisure activity in Japan. Judo became an Olympic sport in 1964 and many Japanese have been gold medallists including the female competitor, Tamura Ryoko, at the Sydney Olympics.

DID YOU KNOW?
Two recent crazes

Jump rope or skipping and scooter boards are two of the latest crazes to hit Japan. The toy makers, Bandai, have brought out the J-rope which has ball bearings for better skipping! It has become popular with children and adults alike, especially in women's keep-fit classes and Bandai have organized classes and tournaments. Scooter boards are as popular in Japan as they have been in other Western countries and you can buy two- or three-wheeled versions.

Clubs, associations and traditional arts

Clubs and associations exist for a huge variety of leisure and sporting activities and the Japanese are keen team players. Most schoolchildren are expected to take part in clubs after school and the choice includes martial arts, sports, orchestra, brass band, traditional instruments, origami, dance and English club. Traditional arts such as tea ceremony, flower arrangement and Japanese dance are popular with older women and were once seen (but less so now) as an important part of a young girl's preparation for marriage. Golf is particularly popular with working men – 17 million Japanese people play – but club membership is very expensive and many people use the ubiquitous golf drives to perfect their swing. Hiking, climbing and fishing clubs are all popular outdoor pursuits and in May 1999 Japan's Noguchi Ken became the youngest person ever, at the age of 25, to climb the seven summits (the highest peak on each of the seven continents). Finally, **bonsai** (*miniature tree*) growers devote many years to this art and display their trees on stands outside their home. These trees can last for hundreds of years and are passed down through generations.

Gambling

The only sports in which gambling is allowed are horse racing, cycle racing, motorboat racing and motorbike racing, the most popular being horse racing. **Pachinko**, a game which combines elements of pinball and slot machines, is played by an estimated 30 million people and is a very lucrative industry. It is not strictly (or legally) a gambling game because the pachinko balls you win can only be exchanged for prizes such as CDs and pencils. However, you can take your winnings round the corner from the **pachinko** parlour and exchange them for money!

Traditional board games

Mahjong originated in China and came to Japan in the 1920s. It is played with four players who collect small tiles into sets (rather like playing cards). **Mahjong** parlours (**jansō**) can be found all over Japan and the game is especially popular with men, who smoke and play late into the night. **Shōgi** is a type of chess but players can also use their opponent's captured pieces as their own. **Go** is played on a wooden board divided into squares. The two players have either round black or white stones and try to take more territory than their opponent through a series of moves and captures.

Taking it further

Books

Made in Japan, Akio Morita and Sony (New America Library, 1997)

Gucci on the Ginza: Japan's New Consumer Generation, George Fields (Tokyo and New York, Kodansha International, 1989)

Japan in your Pocket: Vol. 14, Japanese Inn and Travel (Japan, JTB, 1990)

Lonely Planet Guide to Japan (Australia, Lonely Planet, 1997, **http://www.lonelyplanet.com**)

Grand Sumo: The Living Sport and Tradition, Lora Sharnoff (New York and Tokyo, Weatherhill, 1989)

Bonsai: The Complete Guide to Art and Technique, Paul Lesniewicz (Dorset, Blandford Press, 1984)

Information

http://jin.jcic.or.jp Choose **Japan Access** from the menu for information on sports, arts, the economy and employment. Select **The Virtual Museum** for views of traditional Japanese culture and pastimes. Select **Puzzle Japan** to play crosswords and puzzles and **Trends in Japan** for news items on economy, business and sports.

Contact the Japan National Tourist Organizations (JNTO) in your country **http://www.jnto.go.jp** for information about travel in Japan. Addresses also available from the cultural centres (JICC) attached to Japanese embassies (see Taking it further in Unit 1).

Watching traditional sports – JNTO in Japan publish a booklet called *Traditional Sports* which has details of tickets and dates for sumō and martial arts tournaments. They can also give information about baseball games at the **Kōrakuen** Stadium in Tokyo and J-League football at Tokyo's National Stadium.

Contact your JICC for information about classes in traditional Japanese arts.

Statistical information for Units 9 and 10 from *Japan: A Pocket Guide*, Foreign Press Centre, Japan (annual publication). Also available as *Japan: A Web Guide* at **http://www.nttls.co.jp/fpc/e/shiryo/pocket**

Japan 2000 (etc.) An International Comparison, Keizai Koho Center, Japan: **http://www.kkc.or.jp**

GLOSSARY

働く **hataraku**	*to work*
遊ぶ **asobu**	*to play*
会社 **kaisha**	*company*
産業 **sangyō**	*industry*
主婦 **shufu**	*housewife*
サラリーマン **sararīman**	*salary man, employee*
課長 **kachō**	*section manager*
部長 **buchō**	*department chief*
失業 **shitsugyō**	*unemployment*
暇な時 **himana toki**	*spare time*
趣味 **shumi**	*hobby*
休み **yasumi**	*rest, holiday*
旅行 **ryokō**	*travel*
スポーツ **supōtsu**	*sports*
サッカー **sakkā**	*football*
野球 **yakyū**	*baseball*
相撲 **sumō**	
武道 **budō**	*martial arts*

the Japanese people

In this unit you will learn

- **about Japanese stereotypes – the truths and the myths**
- **about current social trends and concerns**
- **about social customs and obligations**
- **some useful tips for doing business with the Japanese**
- **what to do when you visit a Japanese home**

What are today's Japanese people really like? What is it that defines somebody as 'Japanese'? Is it possible to describe the 'typical Japanese person'? This unit attempts to address these questions and to look at Japanese society today.

Stereotypes

Japan often seems very distant and exotic to people in other countries, especially outside Asia. It is so much easier and quicker to travel abroad nowadays but nevertheless, Japan is not yet a mainstream tourist destination and is still a relatively expensive country to visit. As a result, people may have impressions of Japanese people based on limited actual experience. Let's look at a few stereotypical images and statements commonly made about Japanese people and see what, if any, is the truth behind them.

Japanese people are very polite

Japanese people bowing to one another

Showing respect for others, in particular your superiors, is a very important aspect of Japanese society. The upside of this is that social relationships, at least on the surface, tend to be very harmonious and visitors to Japan are treated with great respect and kindness. The downside is that politeness is also used to create distance, making it more difficult to really get to know a Japanese person. Long-term foreign residents in Japan sometimes complain that, after years of living there, politeness is still used as a barrier to closer friendships. There are also special forms of polite language – honorific Japanese – for when you speak to superiors or people you don't know well (see pp. 36–8). Speaking your mind is also considered bad form in Japan and there is a belief that if you have to resort to words to express feelings then you are not really communicating. Understanding someone through intuition and non-verbal communication is seen as more effective but this can create problems when, for example, carrying out complex business deals with non-Japanese people.

Japanese people don't have a sense of humour

The simple response to this is, yes, they do! Japanese people love to have a laugh and to share a good (or bad) **jōdan** (*joke*) just like everybody else. There is a huge variety of comedy on television including light-hearted chat shows, celebrity quizzes and stand up comedians. Some of the humour is fairly slapstick but there is more subtle humour too, evidenced by some recent films such as *Shall We Dance?* and *Tampopo* (see p. 131 for more).

Japanese have inscrutable smiles

To a certain extent this is true, at least from a Western viewpoint. Japanese people certainly smile and laugh when they are happy or amused, but they may also use a smile to cover up confusion or embarrassment. An apology accompanied by a smile can come over to a non-Japanese person as being insincere but it is simply a way of hiding embarrassment. Japanese people may also smile and nod while you talk to them but don't take this to mean that they are in agreement – it may merely be a way of showing you that they are listening.

It's rude to look directly at a Japanese person

The answer to this is yes and no. In Western society, if someone does not look another person in the eye it is often interpreted that they have something to hide or are a bit 'shifty'. In Japanese society, showing respect for others is very important and staring somebody, especially a superior or stranger, boldly in the eye can be interpreted as disrespect. However, looking at a friend while you talk to them is normal practice although people may look away when discussing more personal or difficult issues (this is not restricted to Japanese people, of course).

There is no word for 'no' in Japanese

There are several ways of saying no including **iie** (*no*) or **chigaimasu** (*that's incorrect*) but saying 'no' directly is considered rude and people are more likely to use hesitation and phrases such as **muzukashii desu ne** (*it's a bit tricky*) or **kangaete mimasu** (*I'll think about it*). This is a way of avoiding conflict and is also an example of non-verbal communication – the 'no' has to be filled in. Of course, this avoidance of a direct 'no' is not confined to Japanese society alone!

The Japanese are a cruel race

This perception largely results from World War II and especially the horrors suffered by prisoners of the Japanese and those living in countries occupied by Japan (see p. 228). Without a doubt, there were many extreme and cruel deeds carried out under the guise of war (and such acts were not limited to the Japanese) but there is certainly no evidence of 'inherent cruelty' when you look at the Japanese today. At worst they tend to be rather ignorant and badly informed of events around World War II but Japan today is a pacifist nation, making important contributions to world events (see Unit 12).

Japanese couples are only allowed to have one child

This misperception has arisen because of a confusion between China and Japan: Japan, unlike China, has never enforced limits on the number of children per family. In fact, there is more concern currently at Japan's very low birth rate – just 1.38 per family.

There are a number of other misperceptions of Japanese people, sometimes fostered or at least not discouraged by the Japanese themselves who may enjoy the air of mystery which is attached to them by non-Japanese people. However, it is when you get to know Japanese people as individuals and as friends, that the stereotypes fade and the 'infinite variety' of Japanese people shows through.

The 'uniqueness' of the Japanese

The Japanese have a very strong national identity, possibly the result of being an island nation and closed to the outside world for over 200 years. There are a number of books written by Japanese which discuss and promote the 'uniqueness of the Japanese race' and older Japanese people were educated under the militaristic government of the 1920s and World War II period which promulgated extreme nationalistic ideals. Countries that suffered under the Japanese in the first half of the 20th century such as Korea, China and the war veterans of the Allied forces are quick to protest when government representatives express extreme national sentiments such as Prime Minister Mori Yoshiro's reference to Japan as a '*divine nation centred upon the emperor*' or Prime Minister Koizumi Junichiro's visit in 2001 to a shrine dedicated to the memory of Japan's war heroes (see also p. 94). For most ordinary Japanese people, and particularly those born since the war, there is a far greater awareness and understanding of other countries and cultures and so a gradual fading of the 'them and us' distinctions. The issue remains sensitive, however, and the theme of uniqueness is still a popular topic in Japanese society.

Social trends

Population (jinko 人口)

Japan's population steadily increased during the 20th century but has slowed down in recent years. The total population was 127 million in 2000 and Japan has one of the highest population densities in the world (see following table).

Selected countries	People per km^2 (2000 figures)
Bangladesh (1996)	834
South Korea	471
Japan	336
UK	244
China	133
USA	29

Source: *Japan 2003: An International Comparison* (Keizai Koho Center)

In addition, with 75 per cent of the land taken up with mountains and forest, and the movement of people from the countryside to the cities, the population density of Japan's large cities is even greater. Tokyo has 5,400 people per km^2 and 20,000 in the central part!

Japan, like other industrialized countries, has falling birth and mortality rates while the elderly population are living longer.

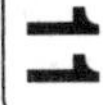

The average number of children per family is 1.38, one of the lowest birth rates in the world. At the same time, it is predicted that the 65+ age group will form one-quarter of the population by 2015. Similar patterns are being repeated across the world and Japan is not alone in having to face the issues of an increasing number of pensioners being financially supported by a decreasing number of earners and tax payers.

The family (kazoku 家族)

The issue of extended versus nuclear family is still a lively topic for debate in the media. There are those who recall the 'good old days' when people lived in larger families as part of a tight-knit community and looked after each other. There are others, women in particular, who complain bitterly of the overbearing, ever-criticizing **shūtome** (*mother-in-law*). And yes, the Japanese enjoy mother-in-law jokes just as many other countries do! Before World War II a system known as the **ie** (*family*) system tied people into households in which the males were always the head of the family, women were obedient to husbands, children to fathers and fathers to parents. Households were extended family units in which the eldest members received great respect. The eldest son normally inherited the family home and, with it, the duty of looking after his parents.

The **ie** system was abolished after World War II and replaced by the 1947 Civil Code which made wives equal to husbands, at least in legal terms. Gradually, as more people moved to the cities and more women went to work, the number of extended (three-generation) families fell from nearly half of all families in 1955 to one in eight by 1994 and nuclear families became the norm (presently about 60 per cent). Single households (young or elderly people living alone or divorced people) have increased and now account for nearly one-quarter of all family units. The size of the average family has also dropped from 5.6 people in 1950 to below three in the 1990s. Many couples say that they would like more than one child but simply cannot afford the costs of housing and rearing children and an increasing number of couples are choosing not to have children at all or to delay the decision. One fact with which the Japanese media are in agreement is that family life has changed drastically in the last 50 years and some of the old obligations to extended family unit and community have been replaced with more independent and individual choices within the nuclear family set-up.

Marriage and divorce (kekkon to rikon 結婚と離婚)

Miai kekkon (*arranged marriages*) accounted for two-thirds of all marriages in the 1940s but nowadays the rate is below 30 per cent. People may still choose to have a **miai** or **omiai** (*arranged meeting*) because it is a convenient way of meeting someone (rather like computer dating) or to please their family. A **nakōdo** (*matchmaker*), often a friend of the family, a boss or a well-regarded person in the community, sets up the **miai** between the potential couple and their parents. Either of the parties can pull out after this stage and people may have a number of **miai** before meeting the person they marry. Once the couple begin dating there is an expectation that they will marry. The **nakōdo** is an important guest at the wedding. **Ren'ai kekkon** (*love marriages*) are the norm nowadays but an honorary **nakōdo** is usually still invited.

Japanese people, along with those in other industrialized nations, are getting married later (currently 26.7 years for women and 29 for men). People's expectations of marriage have changed, too, and women in particular, many of whom now work, expect their husbands to take a greater part in housework and child rearing. Expectations and reality are still often far apart as can be shown by these statistics on housework sharing by couples who both work (hours and minutes a day).

	Husband	1986	1996	**Wife**	1986	1996
Housekeeping		0.05	0.07		3.16	3.35
Childcare (under 6)		0.01	0.03		0.15	0.19

Source: Statistics Bureau and Statistics Centre

Very few Japanese people co-habit (less than 2 per cent of couples) and marriage remains a popular choice. However, **rikon** (*divorce*) is on the increase although still relatively low – currently less than one marriage in three ends in divorce (one in two ends in divorce in the UK and USA). A significant number of marriages fail within the first five years but another critical point is for couples in their 40s and 50s who have reared their children. Reasons cited for this trend is that women nowadays are more financially independent and that people, in the knowledge that they will live longer, are reassessing their options!

DID YOU KNOW?
Names and signatures

Until the Meiji restoration (1868) only upper-class Japanese people had family or surnames (**myōji**). Commoners were called by their first name (**namae**) and sometimes by a name indicating their trade or where they lived (e.g. **Tanaka** means '*middle of the ricefield*'). From 1875, all Japanese had to adopt a surname and certain names were particularly popular. The most common Japanese surnames are **Satō** and **Suzuki**.

The traditional way that Japanese people sign their name is with a **hanko** (personal seal). A person's name in **kanji** is engraved onto the end of a wood, bone or plastic block, this is dipped into red ink and stamped onto official documents. Both companies and individuals have **hanko** which have to be officially registered.

Young people (wakamono 若者)

'Imadoki no wakamono' (*the youth of today*) is a not infrequent lament of older Japanese people as they observe the young experimenting with every fashion trend such as bleaching, dying, perming and extending their hair, plastering on makeup or tottering through the streets in huge platform boots. Fashions change frequently and the Japanese youth are not afraid to express their own individuality, causing concerns among older generations that the traditional values of social harmony and group conformity are being forgotten or replaced by a 'me, me, me' culture which threatens to corrupt the smooth-running and caring Japanese society familiar to older people. Of course, complaints about 'the youth of today' are hardly new in any society but without a doubt, younger Japanese people have very different expectations and desires than did their parents and grandparents, they also have more job insecurity and many are turning their backs on conventional careers and rejecting the path of duty which their parents followed. It remains to be seen whether this is just a delaying tactic and that young people will eventually bow down to the expectations of society or whether Japanese society itself is in flux and a new Japan is in the making.

Old people (toshiyori 年寄り)

The increasing ageing population is a cause of great concern for the Japanese. At the same time that most people are choosing to live in nuclear family units, the sense of obligation to elderly relatives is still very strong. The rate of suicide among the elderly has increased (see p. 168) and children are having to make difficult choices between caring for their parents at home or putting them into homes where the standard of nursing care varies hugely. The Ministry of Health and Welfare introduced the Gold Plan in 1989 aimed at improving care for the elderly with targets such as increasing the number of home helpers and of beds in special care homes. The age at which people can receive employee pensions is also being raised from 60 to 65 to cope with the increasing number of people claiming.

Social issues

Sex and pornography

Visitors to Japan often express surprise at the prevalence of openly pornographic images and pictures in the media and on video shop shelves. Japan has obscenity laws prohibiting, for example, the showing of pubic hair or full frontal nudity but, in reality, the Japanese are fairly tolerant of sexual images in the media. **Manga** (*comic books*), for example, often portray women as victims of violent or sexual attacks and this doesn't seem to raise much concern. Prostitution (**baishun**) was legal in Japan from the 12th century but was banned in the 1950s and exists today (illegally) within the entertainment industry, organised by the yakuza (see p. 211). In hostess bars, massage parlours and soapland (Japan's version of Turkish baths), a range of 'services' are usually available. In fact, the sex industry is worth 1.4 trillion yen (about $10 billion) a year! The Japanese are protective about young people's exposure to pornography and there have been concerns over recent reports that streetwise Japanese schoolgirls in large cities have found a new way of acquiring spending money by sleeping with businessmen. Finally, on the outskirts of every city and town in Japan are the love hotels, distinguishable by lots of gaudy lights and a variety of shapes and themes such as ships or stars and stripes (some complete with a Statue of Liberty on the roof!). There is a choice of themed rooms which are available by the hour and used by a variety of couples including married couples who want some 'quality time' away from home.

Birth control and abortion

Historically in Japan, the use of abortion and infanticide for unwanted pregnancies were widespread and accepted practices but from the Meiji period (1868) they were banned and under the military governments of the 1920s and 1930s, procreation was actively encouraged and birth control made illegal. Since the war, Japan has held a seemingly contradictory stance on birth control and family planning. On the one hand, abortion is legal and available on demand. On the other, the pill has not been available (except for medical reasons) ostensibly because of concerns over the side-effects but, more controversially, it has been seen by right-wing thinkers as dangerous to the moral fibre of Japanese society. This has been considered a hypocritical moral stance by many outside observers because the most common forms of contraception have been the condom and the rhythm method, resulting in a high rate of abortions (0.5 million per year). In addition, objections to the pill haven't stopped Japan from producing and exporting it in large quantities. Only since the late 1990s has the pill become more widely available.

Women

The word for wife in Japanese is **okusan. Oku** means interior or inside and **okusan** can be translated as 'the one indoors'! Up until the end of World War II, the wife's role was to manage the home and to serve her husband and parents-in-law. The post-war constitution made women equal to men but the old system lingered on, no longer in law but in attitudes. Unit 10 (p. 187) looks at women in the workplace, but what about Japanese women in today's society? They have not been particularly active in women's movements and campaigns for equality and may not seem very liberated. On the TV, for example, they often play the 'lovely assistant' role to the male host, giggling at his jokes and agreeing with all his statements. Women's language also, with its polite and respectful expressions and structures, puts women in a deferential role to men and there are a small number of radical feminists who refuse to use this language and use 'men's language' and slang instead. Young Japanese women, however, are enjoying the benefits of better education, better jobs and, in general, a greater degree of equality than previous generations and it will be interesting to see what impact this has on women's expectations and life choices in the future.

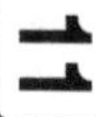

Immigrants and ethnic minority groups

Japan's belief in itself as an ethnically pure race has caused a number of problems for foreign residents over the years. This has been less so for people from Western countries who tend to have a more elevated position in Japanese society, particularly those who go there to teach English. Long-term Western residents complain that it is hard to gain true acceptance in Japanese society and that, however long they stay, they stand out as the **gaijin** (*foreigner* or *outsider*). Black Westerners have even greater problems of acceptance and encounter much ignorance and poor racial awareness in Japan. However, the treatment of Korean and Chinese residents has been particularly severe and exclusive. The Korean community is the largest minority in Japan and, together with the Chinese community, accounts for almost 60 per cent of the 1.8 million foreign residents. Most have lived in Japan since they were brought over as forced labourers during the war and some are second and third generation, born in Japan and with no connections to their former countries. However, under Japanese law, those born in Japan are only granted citizenship if one parent is Japanese. In 1982 permanent residency (but not citizenship) was granted to those brought over to Japan during the war and their children (and later extended to third generations). Nevertheless, certain jobs are only open to Japanese citizens and, over the years, Koreans and Chinese have suffered much discrimination and high unemployment. A particularly contentious issue was the alien registration law (**gaikokujin tōroku**). All non-citizens in Japan (apart from those on tourist visas) have to register with the local government and provide a fingerprint. Many Koreans during the 1980s refused to be fingerprinted, complaining that they were being treated like criminals and that it was an infringement of their human rights. In 1993 the Japanese government conceded and abolished fingerprinting for all permanent residents.

Japanese people who emigrated in the early 20th century, particularly to the Americas, were granted the right to be Japanese residents from 1989 and as a result the number of Brazilians of Japanese descent returning to Japan has increased. Immigration laws in general are strict and only skilled workers can potentially be granted work visas. However, there is a shortage of manual workers resulting in many illegal immigrants, particularly from the Philippines, Thailand, Peru,

Indonesia and Pakistan. The other illegal trade is the employment of women from Asian countries as bar hostesses in the entertainment industry. (See pp. 6, 19 and 23 for information on other minority groups.)

Crime, drugs and the yakuza

Although Japan has its high-profile crimes and murders such as the salin gas attack on the Tokyo underground (see p. 103) and the murder of a British woman by a Japanese businessman in 2000, in general it is a very safe country with the incidence of serious crime about one-fifth of that in Europe and the USA. There are **suri** (*pickpockets*) in large cities and it is necessary to take sensible precautions but, in general, both men and women can feel relatively safe even late at night. However, there is a huge underworld of organized crime run by the **yakuza,** Japan's mafia or gangsters. They have a history going back over 250 years and have an amazingly high profile when compared to gangsters in other countries. They carry **meishi** (*business cards*) and each gang (there are about 3,300 in total) has its own logo. The police estimate that there are about 90,000 yakuza, almost five times the number of mafia in the USA. They see themselves as a kind of modern-day samurai, and follow strict codes of conduct and loyalty based on **bushidō** (the warrior code). They are distinguished in two particular ways – the incredible tattoos that often cover the whole body and **yubitsume** (*finger cutting*). This is a punishment to a gang member who has been disloyal – to make amends the offender cuts off the first joint of his little finger and presents it to the gang leader.

The yakuza's main income is through drugs, gambling, prostitution, pornography and debt collection but as Japan's economy has grown and diversified so have the yakuza and they have also made huge investments in stocks, shares and real estate. Some of these investments, including overseas deals, have been through reputable Japanese companies, calling into question the 'turn a blind eye' approach of both Japanese businesses and politicians. Indeed, the yakuza have been very prominent in right-wing politics and have been important fund raisers for parties such as the LDP. They are mainly associated with extreme right-wing politics, calling for the rearming of Japan, the redeification of the emperor and the return of the Northern Territories to Japan (see p. 226). Fighting and murders tend to be within and between gangs and to have no impact on ordinary people's lives. In fact, yakuza have been given a very romantic image and often feature in **manga** (*comic books*) and films. However, concern has grown in recent years over their illicit activities, particularly in drug dealing. The most widely available drug is **shabu** (*methamphetamine*), imported from Taiwan and South Korea and with an estimated 0.5 million users. Cocaine is another more recent import. The government began to take steps towards limiting yakuza activity in 1991 with the introduction of laws aimed at confiscating possessions linked to illegal drugs profits but it is yet to be seen whether these laws will be strictly enforced.

Social customs and obligations

Japanese society is often described as a vertical or hierarchical society because in many of the key areas of life such as work and community, social relationships are built on a respect for elders and superiors. Through this system, people are tied into reciprocal relationships in which **giri** (*social obligation*) plays an important role. For example, a junior in a company may want to go home to his family at the end of a long day but have to carry out his **giri** by going drinking with his boss. Another aspect of Japanese society is the importance of harmonious relations and group solidarity. Even if a person's private views differ from the group's, decisions are reached through consensus. Japanese people tend not to speak their mind especially if it might cause conflict and one aspect of this is known as **honne** (*real thoughts* or *motives*) and **tatemae** (*stated reasons*). An example is when a visitor has outstayed their welcome. The host might insist that they stay longer (**tatemae**) when in fact their true motive (**honne**) is to ensure that they leave. Japanese people often use such non-verbal communication to convey their true feelings and this can be easily misunderstood by non-Japanese people.

Exchanging gifts

Gift giving in Japan has an important function in business – it is a way of thanking clients for their continued custom and of keeping in favour with key contacts. There are two main gift-giving seasons: **chūgen** in July and **seibo** in December. At these times, gift packs of fruit, wine, tinned food and whisky appear

in department stores and supermarkets. Many Japanese people fill out forms in the store and the gifts are delivered for them but they will deliver gifts in person to those to whom they are particularly indebted, for example, a teacher who has helped their child prepare for an entrance examination. **Chūgen** and **seibo** gifts do not have to be reciprocated but when gifts are received for family occasions such as births, weddings, illness or deaths, a gift worth half the value is given in return. This custom is called **hangaeshi** and it may seem rather calculating to an outsider to witness a Japanese family working out the cost of a gift in order to return roughly half the value.

DID YOU KNOW?
Superstitions

Japanese people, like all other nations, have their superstitions. Did you know, for example, that the number 4 is unlucky? This is because one of its pronunciations is **shi** which also means *death*. You won't find a room number 4 in places such as hospitals and hotels. There are certain days throughout the year which, according to Buddhist calculations, are considered lucky or unlucky and are marked on Japanese calendars. People consult these calendars or a Buddhist priest when deciding, for example, when to get married. **Taian** are particularly auspicious days for getting married and wedding halls are booked up months and years in advance. In contrast, wedding halls resort to offering huge discounts on **butsumetsu** days which are good for funerals but not marriages.

Doing business with the Japanese

Building up trust and good relationships is extremely important to Japanese companies when considering potential business deals. Westerners, used to 'pulling off deals' in much more aggressive or pushy ways, can find themselves wrong-footed when dealing with Japanese business people and many non-Japanese companies have expressed frustration with the apparent slowness in reaching deals and agreements. The following 'dos' and 'don'ts' will help to clarify some points of Japanese business etiquette.

Don't 'cold call' – business relationships in Japan normally begin through some kind of introduction. Arranging an appointment should then be done by phone and not by turning up in person.

Do take **meishi** (*business cards*) to the first business meeting. They are an important part of Japanese business etiquette because they help establish the position of a person in the company and therefore how they should be addressed and spoken to (see honorific language on p. 36). The language aspect may be less applicable for non-Japanese business people but establishing a person's rank is still very important.

Don't fold or write on the **meishi** you receive. A **meishi** should be treated with the same respect as the person giving it. **Don't** put it in your back pocket.

Once negotiations are underway, **don't** expect instant decisions. Decisions are made in Japanese companies through consensus, and directed by the more senior managers. Initial meetings may not include senior staff and may simply be fact-finding missions. 'Yes' will probably not mean '*yes, we will do business with you*' but '*yes, I hear what you say and will go and discuss it with others/ my seniors*'. This misunderstanding has led to confusion and frustration on the part of non-Japanese businesses in the past although increased contact with Japanese companies has helped to raise awareness.

Don't be confrontational or too direct, particularly about more tricky issues. Keeping social harmony is an important part of Japanese business practice (and of other areas of life too) and you need to find more indirect and 'humble' ways of getting your point across. This may be frustrating at times but will pay off in the long run and the Japanese are very good at knowing the meaning behind what is actually being said.

Do entertain important established Japanese clients at least once or twice a year. **Settai** (*business socializing*) is an essential part of the business relationship and an important way to build trust.

Settai (entertaining business clients)

Japanese companies use entertainment to cement relationships with established clients rather than to attract new business. The protocol of who to invite is very important and the status of the clients invited should match those attending from the host company. For example, if the **kachō** (*section head*) or **buchō** (*department head*) of the host company is to be present, then the equivalents are invited from the client company. A typical evening would include dinner at a high-class restaurant with plenty of alcohol, traditionally beer and sake, but wine is very popular nowadays. Both business and social topics are talked about and then the group will move onto one or more bars, the evening often ending with karaoke where modesty about your singing voice has no part – everyone is expected to do a turn, sometimes to the background of mildly pornographic videos. By this point in the evening there will be many **yopparai** (*drunkards*) among the group, making people braver about voicing opinions than when sober. However much someone may make a fool of themselves, it is not talked about the next day and it's back to 'business as usual'.

Visiting a Japanese home

Visitors to Japan often worry that they are going to offend a Japanese person mortally by some unforgivable *faux pas* but, in reality, Japanese people are very understanding of foreigners' 'blunders' – although getting it right is far more satisfying and will be met with delighted approval. Here are some 'dos' and 'don'ts' when meeting and mixing with the Japanese.

Don't blow your nose in front of people – this is considered very rude. Retreat to a corner of the room, turn your back to the group and blow discreetly!

Don't mind if Japanese people slurp while eating noodles. This is not considered to be bad manners although recent research has shown that young people, no doubt influenced by Western customs, are less inclined to slurp these days.

Do remove your shoes before entering a Japanese home, remove slippers in any **tatami** mat rooms, and put on toilet slippers as you enter the toilet. And do remember to remove the toilet slippers – if your host looks horrified when you return to the living room, you probably still have them on (and you won't be the first foreigner to do so!).

Do sit in the formal **seiza** (kneeling) position when you first sit down in a Japanese home. Formal greetings and bows are normally done from this position and your host will invite you to relax after a short time. When 'relaxing', men usually sit cross-legged and women with their legs to one side.

Sitting formally; bowing from kneeling; sitting cross-legged; women with legs to one side

Japanese people will understand if you need to stretch your legs out but **don't** point your feet towards anyone as this is considered to be very bad manners.

Don't leave your chopsticks sticking up in your bowl of rice because this is how rice is offered to deceased ancestors in Buddhist ceremonies! Place them on the **hashioki** (*chopsticks stand*) or across one side of your rice bowl when you are not using them.

Do take a gift (a souvenir of your country is always a good idea) when you visit a Japanese home but don't be surprised if it isn't opened in front of you because this is not the usual custom. This does not stop you explaining something about it if necessary.

Don't overstay your welcome. Japanese people are very polite and will ask you to stay longer but use your common sense about what is a reasonable length of stay rather than waiting for signals from your hosts. If green tea is served, this is usually a signal to leave.

Taking it further

Books

Two novels (available in Japanese or translation) by the contemporary female writer, Ariyoshi Sawako deal with issues raised in this chapter. The first, *The River Ki* (Tokyo and New York, Kodansha International, 1986; in original, ***Kinokawa***, 1959), gives a detailed portrait of family life and the changes over the past 100 years and the other, *The Twilight Years* (***Kōkotsu no hito***), is a very contemporary and insightful novel, looking at the issues of old age. (Tokyo and New York, Kodansha International, 1972)

The Chrysanthemum and the Sword: Patterns of Japanese Culture, Ruth Benedict (available in Japanese translation as ***Kiku to katana***). A classic study of Japanese society written by an American anthropologist in 1946 (reprinted, Boston, Houghton Mifflin, 1989)

Doing Business with Japanese Men: A Woman's Handbook, Christalyn Brannen (Stone Bridge Press, 1993)

Passport Japan: Your Pocket Guide to Japanese Business, Customs and Etiquette, Dean Engel (World Trade Press 1996)

What is Japan? Contradictions and Transformations, Taichi Sakaiya (Kodansha International, 1995). A book about Japan from the Japanese perspective

The Anatomy of Self: The Individual versus Society, Takeo Doi (Tokyo and New York, Kodansha International, 1986)

Information

Japan Information Network (see Unit 1). Select **Statistics** on the menu for a variety of statistics on society, population and trends, **Japan Insight** for in-depth articles on recent trends and **The Japan of Today** for an online databank of today's Japanese society.

Films give a great insight into a country's society and thinking – see Unit 7 for suggestions.

GLOSSARY

社会 **shakai**	*society*
人間 **ningen**	*humans*
日本人 **nihonjin**	*Japanese people*
外(国)人 **gai(koku)jin**	*foreigners*
人口 **jinkō**	*population*
ステレオタイプ **sutereotaipu**	*stereotype*
冗談 **jōdan**	*joke*
レイシズム **reishizumu**	*racism*
結婚 **kekkon**	*marriage, wedding*
離婚 **rikon**	*divorce*
恋愛 **renai**	*love*
お見合い **omiai**	*arranged marriage*
若者 **wakamono**	*young people*
年寄り **toshiyori**	*old people*
男性 **dansei**	*male*
女性 **josei**	*female*
家族 **kazoku**	*family*
やくざ **yakuza**	
義理 **giri**	*social obligation*
本音 **honne**	*real intention, motive*
建前 **tatemae**	*stated reasons*
歳暮 **seibo**	*year-end gift*
中元 **chūgen**	*July gift giving*

12 Japan in the wider world

In this unit you will learn

- about the influence of Japan abroad and Japan's attitude to foreigners
- about Japan's trading links with other countries
- about international issues including compensation to war victims and whaling
- about predictions for the future

Japanization

By now, you will have realized that Japan has a unique culture of which people are intensely proud. However, the Japanese have been very open to foreign influences and cultures from their earliest history. And whereas countries such as France get very hot under the collar about the 'corruption of French society' by foreign cultures and languages, the Japanese have their own style of 'borrowing' from other cultures and making these borrowings Japanese in a process which could be called 'Japanization'. A good example is the famous Scottish folksong 'Auld Lang Syne'. The Japanese have their own words for this song which they call **'Hotaru no Hikari'** and associate it not with New Year but with school and university graduation ceremonies. Many Japanese assume that the song is Japanese in origin. This process of 'Japanization' has both positive and negative aspects. Openness to outside influences has given Japanese culture its rich and varied nature but paradoxically, the Japanese have been fairly ignorant and badly informed about foreigners and foreign countries. Older Japanese people, whose knowledge of the world outside Japan may be confined to old-fashioned school books and black and white movies, may still believe that London is always foggy, British men wear bowler hats and all Americans chew gum! Young Japanese people, especially those living in cities, tend to be much more knowledgeable and 'streetwise'. Parents must look on in quiet despair as their teenage children experiment with all the latest fads and trends sweeping across the global village such as multiple body piercing, hair dyeing (bright orange is a current favourite) and nylon tattoos. Nevertheless, Japanization can have a negative effect on young people too. Many brought up on McDonald's burgers believe it to be a Japanese company and tradition!

Internationalization (kokusaika 国際化)

In the 1990s, a large sign in Japanese and English greeted all passengers arriving at Narita Airport in Tokyo with the word **kokusaika** (*internationalization*). It was a bold statement designed at affirming to both visitors and Japanese people Japan's outward-looking stance and its embracing of the outside world. Indeed, there have been rapid changes in this direction, particularly in the 1980s and 1990s. It was only a matter of years ago that even in some of the larger cities, **gaijin** (*foreigners* or *outsiders*) would be stared at and commented on (**gaijin da!** *It's a foreigner*) and many Japanese people had never seen a Westerner in real life. Japanese people were quite convinced that their language was far too difficult for foreigners to speak and many long-term foreign residents frequently found that their efforts at speaking Japanese face to face were met with uncomprehending looks and embarrassment even when they had no problems communicating over the phone. Such experiences may not have gone away altogether but there are many more foreigners in Japan nowadays and just about every schoolchild has been taught by a JET (Japanese English teacher) from a range of English- and French-speaking countries. There are many more foreigners on TV too who speak excellent Japanese and are confident contributors on chat shows, celebrity quizzes and news programmes. And Japan has become much better at promoting the cultures of other countries – 1998, for example, was both the 'Year of France' and a UK Festival in Japan, with opening ceremonies attended by the British Prime Minister, Tony Blair, and the French President, Jacques Chirac.

The exoticism of the West

Japanese people, and women in particular, have often had a poor self-image and have seen the blond hair, white skin and big eyes of the 'typical' Westerner to be far more desirable. Clothes for the Japanese market are frequently modelled by Western models, **manga** (*comic book*) heroes and heroines typically have big eyes, long legs and Western-style bone structure and it is even possible to have an operation to give the eyes a more Western shape. The Japanese president of McDonald's, Japan, even famously said in a book called *Behind the Arches* that Japanese people were short and yellow skinned because of eating rice and fish for 2000 years and '*if we eat McDonald's hamburgers and potatoes for 1,000 years we will become taller, our skin become white and our hair blonde*'! It is not clear how many Japanese were actually taken in by this outrageous statement but it was designed to promote the virtues of the product. However, alongside this adulation of the Western image, Japanese people are very proud of their own heritage and the young, in true 'Japanization' style, are picking from Western and Japanese trends to create their own unique look and are much more confident about their self-image and about expressing their individuality. Futhermore, this 'Western image' is very narrow and does not include, for example, black Westerners about whom there is a lot of ignorance and bias in Japan.

The exoticism of the East

Japan has a very exotic image to the outside world. There is a fair amount of ignorance about where Japan is and what it is like and a number of misperceptions and out-of-date images such as geisha girls, ninja spies and samurai chopping people's heads off! More modern perceptions have stereotyped Japan into a workaholic, humourless society, overstacking the world's shelves with a glut of home appliances, cars and cameras. However, interest in and education about the real Japan has grown considerably in recent years and a stroll around a medium sized city in the UK, USA, Europe or Australia will reveal a wealth of Japanese culture including karaoke bars, sushi restaurants, department stores, exhibitions and gardens. TV channels broadcast a host of programmes about Japan, cinemas have Japan seasons and show Japanese films in the mainstream schedules too, newspapers discuss issues like education and the economy, and many countries have national Japanese events such as Japan 2001, a year-long arts festival in the UK. There are also official bodies created by the Japanese government to promote Japan abroad such as the **Kokusai Kōryū Kikin** (*The Japan Foundation*) and organizations in individual countries such as the Japan Society. Many more Japanese people are visiting and working abroad and increasing numbers of foreigners are visiting and working in Japan, too.

Trading with other countries

One key factor in Japan's post-war 'economic miracle' was its highly competitive and lucrative export market. Japan's main strategy was to import raw materials such as metal ores and export finished products such as electrical goods for the home, cars and car parts. As trade surpluses grew, this became the cause of much trade friction during the 1980s, particularly with the USA. Japan agreed voluntarily to restrict exports to the USA but when, for example, Japanese car production overtook that of the USA in 1980, demonstrations by American car workers about the threat of Japanese exports and the dumping of

Japanese products on overseas markets sprang up around the USA. Japan also reached agreements with the USA on reducing tariffs and opening up opportunities for USA imports such as beef, oranges and rice (this last one still a very contentious issue with Japanese politicians and farmers who have enjoyed protected rice prices, see p. 109). The EC (European Community) also made moves to limit Japanese exports and in 1984 Margaret Thatcher entered into negotiations with Japan to encourage Japanese investment and the establishment of Japanese manufacturing plants in the UK.

During the 1990s, following a number of trade negotiations including difficult talks through GATT (General Agreement on Tariffs and Trade) and subsequently the WTO (World Trade Organization), Japan's trade pattern began to change. Japan started importing more manufactured goods such as machinery and foodstuffs such as fish, meat and alcohol, and to decrease the imports of raw materials. At the same time, Japanese companies shifted some production from within Japan to the USA, Asia and Europe in order to avoid trade friction and

Japan's main trading partners

Country	% of Japan's imports	Main items	% of Japan's exports	Main items
USA	23.9	Meat, fruit, cars, semiconductors, planes, communications equipment	30.5	Cars, electrical goods, office machinery, chemicals
China	13.2	Fish, vegetables, textiles, electrical machinery	5.2	Textiles, metals, general machinery
EU*	13.9	Wine, whisky, cars, chemicals	18.4	Cars, chemicals
Korea	4.3	Electrical machinery	4.0	Electrical machinery, chemicals
Australia	4.6	Meat, milk, metals	2.1	Cars, electrical goods

* In the EU, Germany is the biggest trading partner and Japan's fourth trading partner overall (imports: 3.8%; exports: 4.9%).

Source: Japan 2000: an international comparison

export restrictions, and to improve overseas relations. As of 1999, exports accounted for only 10 per cent of Japan's GNP (gross national product) and investment overseas had grown to $54 billion by 1997. Two-thirds of Japanese industries set up overseas are non-manufacturing such as services and finance, and the main countries are USA, Asia and the EU (with the UK accounting for almost half of European Union investment). Investment has begun to fall slightly as companies make cutbacks following Japan's recession and the general Asian financial crisis.

DID YOU KNOW?
Foreign status symbols

The Japanese love foreign products, particularly the designer-label and brand-name varieties which carry prestige and status. The BMW and the Mercedes are the ultimate status cars, the 'in-the-know' Japanese tourist wouldn't leave home without their Louis Vuitton luggage and you are certainly onto a winner if, on a visit to Japan, you take bottles of malt whisky for male acquaintances! Gucci, Clinique, Paul Smith, The Body Shop, Benetton, Häagen-Dazs, Toys 'Я' Us . . . the list is a long one and constantly being added to. Not forgetting the British Mini which has the status of a cult car in Japan, with bigger sales than in the UK! And the Japanese love going abroad to buy luxury foreign goods, naming France, Hong Kong and Italy as the most fun places to shop in.

The Japanese abroad

There are about half a million Japanese people living and working temporarily abroad, made up of company employees and families, students and government employees. Together with the almost 300,000 Japanese living permanently in other countries and the 16 million Japanese tourists each year, there is a considerable proportion of the population who are getting exposure to other cultures and peoples. A typical pattern is that of a Japanese company such as Toyota or Nissan which will build a manufacturing plant overseas, employ a gradually increasing workforce from the local area but also initially place managers from the parent companies in Japan to help set up the bases abroad. The Japanese employees may be single or married men. If they have families, many, but not all, will accompany the husband and, as a result, some substantial Japanese communities have developed in areas of the USA, UK and France, to name a few. Japanese employees typically stay for three to five years and the postings are seen as a step up the career ladder. Interest in Japanese culture and language within the local community tends to increase around these communities and lasting friendships between Japanese and other nationalities have been established. Japanese children will either attend special Japanese schools or, especially in English-speaking countries, a local school because many parents are keen for their offspring to have the chance to learn another language. However, it is also felt to be important that these children keep up with their Japanese school education, and so **monbukagakushō** (the Ministry of Education) have set up Saturday schools called **hoshūkō** where children learn Japanese language and mathematics. These children, having experienced different styles of teaching and discipline abroad, often find it difficult to settle into the Japanese system when they return home and some programmes have been set up recently in Japan to help these returnees.

International issues

Japan's self-defence forces

Under the Potsdam Declaration of 1945 and the subsequent Constitution of Japan, Japan's armed forces were to be dismantled permanently. However, world events, namely the Korean War in 1950 and the beginning of the cold war between the USA and the Soviet Union, caused America to reconsider Japan's position in Asia and, most importantly, its ability to defend itself from what America saw as the threat of Communism. This resulted in two separate agreements. The first of these was the Security Treaty of 1951 between the USA and Japan which allowed US troops to use bases in and around Japan to protect Japan and Asia. In return, Japan ended its status as a defeated nation, resumed international relations and, at the same time, signed the San Francisco Peace Treaty with the Allied nations which stated in article 51 that Japan '*as a sovereign nation possesses the inherent right of individual or collective self-defence*'. This appeared to be in direct conflict with article 9 of the Constitution which states that '*land, sea, and air forces, as well as other war potential, will never be maintained*'. The Japanese government continues to maintain that this did not prohibit the use of forces for defence although other political parties have frequently made challenges in the supreme court.

Worldwide changes following the collapse of the Berlin Wall in 1989 have brought about new constitutional issues for the Japanese government. Up until 1992, Japan had played no active role in UN (United Nations) peace-keeping operations although it had contributed large financial donations ($13 billion raised from new taxes were contributed to the Gulf Crisis in 1990–1) and had participated in civilian operations such as being observers at elections. It was the Gulf Crisis which brought matters to a head because Japan found itself being criticized by the international community (despite its financial contributions) for being too slow in offering what was considered too little assistance. This triggered a new public awareness and increased pressure for a new law that would enable Japan to have a greater international role. Finally, the International Peace Cooperation Law was enacted in 1992 which, although it has a number of restrictions, has allowed Japanese forces to participate in UN peace-keeping operations such as in Angola, El Salvador and the Golan Heights. A number of Japanese people play key roles within the UN, such as Ogata Sadako, who was the UN High Commissioner for Refugees.

Other issues yet to be resolved include the Security Treaty with the USA, brought about at the beginning of the cold war, which is beginning to seem out of step with the post-Soviet world order, and the continuing presence of US military bases in Japan. Also, Japanese people are questioning more and more the amount spent on arms and personnel. An upper limit of 1 per cent of the GNP (gross national product) was set in 1976 on defence spending but since the 1980s this hasn't always been upheld in practice and, with the near collapse of Japan's economy in the 1990s, people have become more aware and critical of government spending. The issue of the self-defence forces is not one which will go away and will continue to be a subject of political and international debate in future years.

The Northern Territories (hoppōryōdo 北方領土)

Japan and the Soviet Union were technically in a state of war until they signed a joint declaration (but not a peace treaty) in 1956 because of the dispute over islands north of Hokkaidō which have been occupied by the Russians since the end of World War II. In 1991 President Gorbachev was the first Soviet leader to visit Japan and it seemed that a resolution to the issue over the sovereignty of the Northern Territories and the drawing up of a peace treaty was at hand. However, the break-up of the Soviet Union put an end to this. Negotiations have been underway with Russia since and in 1998 Prime Minister Obuchi was the first Japanese prime minister to visit Russia in 25 years but, at the time of writing, there has been no resolution to the problem or signing of a peace treaty.

Foreign aid and relations

In 1998 Japan's ODA (official development assistance) totalled $10.73 billion making Japan the highest aid provider (although 11th when the donation is measured as a percentage of GNP). Japan is responsible for almost half (46 per cent) of ODA in Asia, with the largest amounts in 1999 going to Indonesia, China, Thailand, Vietnam and India. Japan is also the provider of about one-fifth of aid given to Latin America and one-sixth of that given to the Middle East. Recent disasters at which Japan has provided medical and other support include the 1999 earthquake in Turkey and the 2000 floods in Mozambique and Zimbabwe. Japan is also UNESCO's largest financial contributor.

The end of the cold war, on-going globalization of the world's economies, and increasing interdependence between groups of countries have had an important impact on Japan's international relations. In recent years, there has been a growing movement towards economic cooperation between countries of the Pacific Rim region, namely Australia, Canada, New Zealand, Mexico, USA, Japan, South Korea, China and the six ASEAN nations (Association of South-east Asian Nations – Malaysia, Singapore, Indonesia, Philippines, Thailand and Brunei). Currently the main concern is to revitalize the economies of Japan and other Asian countries.

Japan has also had to work hard at building good relations with China and South Korea in the post-war period, with the Koreans in particular having bitter memories of their period of colonization by the Japanese. The 1978 China–Japan Peace and Friendship Treaty was reaffirmed in 1998 by the first visit of a Chinese president to Japan. China is Japan's second largest trading partner and Japan is China's largest trading partner.

Also, in 1998, the South Korean president visited Japan and both countries signed a declaration of partnership with 2002 named as the 'Year of People-to-People Exchange between Japan and the Republic of Korea' (as well as being the year of the joint hosting of the football World Cup). The history textbook issue (see p. 164) does continue to be of concern to both China and South Korea and this, along with the perceived lack of an official apology from Japan about the war (see next section) still reignites bitterness about the war. Finally, relations with North Korea have not yet been normalized and issues remain, such as the alleged abduction of ten Japanese citizens into North Korea.

Compensation to war victims

War veterans and civilians of Asia, Europe and the USA who were captured by the Japanese during World War II have some harrowing memories of internment camps, the Burma Death Railway and cruel acts carried out by Japanese soldiers. Almost all saw fellow soldiers and friends die and many have carried bitter feelings towards the Japanese through the years. One clause of the 1951 San Francisco Peace Treaty stated that Japan would pay reparations to any former enemy who demanded it. Japan began by paying $1.15 billion in goods to Burma, the Philippines, Indonesia and South Vietnam. Each government came to its own arrangement but there are those war veterans who feel that they were not compensated enough for what they suffered and groups are still campaigning to their own government and to Japan for fairer settlements. The other contentious issue is the lack of an official apology from the Japanese about their role in the war. Over the years, both prime ministers and emperors on official visits abroad have used wording such as 'sincere regret' for the 'unfortunate past' and in 1990 Emperor Hirohito expressed 'deep regret' for the 'suffering' the Korean people had endured but for many, these words do not constitute an official apology or evidence that Japan has recognized the full impact of its wartime actions. However, there are a number of organizations and missions aimed at bridging some of the rifts which remain between former prisoners-of-war and Japan. These include reconciliation meetings between war veterans and former Japanese soldiers, and visits to Japan by former prisoners-of-war and their descendants. When the Chinese president visited Japan in 2000, he said that the Japanese public were not to blame for Japan's wartime aggression in China. Some war veterans distinguish between the Japanese soldiers of the war period and the Japanese people today, others find it much more difficult to forgive and forget.

The environment

There are two particular international issues concerning Japan and the environment: nuclear power and whaling. The Japanese government has seen nuclear power as an essential source of energy in a country which has virtually no natural resources. Currently, there are 51 nuclear reactors in Japan with five more under construction, putting the country third behind the USA and France. Furthermore, whereas other countries are revaluating their use of nuclear power following a number of serious accidents, the Japanese government is planning to build up to 20 more reactors by 2010 and to increase dependence from 12.9 per cent to 17.4 per cent of the total energy supply. In comparison, there are no plans to increase the production of hydroelectric power which stands at 3.8 per cent. However, after a serious accident at a nuclear power station in Tokaimura, a small city in Japan, Japanese people, who previously had made few objections to nuclear power, have begun to ask questions about the government's plans for expansion and the location of power stations in residential areas.

Traditionally, Japan has hunted whales for the meat, which is considered a delicacy, and for the oil to make fuel, margarine and soap. In the immediate post-war period, food was scarce in Japan and whale meat was an important source of protein. Since then commercial whaling increased to such a degree that by the 1970s most species were threatened with extinction and there were only 1,000 blue whales left. Therefore, the IWC (International Whaling Commission) called for a moratorium on whale hunting in 1982 to which the four whaling nations – Japan, Norway, Peru and the USSR – all objected. Japan was pressurized by the USA to withdraw its objections and by 1988 had discontinued commercial whaling altogether. Japan has continued its research whaling for scientific purposes against the objections of organizations such as Greenpeace and, as the whale population has increased, Japan and Norway have begun discussing putting an end to the moratorium.

Other issues which face Japan regarding the environment include the disposal of household and industrial waste which has been increasing year on year. New landfill sites are scarce and some have been created by building artificial land into the sea. In 1991 household waste amounted to 1,110 grams per person per day and has continued to grow. Sixty per cent of general waste is packaging, for consumer goods tend to be 'overpackaged' in numerous layers and types of packaging. The 1997 packaging recycling law was aimed at addressing this problem. Added to this was the 2001 household electrical appliance recycling law, another area in which Japan is a highly 'throwaway' society. The law compels retailers to take away old appliances and manufacturers to reuse the materials. Japan also uses huge amounts of imported wood for items such as **waribashi**, the throwaway chopsticks used by all Japan's many eating places. In terms of the global environment, Japan is a signatory to the Vienna Convention aimed at protecting the ozone layer and the global warming and biodiversity conventions. The 1997 Convention on Climate Change was held in Kyoto and has enacted a number of laws designed to reduce air pollution and CO_2 emissions and to ban CFCs. Japan also works with countries such as the USA and China to protect migratory birds.

. . . And the future?

Japan is no longer an island nation except in the literal meaning. Membership of the global village will continue to exert a range of cultural, social, economic and other influences on the development of the country and its people. Japan's management of its economy, for example, has implications for all the world's economies and, although the economy shows signs of improvement, there is international pressure on Japan to put its house in order. The crisis is certainly not yet over while banks and other companies continue to file for bankruptcy and the amount of bad loans piles up. There is pressure from within Japan too, as people have become far less tolerant, for example, of public funds being used to bail out private companies. In other areas of life also, the Japanese, who traditionally have taken a fairly passive and consensual role, are demanding to be better informed. For example, cases of medical malpractice have been on the increase and so patients are asking to know more about their illness and treatment, if only to avoid unnecessary expense. Japan needs to join in more fully with the information technology revolution, too, in which the USA and other Asian countries have moved much faster. However, over its long history, Japan has embraced and absorbed new ideas, new influences and new situations and so it wouldn't be unreasonable to predict that recent and future developments can only add to the rich and varied tapestry which makes up Japanese language, life and culture.

Taking it further

Years of Trial: Japan in the 1990s (Japan Echo Inc. 2000). Selection of essays looking at changes in Japan and its direction in the 21st century

Japan Quarterly, published by Asahi Shimbun (newspaper) about current issues affecting Japan. E-mail **serials@jptco.co.jp** for more information

You can keep up to date with current affairs in Japan through the *Japan Times* website: **http://www.japantimes.co.jp/**

The Japanese Overseas: Can They Go Home Again?, Merry White (New York, Free Press; London, Collier Macmillan, 1988)

Finally, if you want to exchange views online or read discussions of current Japanese themes, log onto the JIN website (see Unit 1) and select **JINPlaza**.

GLOSSARY

戦後 **sengo**	*post-war*
国際化 **kokusaika**	*internationalization*
西洋 **seiyō**	*the West, Western countries*
アジア **ajia**	*Asia*
ヨーロッパ **yōroppa**	*Europe*
アメリカ **amerika**	*America*
英国 **eikoku**	*England/Britain*
オーストラリア **ōsutoraria**	*Australia*
ニュージランド **nyūjirando**	*New Zealand*
カナダ **kanada**	*Canada*
貿易 **bōeki**	*trade (foreign)*
外国 **gaikoku**	*foreign, abroad*
北方領土 **hoppōryōdo**	*Northern Territories*
環境 **kankyō**	*environment*

appendix 1

A timeline of Japan's history

Date (from)	Era name	Key figures/events/ developments	Key places to visit
30,000 BC	Paleolithic	Stone tools, Japan still connected to mainland Asia	Tokyo National Museum; Fukui Cave, Kyushu
10,000 BC	Jōmon	Cord-decorated pots, clay figurines	Aomori Prefectural Museum
300 BC	Yayoi	Korean and Chinese influence; rice, iron and bronze	Yoshinogari tomb, Kyushu; Oyu stone circles
AD 300	Kofun (tomb)	Keyhole-shaped tombs, haniwa clay figures, kanji (writing system), Buddhism	Nintoku tomb, Osaka prefecture
AD 710	Nara	Chinese culture and town planning (grid system)	Great Buddha at Nara
AD 794	Heian (Kyoto)	Aristocratic culture; Murasaki Shikibu writes *The Tale of Genji*; rule of the Fujiwara family	Kyoto; Byōdōin Temple near Kyoto

Date (from)	Era name	Key figures/events/ developments	Key places to visit
AD **1185**	Kamakura	First shogunate (military government) first shogun: Minamoto Yoritomo; Zen Buddhism	Daibutsu (Giant Buddha) at Kamakura
AD **1333**	Muromachi	Muromachi shogunate established by Ashikaga Takauji; first Europeans in Japan; arts develop such as tea ceremony, flower arranging, theatre (noh and kyōgen)	Kinkakuji (gold) and Ginkakuji (silver) pavilions in Kyoto
AD **1568**	Azuchi-Momoyama	Three key figures: Oda Nobunaga, Toyotomi Hideyoshi, Tokugawa Ieyasu; political unification; decorative arts	Nagasaki (European influence) Takamatsu Castle (Kagawa prefecture) and Himeji Castle
AD **1600**	Edo	Tokugawa shogunate; seclusion from foreign contact; class system; Confucianism; William Adams, Commodore Matthew Perry; kabuki and bunraku theatre	Tokugawa Shrine at Nikko; Edo Mura reconstructed village in Nikko
AD **1868**	Meiji	Meiji restoration; imperial rule restored; Western influence in government, education, dress, communications, arts; expansion into Asia and Russia	Meiji Mura (outdoor museum) in Aichi prefecture

Date (from)	Era name	Key figures/events/ developments	Key places to visit
AD **1912**	Taisho	Rise and restriction of left wing and communism; World War I allied with Britain and economic boom; 1923 Tokyo earthquake; restriction of freedom of speech and public meetings	
AD **1926**	Showa	Emperor Hirohito; military expansions and domestic political repression; World War II then occupation; Constitution; Japan becomes second largest economy in the world	Hiroshima and Nagasaki Peace Museums
AD **1989**	Heisei	Emperor Akihito; Akiyama Toyohiro is first Japanese in space; economic 'bubble' bursts; financial and political scandals; Hanshin earthquake	Contemporary architecture in Tokyo, e.g. Metropolitan Government offices

Three Japanese recipes

The following recipes are in addition to the information given about Japanese food in Unit 6. These dishes are fairly simple to make and very tasty, so enjoy them!

Sukiyaki

Meaning 'grilled on a spade' (see p. 113), this dish is a very flavoursome stew which is normally cooked at the table in a cast-iron skillet or frying pan. If you have a gas or electric burner for the table top, this is perfect; otherwise you could start the cooking off on the stove and then put the pan in the middle of the table over a table-top warmer (using as many night lights as possible) or a fondue stand.

Zairyō (ingredients – for 4 people)

500 g (1 lb) of prime beef (rump, sirloin or tenderloin)

1 block of tofu (about 200 g or 7 oz)

200 g (7 oz) **shirataki** (jelly-like noodles or use fine egg or rice noodles instead)

8 fresh **shiitake** or other large mushrooms

100 g (4 oz) Chinese leaf or fresh spinach

2 thin leeks

suet or vegetable oil to grease the pan

1 onion

4 eggs

Warishita (cooking broth)

150 ml (5 oz) cup **sake** (rice wine) or dry white wine

1 tablespoon sugar

150 ml (5 oz) **mirin** (sweet cooking rice wine) or sweet sherry

150 ml (5 oz) soy sauce

300 ml (10 oz) instant **dashi** (Japanese stock or use fish stock cube)

Tsukurikata (method)

1 Slice the beef as thinly as possible. If you freeze it for a few hours first, it is easier to do this.
2 Cut the tofu into 2.5 cm (1 inch) cubes, rinse in cold water and drain.
3 Parboil the **shirataki** (or other) noodles in boiling water for 2 minutes and drain.
4 Take the stalks off the **shiitake** mushrooms and cut a cross shape onto the tops.
5 Separate and wash the Chinese leaf then cut into quarters. (If using spinach, wash and leave whole.)
6 Wash the leeks and cut diagonally into 2.5 cm (1 inch) slices.
7 Arrange the beef slices on one plate and the other ingredients on another.
8 Mix and heat the **warishita** ingredients until the sugar melts and pour into a jug.

Cooking and eating

1 Place the frying pan on the burner and melt the suet or oil, making sure it covers the bottom and sides evenly.
2 Put in a few slices of beef, quickly brown them on both sides then add some broth.
3 Begin to add the other ingredients, starting with the harder vegetables which will take longer to cook.
4 Each person breaks and mixes an egg into a bowl, picks out meat (it will only take a minute to cook) and vegetables as they wish with their chopsticks, dips the food into the egg and eats it. The egg cooks with the heat of the food and adds to the flavour but if you don't like the idea of raw egg, the food and sauce is still delicious without it.
5 Add more broth as you need it and water if the flavour becomes too strong. Keep adding and cooking the ingredients as you need them.

Yakisoba (stir-fried noodles)

Yakisoba is quick and easy to prepare and a great favourite with adults and children alike. It is very popular as **yatai** (street food), cooked on hot griddles at shrine festivals and fairs (see p. 116).

Zairyō (ingredients – for 4 people)

1 packet (2 blocks) soba or egg noodles (cooked and drained)

200 g (7 oz) chopped white cabbage

100 g pork, chopped into bite-sized pieces*

1 sliced onion

yakisoba sauce (from supermarket) or Worcestershire sauce

1 sheet of **nori** (seaweed), shredded (optional)

* For vegetarians, replace pork with strips of carrot.

Tsukurikata (method)

1 Heat oil in wok or frying pan and fry onions and pork.
2 Add chopped cabbage, stir and lightly fry.
3 Add the noodles and the sauce (if Worcestershire sauce, sprinkle on as suits your taste).
4 Keep stirring until thoroughly mixed and hot throughout.
5 Sprinkle nori on top and serve.

Yakitori (chicken kebabs)*

Yakitori is another popular **yatai** (street food – p. 114). It is best served on small wooden skewers which you can buy in Japan but the longer wooden or metal skewers will do fine otherwise – but you only need to put on 3 or 4 pieces of meat.

Zairyō (ingredients – for about 12 skewers)

500 g (1 lb) boneless chicken thighs cut into bite-sized pieces

3 spring onions cut into 2 cm ($\frac{3}{4}$ inch) pieces

15 wooden skewers soaked in water

Yakitori sauce

125 ml (4 oz) **sake** (rice wine)

125 ml (4 oz) chicken stock

125 ml (4 oz) **mirin** (sweet rice wine) or sweet sherry

2 tablespoons sugar

250 ml (8 oz) soy sauce

Tsukurikata (method)

1 Simmer the sauce ingredients in a pan for 10–15 minutes until it has reduced by about one-third then put on one side to cool.
2 Thread 3 or 4 pieces of chicken on each skewer with pieces of spring onion in between.
3 Place the skewers in a foil-lined tray, brush them with the sauce and cook under the grill at a high heat.
4 Keep turning and basting the **yakitori** to prevent burning and allow the sauce to soak in thoroughly.
5 Check that the chicken is cooked through (about 10 minutes) then spoon some extra sauce over and serve.

* Vegetarians can replace the chicken pieces with vegetables such as **shiitake** mushrooms, sliced leeks and chunks of green pepper. The chicken stock can be replaced by vegetable stock.

index